Franz Kollmann

Electronic Subscriptions

Franz Kollmann

Electronic Subscriptions

Key Management for Time-bound Access

Südwestdeutscher Verlag für Hochschulschriften

Impressum/Imprint (nur für Deutschland/ only for Germany)
Bibliografische Information der Deutschen Nationalbibliothek: Die Deutsche Nationalbibliothek verzeichnet diese Publikation in der Deutschen Nationalbibliografie; detaillierte bibliografische Daten sind im Internet über http://dnb.d-nb.de abrufbar.
Alle in diesem Buch genannten Marken und Produktnamen unterliegen warenzeichen-, marken- oder patentrechtlichem Schutz bzw. sind Warenzeichen oder eingetragene Warenzeichen der jeweiligen Inhaber. Die Wiedergabe von Marken, Produktnamen, Gebrauchsnamen, Handelsnamen, Warenbezeichnungen u.s.w. in diesem Werk berechtigt auch ohne besondere Kennzeichnung nicht zu der Annahme, dass solche Namen im Sinne der Warenzeichen- und Markenschutzgesetzgebung als frei zu betrachten wären und daher von jedermann benutzt werden dürften.

Verlag: Südwestdeutscher Verlag für Hochschulschriften Aktiengesellschaft & Co. KG
Dudweiler Landstr. 99, 66123 Saarbrücken, Deutschland
Telefon +49 681 37 20 271-1, Telefax +49 681 37 20 271-0, Email: info@svh-verlag.de
Zugl.: Klagenfurt, Universität Klagenfurt, Dissertation, 2008

Herstellung in Deutschland:
Schaltungsdienst Lange o.H.G., Berlin
Books on Demand GmbH, Norderstedt
Reha GmbH, Saarbrücken
Amazon Distribution GmbH, Leipzig
ISBN: 978-3-8381-0693-9

Imprint (only for USA, GB)
Bibliographic information published by the Deutsche Nationalbibliothek: The Deutsche Nationalbibliothek lists this publication in the Deutsche Nationalbibliografie; detailed bibliographic data are available in the Internet at http://dnb.d-nb.de.
Any brand names and product names mentioned in this book are subject to trademark, brand or patent protection and are trademarks or registered trademarks of their respective holders. The use of brand names, product names, common names, trade names, product descriptions etc. even without a particular marking in this works is in no way to be construed to mean that such names may be regarded as unrestricted in respect of trademark and brand protection legislation and could thus be used by anyone.

Publisher:
Südwestdeutscher Verlag für Hochschulschriften Aktiengesellschaft & Co. KG
Dudweiler Landstr. 99, 66123 Saarbrücken, Germany
Phone +49 681 37 20 271-1, Fax +49 681 37 20 271-0, Email: info@svh-verlag.de

Copyright © 2009 by the author and Südwestdeutscher Verlag für Hochschulschriften Aktiengesellschaft & Co. KG and licensors
All rights reserved. Saarbrücken 2009

Printed in the U.S.A.
Printed in the U.K. by (see last page)
ISBN: 978-3-8381-0693-9

Abstract

This work defines and introduces *electronic subscriptions*. It mainly focuses on the broadcast scenario (e.g. pay TV, GPS) with one sender and many receivers. In contrast to prevailing approaches, where an authorization is represented by some predefined bits in a tamper-proof storage unit, solutions based on time-bound keys are given: according to permissions, decryption keys are used with non-changeable expiry dates. The advantage of this concept is manifold. It should be noted that the security of many existing systems exclusively relies on the difficulty of accessing data in tamper-proof devices. If someone has managed to alter some bits in such components, assigned authorizations could be illicitly boosted. However, the solutions in this work are not vulnerable to this attack. Furthermore, for the basic subscription variants the sender does not need to transmit encrypted sessions keys periodically as it is the case in many currently used pay TV systems. Since no interaction with the sender is necessary, the presented constructions provide a key component for preserving the users' privacy.

In literature related approaches can be divided into either Broadcast Encryption or Key Management Schemes. In this context, the relevant published work is summarized and compared with each other. From a technical point of view, features from both research areas are weaved into the presented subscription models. Tailored subscription models and also a more general approach are contributed, which offer differently powerful subscriptions. Unfortunately, such a differentiation of subscriptions requires a variety of keys. Strategies are necessary to reduce the number of keys in a user's key storage. Therefore, several derivation schemes are devised, which make it possible that less powerful keys are computable from more powerful ones. Additionally extensions for interrupted time intervals, subscription upgrades, and revocation techniques are elaborated.

Inspired from the benefits and practicability of the presented subscription models, new applications are shown. In particular subscriptions are used as building blocks for anonymous authentication. Furthermore, applications for electronic vignettes and credit cards are sketched out. Finally, key derivation strategies are exploited in the context of document management so that dependencies between several rights are established. In summary, this work introduces electronic subscriptions and shows its practical relevance with respect of feasibility, scalability, and security.

Contents

1 Introduction   1
    1.1 Motivation 1
    1.2 Contribution and Organization 5
        1.2.1 Contribution 5
        1.2.2 Organization 6

2 Preliminaries   7
    2.1 Graphs 7
    2.2 Efficiency and Complexity 9
    2.3 Security Taxonomy 11
        2.3.1 Unconditional Security 11
        2.3.2 Computational Security 11
    2.4 Cryptographic Mechanisms 12
        2.4.1 Hash Functions 12
        2.4.2 Iterative Design 13
        2.4.3 Keyed Hash Functions 13

3 DRM and Video Protection   17
    3.1 DRM Model 18
    3.2 Lightweight DRM 19
    3.3 Tracing Traitors 20
    3.4 Content Scrambling System 21
    3.5 Digital Video Broadcasting 22
        3.5.1 Encryption 24

		3.5.2 Decryption	26
	3.6	MPEG Video Encryption	26
	3.7	McCormac Hack	28
	3.8	Outlook	29

4 Key Management Schemes — **31**

	4.1	Contribution and Structure	31
	4.2	Problem Definition	32
	4.3	Attacks	33
	4.4	Traditional Key Management Schemes	34
		4.4.1 Akl and Taylor's Scheme	35
		4.4.2 Sandhu's Scheme	39
		4.4.3 Chen, Chung, and Tian's Scheme	41
		4.4.4 Atallah, Frikken, and Blanton's Scheme	43
	4.5	Time-Bound Key Management Schemes	48
		4.5.1 Tzeng's Scheme	48
		4.5.2 Yeh's Scheme	50
		4.5.3 Chien's Scheme	52
	4.6	Comparison of the Schemes	53

5 Broadcast Encryption — **57**

	5.1	Contribution and Structure	57
	5.2	Fiat and Naor's Scheme	58
		5.2.1 Basic Scheme	59
		5.2.2 1-resilient Scheme based on One-way Functions	60
		5.2.3 1-resilient Scheme based on the RSA Problem	61
		5.2.4 Converting 1-resilient into k-resilient Schemes	62
	5.3	Logical Key Hierarchy	64
	5.4	Extended Header Scheme	65
	5.5	Subset-Cover Framework	67
	5.6	Subset-Cover Revocation Algorithms	68
		5.6.1 Complete Subtree Method	69

	5.6.2	Subset Difference Scheme	70
	5.6.3	Comparison	74
	5.6.4	Extensions	75
5.7	Further Schemes		75
	5.7.1	Tree Scheme	75
	5.7.2	Extended LKH	77
	5.7.3	The Biased Subset Scheme	80
	5.7.4	The Bit-Vector Scheme	81
	5.7.5	The Block-by-Block Scheme	81
5.8	Comparison		82

6 Key Derivation — 85

- 6.1 Contribution and Structure 85
- 6.2 Motivation 86
- 6.3 Conceptual Design 87
- 6.4 Extensions for Non-Trees 88
- 6.5 Applying Keyed Hash Functions 89
- 6.6 Applying the AES 91
- 6.7 Applying the Discrete Logarithm Problem 92
- 6.8 Applying the RSA Encryption Scheme 93
  - 6.8.1 Top-Down Key Generation 94
  - 6.8.2 Bottom-Up Key Generation 95
- 6.9 Comparison 96
  - 6.9.1 Remarks 97
  - 6.9.2 Summary 99

7 Subscription Models — 101

- 7.1 Contribution and Structure 101
- 7.2 Motivation 102
- 7.3 General Requirements 103
- 7.4 Assumptions 106
- 7.5 Definitions 108

7.6	Tailored Subscription Models		109
	7.6.1	Subscriptions without Time Limitations	109
	7.6.2	Subscriptions without Access Limitations	110
	7.6.3	Hybrid Key Derivation Trees	110
	7.6.4	Security	112
7.7	The Flexible Subscription Model		113
	7.7.1	FSM$^-$	114
	7.7.2	FSM	116
	7.7.3	Evaluation	119
7.8	Further Security Notes		121
7.9	Comparison		122

8 Extended Features — 125

8.1	Contribution and Structure		125
8.2	Non-continuous Time Intervalls		125
8.3	Revocation		127
	8.3.1	Simple Precautions	127
	8.3.2	1-resilient Revocation Scheme	129
	8.3.3	Framework for Header-based Revoking Schemes	132
	8.3.4	Applying the CS/SD Revocation Schemes	134
	8.3.5	Comparison	135
8.4	Subscription Upgrades		136
8.5	Inheritance of Rights		137

9 Anonymity Aspects — 141

9.1	Contribution and Structure		141
9.2	Anonymous Subscriptions		142
9.3	Anonymous Downloads		143
	9.3.1	Requirements	144
	9.3.2	Simple Protocol	145
	9.3.3	Enhanced Protocols	146
9.4	Legitimate User in the Background		148

9.5 Anonymous Kerberos	150

10 Further Applications 153
  10.1 Contribution and Structure 153
  10.2 Electronic Vignettes 153
    10.2.1 Possible Extensions 156
    10.2.2 Summary and Remarks 157
  10.3 Credit Cards 158

11 Document Rights 163
  11.1 Contribution and Structure 163
  11.2 Motivation 164
  11.3 Partial Encryption 165
  11.4 Access Rights Management 166
  11.5 Read and Write Permissions 167
    11.5.1 Inheritance from Write Permissions 170
    11.5.2 Inheritance from Parent Nodes 170
    11.5.3 Combined Inheritance 171
    11.5.4 Comparison 173
  11.6 Authenticity of Contents and Structures 173
  11.7 Evaluation 175
    11.7.1 Storage 175
    11.7.2 Security 176
    11.7.3 Comparison with Atallah's scheme 176
  11.8 Summary 177
  11.9 Further Extensions 178

12 Summary 181

A XML Security 183
  A.1 XML Access Control 185
    A.1.1 Server Side Evaluation 185
    A.1.2 Access Control based on Encryption 186

A.2 XML Encryption	186
A.3 XML Signature	188
A.4 XML Key Management Specification	190
A.5 XrML	192
A.6 XACML	193

B Abbreviations   **199**

Introduction   1

> *Science must begin with myths, and with the criticism of myths.*
> KARL POPPER

Electronic subscriptions can be considered as time-bound authorizations. This chapter describes and motivates related application areas and gives some examples where electronic subscriptions may contribute a practicable solution.

1.1 Motivation

Digital rights are subject to strongly discussed debates. In comparison to the analog world, the effort of copying and distributing digital contents is negligible. File sharing platforms have sped up the transfer of digital media and hence these platforms soon gained popularity. While users enjoy free downloads of digital media, the rights of the media owners are often ignored. Defining and enforcing rights on digital contents are differently complex to realize. For the first task several languages exist, which make it possible to formulate complex rights on digital contents. However, enforcing rights is much more difficult. Many approaches to enforce digital rights are completely broken today (e.g. DVD). It remains an open question whether there will be DRM systems in future, which satisfy both, the content providers and the consumers. In the following examples, digital rights management plays an important role. Due to the relevance to the present, concepts and techniques concerning DRM are considered separately in Chapter 3.

Pay TV: Pay TV systems usually consist of one sender and many receivers. Consider the transmission of videos like the soccer world championship or the Olympic Games. Here we are faced with a worldwide audience where the live transmission is a crucial requirement: time delays or interrupted data flows are unwanted. Thus, the service provider must expect to serve a huge number of participants concurrently. Traditional access control systems, where users are supposed to log in and authenticate themselves, will probably be overloaded. It can be assumed that such systems cannot cope with such requirements. Generally, if an authorization should be restricted to certain contents and temporal periods, the subscription-based approaches as described in this work are applicable. When the users' anonymity is an additional requirement, one can make substantial profit from these concepts.

Electronic payment systems: Realizing electronic payments has attracted many researchers over several years. In the long run, even highly promoted secure electronic payment systems like Cybercash [BoCY96] (initiated by VISA) and the Secure Electronic Transaction (SET) [MaVI97], which was supported by Mastercard, VISA, IBM, Microsoft, Netscape, Verisign and others, have failed. One of the main reasons for their rejection is the fact that these systems suppose the client to generate signatures. This in turn requires special hard and software components, which are hardly accepted by the users. Besides, the secret keys of the clients have to be protected. Furthermore, the verifier needs to evaluate the signature from the client. Thus, the verifier must authentically know the public key of any participant, who may join or leave. All in all, secure electronic payment systems could not fulfill the initially high expectations whereas the concept of maintaining private and public user keys did not get the desired acceptance.

Today the problem of untrustworthy financial transactions is often solved by a trusted third party (e.g. PayPal). In principle, the customer selects goods from a shop and pays the trusted third party for the required price. Then, the trusted third party informs the shopkeeper about the payment and transfers the money to the shopkeeper only after goods are delivered to the customer. This concept provides some interesting features: on the one hand the customer can be sure that the shopkeeper is not fooling, i.e. taking the money without delivery. On the other hand the shopkeeper is assured to get the money, because the trusted third party holds the money in trust. Besides, the customer does not need to reveal the data about his or her bank connection to the shopkeeper. However, a trusted company is necessary and the requirement for anonymity is only partially addressed.

David Chaum proposed the idea of blind signatures [Chau81]. Inspired from this concept he founded the company *DigiCash* in 1990, which promoted the anonymous payment system *eCash*. However, the system did not succeed and finally the company went bankrupt. Nowadays the "anonymity gap" is filled with initiatives like the *Paysafecard*, which is a payment system that uses prepaid cards. The cards are characterized by a secret 16-digit number, which is printed on them.

1.1 Motivation

During the payment, the number is filled in corresponding fields of Paysafecard-powered online shops. In comparison with others, this concept is based on simple ideas that have approved in practice over several years. However, the cards are limited to some predefined amounts of money, namely 10, 25, 50 and 100 Euro. The Paysafecard provider records remaining balances and allows a combination of up to nine cards.

Electronic subscriptions take some of its motivation from the simplicity of the Paysafecard example. Instead of money limits, they are characterized by temporal restrictions. This has several benefits. First, the overhead for recording balances becomes unnecessary. Second, the problem of the card combination disappears. It should be remarked that the anonymity aspects still remain. In this work solutions for securing financial transaction based on credit cards are presented.

Electronic toll systems: During 1994 and 1995, the German government performed a field study on a German highway section in order to test several ICC-based toll systems for their suitability [RaEf99]. As a requirement, the systems should not influence the traffic flow. In addition to this, changing the lane and high speed should not become possibilities to escape from registration. Assuring the user's anonymity has evolved into a main challenge. This is best done with prepaid cards. Among fixed installed registration systems, also GPS-based systems were analyzed. Besides, prepaid and postpaid billing systems were experimentalized. However, the results could not meet the high expectations: from 13 systems only 3 were considered to be suitable. Nevertheless, some toll system providers still underestimate the complexity of such systems [Skro03].

Hereby, simple, practicable and robust approaches are required. To produce electronic vignettes, the concept of electronic subscriptions can be applied. According to the conventional vignette in the real world, the electronic variant offers time-bound authorization where the anonymity of the card holder is preserved.

Anonymous authentication: Instead of proving one's identity, there are situations where it is sufficient to show the membership of a legitimate user group (without showing one's identity). When the membership should be temporal limited, the subscription models can provide a solid solution to this problem. For instance, suppose one has acquired a software license (e.g. anti-virus software) and the licensee is allowed to update the purchased software up to a given time. The update packages are offered by the software company. In case of an anti-virus software, the update could cover new material for detecting the latest viruses. Only those that have an according subscription can make use of the updates. Several protocols are devised that contribute solutions to this problem.

Final remarks: Under which conditions can we fully benefit from the electronic subscriptions? The subscription models are suited for the broadcast scenario with an innumerable amount of users that may concurrently use services, while it is required that the anonymity of the users is preserved. However, even if only a few from these conditions are fulfilled, they might be favored over others.

It should be remarked that the security of many systems (e.g. pay TV) is based on the reliability of tamper-proof devices like smart cards. It is generally assumed that smart cards ensure the confidentiality and integrity of their stored data. The fact that smart cards have already been successfully attacked is often neglected. Note that techniques like dummy operations or code obfuscation only have a short-term success. Lessons learnt from the past, one should not rely on "security by obscurity". A good summary of currently used attacks on smart cards is described in [Bar-04]. For a realistic estimation, it has to be expected that, concerning attacks on tamper-proof devices, progress will continue. Many card providers face this problem by replacing issued cards periodically by new ones. However, a good concept will inherently provide robustness such that compromised cards do not reveal more information than the card holders are already entitled to. Therefore, a well designed system should prohibit that an attacker can modify permissions for compromised subscriptions. Generally a disclosure of card-held secrets should not lead to a breakdown of the whole system.

Certainly, once a key is compromised, it can be distributed to others. That is why a crucial system key should never be stored in an issued smart card. The potential distribution of secrets evolved into a serious problem where the entire DRM leadership is working on. In this work several approaches are described that cope with this obstacle. The solutions range from simple precautions to the integration of existing hard-line revocation schemes that cause additional overhead.

As far as the system design is concerned, the integration of extra services after a start-up can be extremely costly. It is advantageous that issues like key updates, revocation, and modular architecture are well considered during the design phase. However, too many features will make a system less practicable. Therefore, one might look for a reasonable trade-off between these requirements.

1.2 Contribution and Organization

Since the contributions of this work span several areas, this section gives a background information about the main topics and the relationship between them. In addition to this, an overview of the organization of this work is given.

1.2.1 Contribution

The dependencies between the major topics in this work are illustrated in Figure 1.1. The main contribution is given by the subscription models. Thereby, tailored variants for practical scenarios but also a more flexible variant are contributed. Among completeness, proofs for the resiliency of the models are given. The subscription models combine benefits from both research areas, key management schemes and broadcast encryption. Substantial work from both fields are summarized and compared with each other in separate chapters.

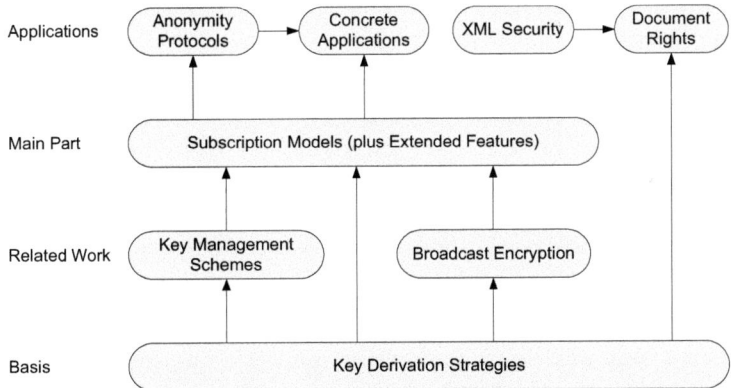

Fig. 1.1: Dependencies between the main topics in this work

Based on subscription models, extensions for non-continuous time intervals, subscription revocation and also upgrades are presented. Revocation techniques cover simple precautions and ad hoc exclusions of existing subscriptions.

Key derivation strategies serve as the basis for all mentioned topics. Hereby technical realizations are discussed and analyzed. Comparisons with respect of their suitability are drawn when the HMAC, the AES, a DLP-based concept, and an

RSA-based approach are used. The chapter concludes with a recommendation reflecting the requirements for the specified key derivation concept.

The last level in Figure 1.1 shows relevant applications. In particular protocols for anonymous authentication are presented. Additionally new applications for creating electronic vignettes and securing credit card based payments are shown. Finally, key derivation strategies are applied such that connections between several rights in the context of document management and XML security are established.

1.2.2 Organization

The overall structure of this work is classified into three main parts: Preliminaries and Related Work, Subscription Models and Extensions, and Applications. Among preliminaries, the first part presents currently used techniques concerning DRM, summarizes significant work, and compares them with each other. The second part describes subscription models and presents extensions on them. Finally the third part shows relevant applications.

Part 1 (Preliminaries and Related Work): Chapter 2 describes preliminaries, Chapter 3 shows currently used DRM techniques, Chapter 4 compares related work concerning key management schemes, and Chapter 5 analyzes approaches in context of broadcast encryption.

Part 2 (Subscription Models and Extensions): Chapter 6 investigates and compares possibilities for realizing a key derivation. Chapter 7 presents the subscription models, which is the main contribution of this work. Chapter 8 shows possible extensions on the described models.

Part 3 (Applications): Chapter 9 contributes new protocols concerning anonymous authentication. Chapter 10 describes two applications, namely electronic vignettes and credit card based payments. Chapter 11 shows applications in context of document management. Finally, appendix A serves as an annex of document management where a summary of essential work concerning XML security is given.

Preliminaries 2

> *Few things are harder to put
> up with than a good example.*
>
> MARK TWAIN

In this chapter some basic terms are defined that are used throughout this work. The chapter starts with a short introduction of graph structures with a special emphasis on trees. Afterwards common terms in the context of algorithms are introduced. Particular measures (due to Landau) are shown that allow limiting the runtime of algorithms. Then definitions for information-theoretic secrecy and computational security are given yielding to security classes for theoretical security and practical security. Finally, some cryptographic mechanisms particularly in the context of hash functions are investigated.

2.1 Graphs

In this work many concepts and mechanisms are based on graph theory. The following section defines some terms in this context; in particular graphs, graph properties, and graph functions.

Let V be the finite set of vertices (or nodes) with $V \neq \emptyset$ and $E \subseteq V \times V$ be the set of edges. A (directed) *graph* G is a pair (V, E). An edge $e = (v_i, v_j) \in E$ starts at v_i and ends at v_j. In this work, a graph is referred to as a directed graph. A *path* p from v_0 to v_n is a sequence of $n+1$ vertices $\langle v_0, \ldots, v_n \rangle$ such that $(v_{i-1}, v_i) \in E$ for $1 \leq i \leq n$. If $v_0 = v_n$, p is called a *cycle*. Generally, if there is a path p from v_i to v_j, then v_j is *reachable* from v_i via p. The *path length* is given by the number of edges. A node $v \in V$ is *adjacent* to a node $u \in V$ if and only if $(u, v) \in E$. A graph is *connected*, if each pair $v_i, v_j \in V$ is connected by a path. A connected graph is *strongly connected*, if each pair $v_i, v_j \in V$ is reachable one from another. A *subgraph* is a graph $G' = (V', E')$ with $V' \subseteq V$ and $E' \subseteq E$. A *connected component* is a maximal connected subgraph.

Let a graph $G = (V, E)$ be given whereby V denotes the finite set of vertices and E is the finite set of edges. We define the following function on G.

$Anc : V \to 2^V$ denotes a function, which maps a node to all its *ancestor* nodes: $v_i \in Anc(v_j)$, iff there exists a path p from v_i to v_j in G with $|p| \geq 1$.

$Des : V \to 2^V$ denotes a function, which maps a node to all its *descendant* nodes. Hence, $v_k \in Des(v_j)$, iff there exists a path p from v_j to v_k in G with $|p| \geq 1$.

$AoS : V \to 2^V$ denotes the *ancestors' or self* function, which maps a node to all its ancestor nodes including itself: $v_i \in AoS(v_j)$, iff v_j is reachable from v_i.

$DoS : V \to 2^V$ denotes the *descendants' or self* function, which maps a node to all its descendant nodes including itself: $v_k \in DoS(v_j)$, iff v_k is reachable from v_j.

$Par : V \to 2^V$ denotes a function, which maps a node to all its immediate predecessors (*parents*): $v_i \in \text{Par}(v_j) \Leftrightarrow (v_i, v_j) \in E$. Hence $Par(v_j) \subseteq Anc(v_j)$ for all nodes $v_j \in V$. If G is a tree then $|Par(v_j)| \leq 1$ for any node $v_j \in V$.

$Chd : V \to 2^V$ denotes a function, which maps a node to all its immediate descendants (*children*): $v_k \in Chd(v_j) \Leftrightarrow (v_j, v_k) \in E$. Hence $Chd(v_j) \subseteq Des(v_j)$ for all nodes $v_j \in V$.

$Leaves : G \to 2^V$ denotes a function, which determines the *leaves* in G. We define a leaf as a node v_i whose set of descendants $Des(v_i)$ is empty.

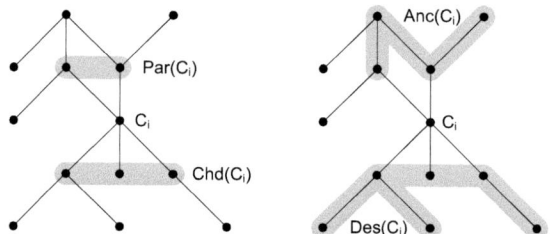

Fig. 2.1: Ancestors and descendants in a hierarchy

A graph G without cycles is called *forest*. A connected forest is called *tree*. A *rooted tree* is a tree satisfying the condition that every node except one (the root node) has exactly one parent node. The root node has no parent node. A node v_i in a rooted tree is called leaf node iff $Des(v_i) = \emptyset$; all other nodes are called *inner nodes*. A *sibling* of a node v_i is a node different from v_i that has the same parent node. A rooted tree is called *binary rooted tree* iff $|Des(v_i)| \leq 2$ for each node $v_i \in V$. A *full binary tree* is a binary rooted tree for which each inner node has exactly two child nodes. A *subtree* T_{v_i} of a tree T is a tree rooted at node $v_i \in V$.

Let $T = (V, E)$ be a rooted tree and $V' \subseteq V$. A *Steiner tree* $ST(V')$ is the minimal subgraph of T that includes only the paths from the root to the leaves $Leaves(T) \cap V'$.

A *poset* (partially ordered set), also called *hierarchy*, is a set P with a binary relation $\leq$ such that for all $a, b, c \in P$ the following statements hold:
i) $a \leq a$ (reflexivity),
ii) if $a \leq b$ and $b \leq a$ then $a = b$ (antisymmetry), and
iii) if $a \leq b$ and $b \leq c$ then $a \leq c$ (transitivity).

A *Hasse diagram* is a graph that represents a partial order $\leq$ on a finite set M as follows: each element in M is represented by a dot whereby for any two elements $p_1 \in M$ and $p_2 \in M$, if $p_2 \leq p_1$ and there does not exist a $p_i \in M$ with $p_2 \leq p_i \leq p_1$, then p_1 is connected with p_2 by an edge (p_1, p_2) such that p_1 is located above p_2 (cf. also [BrSe87]).

2.2 Efficiency and Complexity

For a comparison of algorithms, the growth of their running time and necessary storage is of main interest. An excellent introduction to algorithms is given by the book of Cormen et al. [CoLR90]; in this context also the books [OtWi96, Sedg03, Knut97] are recommended.

The running time of an algorithm is measured by the number of primitive operations it needs on a given input. This can be used to investigate whether an algorithm is more efficient than another one. The O-notation is used to limit the output of a function to an upper bound as follows.

Let $f, g : \mathbb{N} \to \mathbb{R}^+$ be two functions. $f \in O(g)$ if and only if there exist $c, n_0 \in \mathbb{R}^+$ such that for all $n \geq n_0$ the condition $0 \leq f(n) \leq c \cdot g(n)$ is satisfied. $f \in \Omega(g)$ if and only if $g \in O(f)$. $f \in \Theta(g)$ if and only if $f \in O(g)$ and $g \in O(f)$.

A *polynomial-time algorithm* is an algorithm whose running time is bound by $O(n^k)$, where n is the characteristic input size and k is a constant. An algorithm is referred to as *exponential-time*, if its running time cannot be bound by $O(n^k)$.

Polynomial-time algorithms are called *efficient*, while exponential-time algorithms are called *intractable* (also *infeasible* or *inefficient*). It should be noted that these considerations reflect only the asymptotical behavior of large n; the case for small n is disregarded.

In complexity theory considerations are restricted to *decision problems*. These are problems whose answers can be either *true* or *false*.

The complexity class P is the set of decision problems that are solvable in polynomial time. The complexity class NP is the set of decision problems for which a positive answer can be verified in polynomial time.

A *random function* is a function that assigns, independently from any others, a random value y to each input value x (cf. [MeOV96]). Knuth [Knut98] suggested many statistical tests that can give confidence in the randomness of a sequence when those tests are passed. Additionally, the National Institute of Standards and Technology (NIST) specified the NIST Test Suite [RSN+00] for similar purpose.

A function is called *poly-random* (also called *pseudo-random*) if no algorithm that runs in polynomial time can distinguish the output of the function from a random value upon an input of its choice (cf. [GoGM86]).

A *pseudo-random number generator* (PRNG) is a deterministic algorithm, which generates a sequence of numbers (upon an input called *seed*) that "appear" to be random (cf. [MeOV96]), i.e. a polynomially bound algorithm cannot distinguish the produced numbers from truly random numbers.

A function is called *one-way function*, if

  i) from every possible input, the output of the function can be efficiently computed and

  ii) from the exclusive knowledge of a randomly chosen image, computing the corresponding input is *infeasible* even if the function is public.

A function f is called *trapdoor one-way* function, if x can be computed efficiently from $f(x)$ when a certain additional information is given (cf. [MeOV96, Denn82]).

Birthday paradox: Let M be a set of m elements numbered 1 to m. Suppose that n elements are taken randomly from M one after another such that chosen elements are returned to M right after their selection. For $n \approx \sqrt{m}$, i.e. $n \in \theta(\sqrt{m})$, with $m \to \infty$ the probability p that at least one element is chosen more than once is greater than or equal to 0.5.

The birthday paradox is named after the astonishing fact that, when 23 people or more get together, it is likely (with probability greater than 0.5) that at least two of them will have a common birthday.

2.3 Security Taxonomy

The security of a system can mainly be classified as *unconditionally secure* or as *computationally secure*. Additionally there is a further class called *ad hoc security* that focuses on short-term security. This could be interesting for data that loses its attraction after a short time period (e.g. news). However, schemes with serious security requirements provide at least computational security. It should be noted that many asymmetric and symmetric cryptosystems are based on the latter one. The highest confidence is offered by unconditional security (perfect secrecy).

2.3.1 Unconditional Security

Shannon considers the question: "How immune is a system to cryptanalysis when the cryptanalyst has unlimited time and manpower available for the analysis of cryptograms?" [Shan49]. He gives an answer to this question:

A cipher provides perfect secrecy (also called unconditional security or information-theoretic security) if the ciphertexts and plaintexts are statistically independent. This means that intercepting a ciphertext does not reveal any additional information. For perfect secrecy the probability that a particular ciphertext c is the output of encrypting a given message m (with a certain key k) must be equal to the probability that c is the result of encrypting another message $\widetilde{m}$ (with another key $\widetilde{k}$) for any possible messages and ciphertexts:

$$Pr[c = E_k(m)] = Pr[c = E_{\widetilde{k}}(\widetilde{m})]$$

Perfect secrecy is provided by the *Vernam Cipher* (or *One-Time Pad*). It encrypts a plaintext with a truly random bit sequence, which is uniquely chosen for each plaintext and has the same bit length as the plaintext, by an XOR operation.

2.3.2 Computational Security

A scheme is said to be *computationally secure*, if its security is considered to be unbreakable in terms of computational resources. It is called *provable secure*, if its security can be shown to be equivalent to a computational problem like the Integer Factorization Problem or the Discrete Logarithm Problem.

Generally computational security relies on NP problems or NP complete problems. For instance the RSA Problem and the Discrete Logarithm Problem (DLP) (cf. [MeOV96]), which serve as the basis for many cryptographic schemes, are considered as problems of such types (computationally bound).

Definition 2.1: *RSA Problem*: Let n and e be adequate public RSA parameters. From the ciphertext c, which is a number between 0 and n, and the public parameters e and n, find an integer m less than n such that $m^e = c$ MOD n.

Definition 2.2: *Discrete Logarithm Problem*: Let p be a prime and g be a generator of $\mathbb{Z}_p^*$, each adequately chosen. Let y be an element in $\mathbb{Z}_p^*$. Find the integer x with $0 \leq x \leq p-2$ such that $g^x = y$ MOD p.

2.4 Cryptographic Mechanisms

It is assumed that the reader is familiar with symmetric and asymmetric encryption schemes. In this section some mechanisms are presented that use some cryptographic primitives. It starts with the definition of hash functions whereby some basic properties concerning collisions are stressed. Since keyed hash functions serve as a building block for constructing key derivation function (cf. Chapter 6), we examine several approaches for designing keyed hash functions afterwards.

2.4.1 Hash Functions

A *hash function* $h : \{0,1\}^* \to \{0,1\}^k$ is a function that maps binary strings of arbitrary length to k-bit strings (with constant $k \in \mathbb{N}$) called *hash value* or *message digest*. $h(x_1) = h(x_2)$ on two different inputs x_1 and x_2 is referred to as *collision*. h is *weakly collision-resistant* if, given an input x_1, it is infeasible to find a different input x_2 such that $h(x_1) = h(x_2)$. h is *strongly collision-resistant* if it is infeasible to find two different inputs x_1, x_2 such that $h(x_1) = h(x_2)$ (cf. [MeOV96, Stin95]).

Since the property of a strongly collision-resistant hash function holds for variable different inputs, it also covers the special case, when one input is constant. Thus, if h is strongly collision-resistant, h is also weakly collision-resistant.

When talking about hash functions, the one-way property is often of interest. The following proposition elucidates a relationship between strongly collision-resistant hash functions and one-way functions: if h is strongly collision-resistant, it is also a one-way function (for a proof see [Stin95]). In the sequel hash functions are referred to as strongly collision-resistant hash functions, unless declared differently.

2.4.2 Iterative Design

In general keyed hash functions compute hash values from messages by applying a secret key. Predominant hash functions like SHA1 [EaJo01], MD5 [Rive92], and RIPEMD-160 [DoBP96] proceed the input block by block. These algorithms expand an input m (by padding) such that the result can be divided into a sequence of n blocks $m_1, \ldots, m_n$, where each block $m_i \in \{0,1\}^\ell$ has a fixed length ℓ. In each hash-iteration only one input block is processed. Let $h : \{0,1\}^* \to \{0,1\}^c$ be a hash function (note that for some hash functions like SHA-1 the length of the input size is restricted) and let $H : \{0,1\}^c \times \{0,1\}^\ell \to \{0,1\}^c$ be the internal compression function that is applied on each input block m_i. The hash value produced in the i-th iteration only depends on the i-th input block and the hash value from the previous iteration: $h_i = H(h_{i-1}, m_i)$. The starting hash value h_0 used in the first round is defined by some constants (initial vector IV). Figure 2.2 illustrates the main building blocks, which are used in iterated hash functions. The iterative construction concept is known as *Merkle-Damgård construction* [Merk89, Damg89]. Damgård showed that if the applied compression function is collision-resistant, then the hash function based on this construction is also collision-resistant [Damg89].

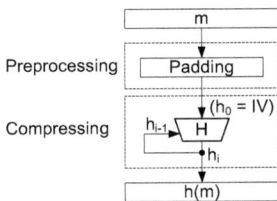

Fig. 2.2: Main components of an iterated hash function

2.4.3 Keyed Hash Functions

Let k be a secret key. Assuming that an iterative hash function is used, designing a keyed hash function as $h(k \,||\, m)$, which is called *secret prefix method* [Tsud92], is not a very good strategy: due to the iteration functionality, a length extension attack [Tsud92, FeSc03] is possible. Without knowing k, from $h(k \,||\, m)$ further keyed hash values can be produced, simply by extending m. Iterative hash functions compute $H(\ldots H(H(H(IV, m_1), m_2), m_3) \ldots, m_n)$ on input $k \,||\, m$, whereas

$m_1 \,||\, m_2 \,||\, \ldots \,||\, m_n$ is the output of the preprocessing unit. Let ext be an arbitrary bit sequence. If the bit length of $k \,||\, m$ is adequate, i.e. for $h(k \,||\, m)$ no padding is necessary, then $h(h(k \,||\, m) \,||\, ext)$ is also a valid keyed hash value for the extended message $m \,||\, ext$. Even if the input $k \,||\, m$ has to be filled up with some padding bits, computing other valid keyed hash values is possible, because the padding bits can be filled up "manually", i.e. the message m is appended according to the specified padding scheme. Thus, for any $h(k \,||\, m)$ an arbitrary bit sequence ext can be appended to m yielding to a valid keyed hash value.

Replacing the arguments and designing a keyed hash function as $h(m \,||\, k)$ seems to be a more secure approach. This variant is referred to as *secret suffix method*. However, Tsudik [Tsud92] describes an attack based on the birthday paradox. In particular an attacker pre-computes a sufficient amount of samples such that the chance for producing a collision for a MAC based on the suffix method is significantly high. For two different messages m and $\widetilde{m}$, if $h(m) = h(\widetilde{m})$ holds then $h(m \,||\, k) = h(\widetilde{m} \,||\, k)$ is true, provided that an iterative hash function h is used and the bit length of the messages are multiples of the input size of the internal compression function.

To counteract both attacks, Tsudik suggests a hybrid variant called *envelope method* where the message is enveloped between two keys k_1, k_2: $h(k_1 \,||\, m \,||\, k_2)$. The internet standard RFC 1828 [MeSi95] specifies an implementation of this method as $\text{MD5}(k \,||\, p \,||\, m \,||\, k)$, where k is a secret key of variable bit length and p denotes some padding bits for fulfilling the next 512-bit block according to the MD5 algorithm. In [PrOo95] Preneel and van Oorschot discuss these constructions in detail. They notice some vulnerabilities of the envelope method. In a subsequent paper [PrOo96] they show how to exploit a key recovery attack.

Some variants concerning the application of a hash function within a hash function are suggested in [KaRo95]. The Nested MAC (*NMAC*) uses two keys k_1 and k_2. It is defined as follows (cf. [BeCK96]):

$$\text{NMAC}_{k_1,k_2}(m) = h_{k_1}(h_{k_2}(m))$$

In [BeCK96] a variant of NMAC called *HMAC* (the Hash based MAC) is described. HMAC is standardized as RFC 2104 [KrBC97]. It uses a nested hash function, two constants $opad = (01011100)^{\ell/8}$ and $ipad = (00110110)^{\ell/8}$, here expressed as binary strings, with ℓ as the bit size of the used key k. HMAC is defined as:

$$\text{HMAC}_k(m) = h((k \oplus opad) \,||\, h((k \oplus ipad) \,||\, m))$$

2.4 Cryptographic Mechanisms

HMAC is shown to be a pseudo-random function as long as the compression function is a pseudo-random function [Bell06]. Recently Kim et al. [KBPH06] showed how HMAC based on MD5, SHA-1, and others can be distinguished from an HMAC with a random function exploiting a forgery attack. The authors emphasize in the conclusion of their paper, "All these attacks do not contradict the security proof of HMAC, but they improve our understanding of the security of HMAC based on existing cryptographic hash functions." [KBPH06]

3. DRM and Video Protection

> *Good people do not need laws to tell them to act responsibly, while bad people will find a way around the laws.*
>
> PLATO

Digital Rights Management (DRM) has been causing a great deal of controversial discussions. Incited by some very restrictive DRM systems, heated debates occurred between supporters and detractors. Nowadays, DRM is strongly involved with mechanisms to protect copyrights. A primary goal is to grant certain rights like reading, playing, viewing, printing etc. to some digital data under certain conditions, e.g. by a financial transaction. To overcome the complexity of rights and conditions, appropriate languages like XrML [xrm] (cf. Appendix A) and ODRL have been developed. However, formalizing and assuring rights in practice are completely different things. The latter is by far the harder part. For example how can a system assure that a specific audio file can be played only three times by a system user? The defined rights have to be evaluated by some DRM components, which then allow or do not allow certain rights. For a seamless rights enforcement, tamper-proof hardware and trusted software components need to be installed. Generally, if someone succeeds in attacking or circumventing such a component, the contents behind that rights enforcement logic can be accessed in an unrestricted manner. The past has showed us many examples where DRM mechanisms have been undermined.

For digital data, producing copies that cannot be distinguished from the original is a trivial task. The ease of making perfect copies has become a main problem in the DRM industry. Additionally, the internet has evolved as a distribution platform where data can be exchanged at almost no charge. Several file exchange platforms have been emerging whose services facilitate users to share movies, music, software, and other digital data, which may violate copyright issues. Lessons learnt from the server-based file-sharing platform *Morpheus*, today's initiatives (like BitTorrent, Shareaza, eMule, Azureus, Limewire, eDonkey, etc.) are usually peer-to-peer platforms, i.e. the storage of illegal goods is shifted to their users. Recent platforms offer mechanisms to protect the anonymity of users and contents.

3.1 DRM Model

Rosenblatt [RoTM01, RoDy03] contributes a general DRM model, which is widely used. For instance, the Windows Media Player utilizes a related DRM concept.

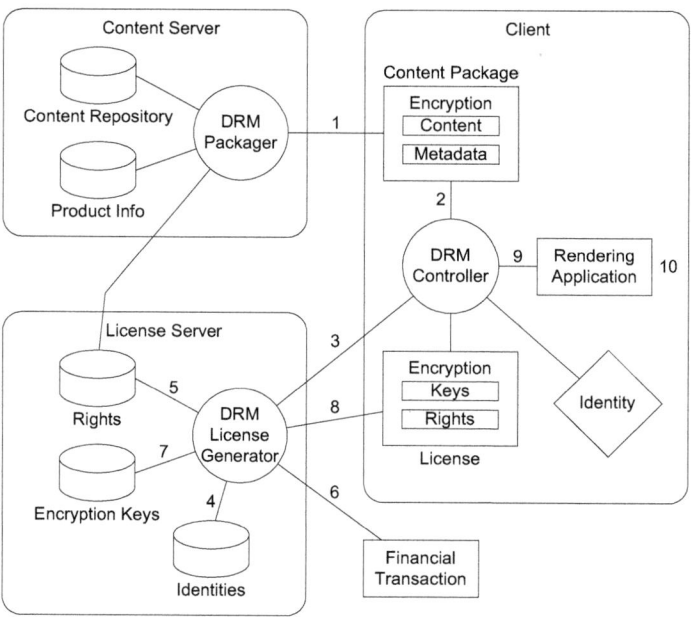

Fig. 3.1: DRM model

Referring to Figure 3.1, there are three participating instances: the client, the content server and the license server. The model assumes that the client is equipped with an appropriate software that can interact with the license server. Initially encrypted contents are offered by the content server for download. When the client downloads encrypted contents and requests for decryption, the content server transmits the corresponding license information to the client. The client's DRM controller evaluates the license and, together with the content request, the user identity is sent to the license server. The license server locks up in its data repositories in order to get information about the user and his or her assigned rights. Then, the license server formulates the conditions for the license, which are generally characterized by the price of the license. After fulfilling the conditions, the license server encrypts the decryption key with the key of the client. The license server generates the license, which consists of the encrypted decryption key, and transmits it to the client. The client decrypts the encrypted components so that the decryption key is revealed, which empowers to decrypt the encrypted content.

3.2 Lightweight DRM

The lightweight digital rights management system, developed at the Fraunhofer institute (cf. [GrAi04]), is an alternative to strict DRM systems and follows the fair use principle. This means that media files can only be distributed when users sign their contents. Thus, it provides a mechanism to trace back the origin of a media dissemination; a copy protection is not supported. Legal consequences are up to the content providers. For a realization of this concept, they use watermarks (cf. [Ditt00, CoDF06, NaDW00]) and hybrid cryptosystems, i.e. RSA for creating and verifying signatures and the AES for content encryption. To make distributors traceable, users have to register at the trust center and henceforth they get a certificate with an identifier. Furthermore, a special software component (LW-DRM client) needs to be installed at the client side. Basically LWDRM offers two file formats: the local media file (LMF) and the signed media file (SMF).

Formats: To create a local media format, the media is encrypted by a randomly generated AES session key. The session key is signed by the private key of the target system (the RSA key pair is derived from hardware parameters). Hence, the LMF binds a media file to an end-user device. Additionally, watermark information is embedded in the file. The left picture in Figure 3.2 shows the creation of a local media file.

To release the local binding and distribute the media content, a user has to sign the media file. First the encrypted session key, which is embedded in the local media format, is decrypted with the private key of the device. After that the session key is encrypted with the private key of the user (not of the device) without hashing it before, which is referred as *signcrypt*. This replaces the local binding by the binding to its user (see right picture of Figure 3.2). Another approach from the Fraunhofer institute is called *Potato System* [NüGr03], which is a selling system. Its intention is to attract users to resell contents by offering percentages.

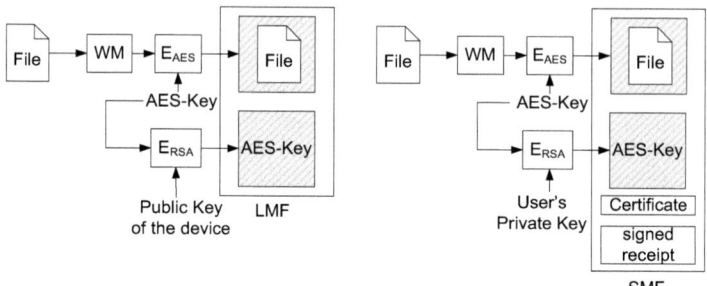

Fig. 3.2: Local Media Format(LMF) and the Signed Media Format (SMF)

3.3 Tracing Traitors

Boneh and Shaw [BoSh95] investigate collusion attacks on uniquely marked data. Anderson and Manifavas [AnMa97] contribute an approach, which marks contents individually during the decryption process. In case of an illicit content distribution, this allows to determine the originator of the distribution. It turns any stream cipher algorithm into an encryption scheme. Thereby, the decryption of a ciphertext with a slightly different key causes a marginal change in the resulting plaintext. With this method individual bits are inserted into retrieved contents during the decryption process. This in turn makes it possible to trace legitimate users who distribute contents without permission.

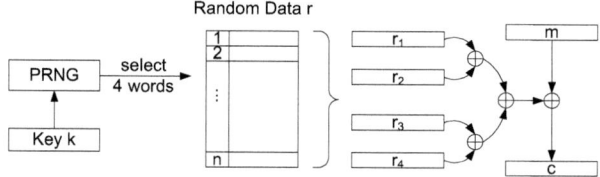

Fig. 3.3: Encryption process of Chameleon

The scheme uses a secret key k for the pseudo-random number generator (see Figure 3.3). Hereby r denotes a huge random data block. Each subscriber gets an individually marked version of r such that any two subscribers uniquely have a marked bit in common. If two subscribers collude, they can find out all but one marked bit that would identify them as illegitimate distributors.

3.4 Content Scrambling System

The content scrambling system (CSS) was developed by Matsushita and Toshiba in the mid 90ies and was anchored in the DVD specification. CSS is a proprietary 40-bit stream cipher that is completely broken today. The hardware components with their keys are listed in Figure 3.4.

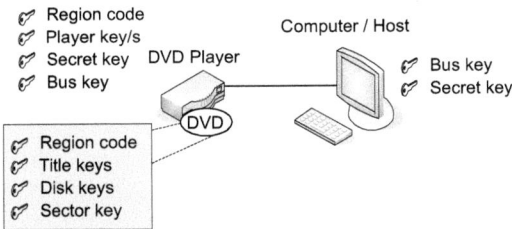

Fig. 3.4: Content scrambling system

To assure that DVD contents can be viewed by legitimate players in intended regions only, the DVD specification defines a bundle of symmetric keys. In particular the following key types are utilized:

Player key: The DVD Copy Control Association has produced a total number of 409 player keys. Only licensed manufacturers are supplied with such keys, which are stored in licensed players. The player keys are used to encrypt the disk keys.

Disk key: Disk keys are used to encrypt the title keys. To verify the support of disk keys, the hash values of the disk keys are stored in the disk.

Title key: Each title on a DVD is encrypted with a title key. The title keys are encrypted with the player key and stored in the DVD. To disable several DVD players to play future DVDs, the title keys are not encrypted with any of the revoked player keys.

Sector key: Each sector is encrypted with a sector key. This key is encrypted with the corresponding title key and is stored in the section header.

Secret key: The secret key is used for mutual authentication between a DVD player and a host. It is further used for negotiation of the bus key (see below).

Bus key: This key is generated during the initial authentication process between a DVD player and a host. Before title and disk keys are sent to the host, they are encrypted with this key.

Region code: The region code should restrict DVD contents to intended regions. Dependent on the region, film debuts are generally delayed. Transferring DVDs from one region to another would undermine the impact of delayed film debuts in other regions. Hence, DVDs are labelled with the region code to which they are intended. The region code enables a DVD player to detect DVDs, which are not allowed to be played in a certain region.

Due to US export restrictions, the key length for CSS was specified for 40 bits only. Additionally, CSS has a weak design, so that the effort for a possible brute force attack on the key length can be diminished. On October 1999 all player keys were published. The CSS is considered to be completely broken today.

The *Content Protection for Prerecorded Media* (CPPM) standard was devised that uses the so-called *C*2 cipher, which is used for DVD-Audio devices [AdGr05]. However, it is restricted to 56-bit keys, which is nowadays insufficient to withstand a brute force attack. Today tools are developed, which undermine the protection mechanism of CPPM [News05, enga05].

3.5 Digital Video Broadcasting

Digital Video Broadcast (DVB) is a broadcasting standard for digital contents. Actually there exist several types of transmissions:

Tab. 3.1: Classifications of DVB

DVB-S:	Transmission by satellites	DVB-C:	Cable transmission
DVB-T:	Terrestrial transmission	DVB-H:	Handhelds
DVB-IPI:	IP infrastructure	DVB-RC:	Return Channel
DVB-SI:	Service Information		

3.5 Digital Video Broadcasting

On October 2007, DVB-T started transmitting videos in Austria [DVB08, DRF08]. There, 85 per cent of digital television used satellite broadcasts, eleven per cent utilized DVB-C connections, and four per cent made use of DVB-T [news] transmissions. Digital TV allows to transmit several programs on a single channel by using a technique called *multiplexing*. The multiplexed data streams are called *bouquets*. Actually, there are two DVB-T bouquets, namely *MUX A* and *MUX B*. MUX A, which is transmitted nationwide, covers the programs *ORF 1*, *ORF 2*, and *ATV*. Additionally the multimedia home platform (*mhp*) *ORF OK MultiText* is offered by MUX A. Since October 2007 MUX B is broadcasted, which consists of PULS 4, ORF SPORT PLUS, and 3sat. At the time of writing, the programs of MUX B can only be received in regional capitals. According to [DVB08] the data rate for each bouquet is given by 14.93 Mbit/s at 8 MHz bandwidth.

In Europe pay TV channels, which are transmitted by DVB systems, are encrypted with the *Common Scrambling Algorithm* (CSA). This algorithm was specified by the ETSI for encrypting MPEG-2 videos and it was appropriated by the DVB consortium in 1994. The CSA is a combination of a block cipher and a stream cipher, where the stream cipher is built upon two linear feedback registers and the block cipher expands a 64-bit key to convert a 64-bit plaintext into a 64-bit ciphertext. Usually the encryption keys change every 5 to 10 seconds. The CSA was kept secretly for several years and was only implemented in hardware. Licensees have to sign a non-disclosure agreement. However, details on the algorithm appeared in the internet; the algorithm was reverse-engineered and was published.

The *Conditional Access System* (CAS) is the interface between the transmitted data stream and the users' set top box. Its main task is to supply the decryption component with the right Control Word (CW), which is 8 bytes long. To run the services on the set top box, the user needs an adequate smart card. Widely used CAS providers like irdeto or Nagravision offer so-called *Conditional Access Modules*, which are connected with the *Common Interface* (CI) at the receiver. One reason for the modular architecture is that components could easily be exchanged while others would remain uninvolved. Consider the case when a weak CAS is replaced by an improved one (e.g. due to security reasons). Then, it is not necessary to upgrade the users' receivers.

Smart cards are inserted into the CAM. They decrypt the encrypted CW, which, subsequently, is passed as plaintext to the decoder. The CW enables the decoder to decrypt received ciphertexts by using the CSA. It should be noted that the transmitted data could be encrypted more than once, which is called *Simulcrypt*.

The CSA was kept secretly and was prohibited to be implemented in software. However, in 2002 a program called *FreeDec* was distributed that implemented the CSA, which was reverse-engineered and published afterwards. The encryption algorithm combines a block cipher with a stream cipher both sharing the same 64-bit key called common key. The following description of the CSA is based on [WeWi04]. In [Wirt05] an attack is presented that breaks the whole algorithm.

3.5.1 Encryption

As shown in Figure 3.5, the encryption consists of a block cipher and a stream cipher. First the plaintext is divided into blocks DB_i of 8 bytes each. If the last block is less than 8 bytes long, the block cipher for that block is bypassed. Such a block is referred to as residue R. Except the residue, the blocks are encrypted by the block cipher in CBC mode, but in reverse order.

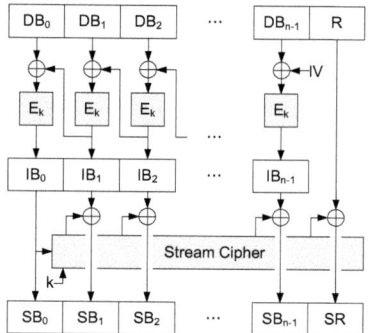

Fig. 3.5: Encryption process of the Common Scrambling Algorithm

Block Cipher: The block cipher takes a 64-bit block from the plaintext together with a single byte from the expanded common key k' to produce a 64-bit cipherblock. The bits of the expanded key k' are given by: $k'_{0,...,63} = k_{0,...,63}$, and $k'_{64i,...,64i+63} = \pi(k'_{64(i-1),...,64i-1}) \oplus \text{0x0i0i0i0i0i0i0i0i}$ with $1 \leq i \leq 6$. Thus, the expanded key has a bit length of 448. The permutation π is listed below.

In each round, the same transformation function ϕ is used. It processes a 64-bit input with a single byte from the expanded key k'. The round transformation is executed 56 times. Let $S = (s_0, \ldots s_7)$ be the state vector that represents the

3.5 Digital Video Broadcasting

Tab. 3.2: Permutation table

i	0	1	2	3	4	5	6	7	8	9	10	11	12	13	14	15
$\pi(i)$	17	35	8	6	41	48	28	20	27	53	61	49	18	32	58	63
i	16	17	18	19	20	21	22	23	24	25	26	27	28	29	30	31
$\pi(i)$	23	19	36	38	1	52	26	0	33	3	12	13	56	39	25	40
i	32	33	34	35	36	37	38	39	40	41	42	43	44	45	46	47
$\pi(i)$	50	34	51	11	21	47	29	57	44	30	7	24	22	46	60	16
i	48	49	50	51	52	53	54	55	56	57	58	59	60	61	62	63
$\pi(i)$	59	4	55	42	10	5	9	43	31	62	45	14	2	37	15	54

internal state of the block cipher for a round. Then the round transformation ϕ that processes S with the corresponding byte k_{r-1} of the expanded key k' for a round r is given by $\phi(s_0, \ldots, s_7, k_{r-1}) = (s_1, s_2 \oplus s_0, s_3 \oplus s_0, s_4 \oplus s_0, s_5, s_6 \oplus P'(k_{r-1} \oplus s_7), s_7, s_0 \oplus P(k_{r-1} \oplus s_7))$ whereas the functions P and P' are two non-linear permutations implemented as S-Boxes.

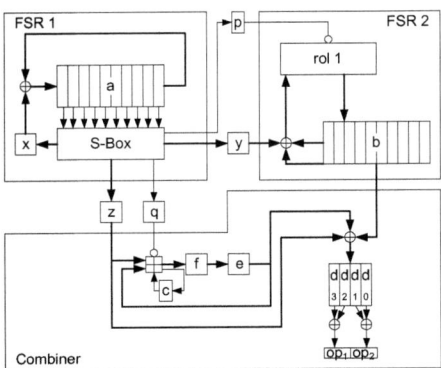

Fig. 3.6: Stream Cipher of the Common Scrambling Algorithm

The state in round r with S_0 as the current 64-bit plaintext block and S_{56} as the output of the block cipher is given by

$$S_r = \phi(S_{r-1}, (k'_{8r-8}, \ldots, k'_{8r-1})) \text{ with } 1 \leq r \leq 56$$

Stream cipher: The stream cipher uses two feedback shift registers and a component that combines the output of both (see Figure 3.6). Per clock cycle two pseudo-random bits are generated. The stream cipher is initialized with the common key k and the nonce IB_0, which is the last output of the block cipher (see Figure 3.5). The registers p, q, and c are registers that can only store a single bit. All other registers cover four bits each. Hereby, $\oplus$ is the *xor* operation and $\boxplus$ denotes the addition modulo 2^4.

3.5.2 Decryption

The decryption process is illustrated in Figure 3.7. For the decryption S_{56} gets initialized with the current cipher block whereas S_0 is the resulting plaintext. The decryption state in round r is calculated by $S_r = \phi^{-1}(S_{r+1}, (k'_{8r}, \ldots, k'_{8r+7}))$ starting at round $r = 55$ and decrementing down to 0. Hereby the inverse function is calculated by: $\phi^{-1}(s_0, \ldots, s_7, k_{r-1}) = (s_7 \oplus P(s_6 \oplus k_{r-1}), s_0, s_7 \oplus s_1 \oplus P(s_6 \oplus k_{r-1}), s_7 \oplus s_2 \oplus P(s_6, k_{r-1}), s_7 \oplus s_3 \oplus P(s_6 \oplus k_{r-1}), s_4, s_5 \oplus P'(s_6 \oplus k_{r-1}), s_6)$.

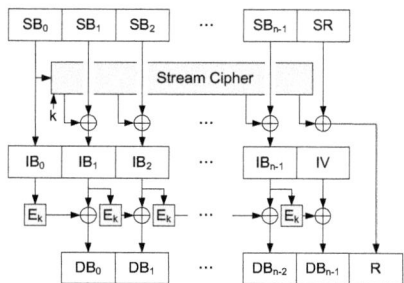

Fig. 3.7: Decryption process of the Common Scrambling Algorithm

3.6 MPEG Video Encryption

In some business models the running time of standardized en-/decryption schemes is considered to be unacceptable. Consider video streaming, where the decryption is performed on low powered resources. Therefore, alternatives need to be devised that might lower one's sight in security aspects. In literature [UhPo05] *Soft encryption* and *Selective encryption* are terms that aim at a trade-off between

3.6 MPEG Video Encryption

speed and security. Generally selective encryption encompasses techniques for encrypting only some parts. Soft encryption embodies encryption mechanisms whose produced ciphertexts are usually breakable, provided that enough efforts are mobilized. However, in some cases contents lose their attraction already after a short period of time: for instance daily news have a short-lived value. If an attack takes too much time, the reconstructed plaintexts might already be worthless. For example, to break the encipherment of encrypted daily news, a day's effort might be unacceptable. In such cases, attackers might lack motivation for breaking ciphertexts that are encrypted by weak encryption mechanisms.

Many research in literature focuses on the integration of encryption techniques in the underlying coding algorithms. To understand the basic concepts of those approaches some knowledge about the applied algorithms is required. The predominant video codec today is MPEG-2, which is expected to be replaced by the H.264 (also called MPEG-4 AVC). Although MPEG-2 and H.264 are based on similar concepts, essential improvements are achieved by the latter one, which outperforms the MPEG-2 standard: according to [Kalv06], H.264 achieves a comparable quality level at one-half to one-third of the MPEG-2 bitrate.

MPEG video coding: In principle MPEG videos consist of a sequence of so-called I-frames, P-frames, and B-frames, whereas I-frames represent pictures that are compressed in a similar way as it is prescribed by the JPEG standard. The remaining frames are predicted from I-frames, either unidirectionally (P) or bidirectionally (B). H.264 defines two further types called switching-I and switching-P, which are used for streaming applications. Both standards divide the I-frames into blocks, i.e. 8×8 pixels in MPEG-2 and 8×8 or 4×4 in H.264. MPEG-2 deploys the so-called Discrete Cosine Transform (DCT) to their blocks where the resulting data is quantized. Instead of DCT, H.264 uses the more efficient integer transform. In general, these quantization processes lead to lossy compressions. The quantized coefficients are scanned in a zigzag manner and compressed afterwards.

Encryption techniques: Early encryption proposals on MPEG videos describe mechanisms to encrypt the quantized DCT coefficients. The presented techniques range from simple permutations to encryptions of components like headers, sign bits, codewords used by the compression algorithm and others. Further strategies investigate the encryption of I-frames and motion vectors. The SEC-MPEG [Stei00] specification evolved inspired from these ideas. This initiative describes five security levels that capture some of the mentioned ideas (cf. [UhPo05]). Other approaches investigate the encryption of components in the color coding. Similar to JPEG, MPEG encodes the colors in their pictures according to the YCbCr model. Some approaches encrypt the luminance and chrominance components of the encoded pictures.

Another interesting research topic deals with the encryption of scalable bitstreams where data is divided into layers. While the base layers contain pictures at a low quality, the upper layers cover information for quality increases. Three scalability types are already supported by the MPEG-2 and MPEG-4 standards:

- SNR scalability: the base layer consists of strongly quantized pictures at the highest possible resolution. Further layers reveal differences between DCT coefficients leading to less quantized versions.

- Resolution scalability: the base layer covers pictures at a low resolution, while the enhanced layers describe differences between the resolutions.

- Temporal scalability: videos with low frame rates are stored in the base layer. Missing frames are captured by further layers.

Two encryption strategies arise in this context: either encryption of the base layer or encrypting the extended layers. Encrypting the extended layers leads to the basic idea of the *Transparent Encryption*.

It should be noted that key management issues were often completely neglected. The next chapter will summarize the significant research on this topic.

3.7 McCormac Hack

In the pay TV example, problems arise when the data, which is sent from the smart card to the decoder box, is tapped. Usually sensitive data like the Control Word (CW) that enables to decrypt the scrambled data is transmitted. The interception and distribution of this information is known as the McCormac Hack [McCo98]. Hereby a single smart card serves multiple decoders. The internet offers an easy and cheap way to carry out this attack. For a simple countermeasure, decoder boxes and smart cards are pairwise accommodated (cf. [KaAm01]): each pair shares a different common secret and thus the set-top box (STB) and the smart card can communicate securely with each other. Trivially this approach withstands a McCormac attack. A similar concept called *smart card marriage* is offered by Irdeto [ird], where smart cards are locked to individual STBs.

3.8 Outlook

Many currently used DRM systems only offer solutions for closed systems. The Coral Consortium is a platform that concentrate on an interoperability framework with the goal that any source can be used on any device independently from the DRM technology of the device. It can be expected that a standardized framework will help to reduce the complexity for DRM developers and it maybe evolve into a key component so that DRM systems will be more accepted by the users.

Actually one can observe a trend to support end-to-end security. In this context the Secure Video Processor (SVP) [svp] is an emerging initiative that supports persistent content encryption until rendering. It uses local scrambling in order to make a distribution of ciphertexts to other devices worthless. End-to-end security is ensured by the integration of personalized secure SVP-compliant media chips, which ensure that keys and compressed contents never appear outside the secure chips. The output device decrypts the ciphertexts and renders the resulting data for the output. The SVP concept also supports revocation techniques that uses certificates whereby the SVP Licensing Authority distributes the certificate revocation list (CRL).

Similar to SVP, High-bandwidth Digital Content Protection (HDCP) is intended to provide end-to-end security until rendering. This technique is integrated in nearly every new output device that uses the High Definition Multimedia Interface (HDMI). In the European Union television receivers that are classified as *HD-ready* have to support HDCP by law.

Key Management Schemes 4

> *Make everything as simple as possible, but not simpler.*
>
> ALBERT EINSTEIN

The access control problem deals with the regulation of access to information for users in different security classes. Generally, security classes are hierarchically structured and can be formalized as partially ordered sets (posets). In practice, there are many examples where people, entities, and information are classified into hierarchically structured security classes. For instance file systems, computer networks, business organizations, military units, and sections in the government are hierarchically structured. In the context of health, salary, and business processes mechanisms are needed that regulate access to read sensitive data. Restricting access to publicly accessible data requires preventive measurements. In the following section, encryption is used as a means of preventive access regulation.

In literature, many techniques and mechanisms are proposed to solve the hierarchical access control problem. However, they are often suited for different requirements. Many of them are based on cryptographic mechanisms. Using encryption mechanisms can help to prevent unauthorized access to publicly accessible data. Suppose that a key is assigned to each security class with which the associated data is encrypted. Then, only those who have appropriate keys (users in corresponding security classes) can decrypt the ciphertexts and henceforth can read the data. When it is required that access should also be granted to descendant classes, relevant users need to be supplied with the keys of these classes. This is also the case when new security classes are to be inserted. With an increase of security classes, the key management problem, in particular to store, retrieve, and protect secret keys, arises. To cope with countless keys, the design of a key management scheme should be carefully elaborated in advance.

4.1 Contribution and Structure

This section presents the significant research on key assignment schemes in literature. The works are described in a continuously uniform way based on graph notation, where some of them are summarized in a more compact manner (e.g. Chen, Chung and Tian's Scheme). The schemes are shown to fulfill the completeness and soundness property (note that in some publications this is disregarded), where it is possible: for example the time-bound schemes are shown to fail against some attacks. On some issues, examples are given in more detail than they are outlined in their publications. For instance, Crampton, Martin, and Wild's improvements of the Akl-Taylor's scheme are discussed in more detail, effects on insertions in Sandhu's scheme are illustrated in a deeper matter, an algorithm for adding shortcuts for posets is shown. The main contribution of this work is a detailed comparison of the schemes in terms of complexity aspects concerning the key derivation and the public data storage as well as effects when keys are updated.

The following key management schemes are based on the idea that granting access to an element can be implemented by encrypting the data with a key and delivering authorized users with that key. Thereby several key derivation strategies are discussed. We investigate the schemes with respect to the completeness and soundness properties and examine the consequences of structural changes in the hierarchies.

The partially ordered sets are illustrated as Hasse diagrams where security classes are represented as nodes in a directed graph. In the sequel the terms *security class* and *nodes* are used synonymously.

This section is organized as follows: first an introduction of the access control problem in hierarchies and a classification of some attacks, which secure schemes have to withstand, are given. Next, the section presents traditional schemes and shows extended approaches afterwards that take time-bound keys into consideration. Finally, a comparison of the schemes concludes this section.

4.2 Problem Definition

Users and their data are divided into disjoint sets $C_1, C_2, \ldots, C_n$, called security classes. Let $C = \{C_1, C_2, \ldots, C_n\}$, then $(C, \leq)$ defines a binary partially-ordered relation. $C_j \leq C_i$ means that users in the security class C_i have a security clearance higher or equal to those in C_j, i.e. users in the class C_i can access data assigned to class C_j, but not vice versa. For $C_j \leq C_i$, C_i is an ancestor of C_j and, respectively, C_j is a descendant security class of C_i. If C_i is a parent node of C_j then C_i is called predecessor of C_j and C_j is a successor of C_i.

The functions *Anc*, *Par* and *Chd* are already defined in Chapter 2. Here some extended graph functions are specified using the definition from prior sections.

$\kappa : V \to K$ denotes the key allocation function, which maps a node to a key from key space K.

Let $C_i \in C$, then id_i denotes the publicly known name of the security class C_i. For all distinct nodes C_i, C_j, if $Par(C_i) = Par(C_j)$ then $id_i \neq id_j$. This means that only sibling nodes, which have the same parent node, must have distinct names. Nodes with different parent nodes may have same names.

The following definitions are based on the work of Atallah et al. [AtFB05]. Let $V = \{v_1, \ldots, v_n\}$ be the set of vertices (nodes), each of which representing a security class in the hierarchy. The set of edges is given by $E = \{e_1, \ldots, e_m\}$. Then $G = (V, E)$ denotes a directed access graph.

Generally the key of a node v_i empowers to access the objects that are covered by $DoS(v_i)$. Keys to subsequent nodes can be computed efficiently, provided that the corresponding key is known.

For $k_1, k_2 \in K$ we write $k_1 \stackrel{G}{\Rightarrow} k_2$, iff there exists a polynomial-time algorithm A such that $A(k_1) = k_2$. For the other case we write $k_1 \stackrel{G}{\not\Rightarrow} k_2$.

Definition 4.1: κ implements an access graph $G = (V, E)$ iff the following conditions are fulfilled:

1. *Completeness*: if v_j is reachable from v_i in G then $\kappa(v_i) \stackrel{G}{\Rightarrow} \kappa(v_j)$.

2. *Soundness*: if v_j is not reachable from v_i in G then $\kappa(v_i) \stackrel{G}{\not\Rightarrow} \kappa(v_j)$.

κ, implementing a non-empty access graph $G = (V, E)$, is *collusion-resilient*, if and only if for any $v_i \in V$ and any set of adversaries, which together have access to the nodes in $V' \subset V$ with $V' \cap AoS(v_i) = \emptyset$, it is infeasible to compute $\kappa(v_i)$.

4.3 Attacks

The security of modern cryptosystems is based on Kerckhoffs' principle [Kerc83], i.e. the security of a cryptosystem solely depends on keeping the keys secret. It is assumed that the crypto-algorithm is publicly known. To formulate this in Shannon's words: the enemy knows the system (Shannon's maxim). Therefore, it is assumed that the used cryptographic mechanisms, including all public parameters, are known to an attacker. A key management scheme has to withstand each of the following attack types, otherwise it is considered to be insecure.

External Attack: For this type of attack an attacker does not have any secret keys at all. Given all publicly accessible ciphertexts and public parameters, the attacker tries to find the plaintexts of the given ciphertexts. This is equivalent to the ciphertext only attack.

Descendant's Attack: Suppose an attacker in class $C_j \in Des(C_i)$ having all publicly accessible ciphertexts, public parameters, and the secret key k_j, which is assigned to C_j. The attacker tries to find the plaintexts in the security class C_i.

Children's Attack: Suppose an attacker has more than one immediate successor key of a security class C_i. He or she tries to find the plaintexts of the ciphertexts in the security class C_i. This type of attack is stronger than the descendant's attack.

Sibling's Attack: Suppose to have more than one secret key each of which is assigned to a security class in $Chd(C_i)$. An attacker tries find the plaintexts of C_i.

Collaborative Descendants' Attack: Suppose to have a group of attackers, which have keys for different security classes, but which have no key of any security class in $AoS(C_i)$. The goal is to reveal plaintexts or secret keys of security classes in $AoS(C_i)$ by using all secret information from all attackers. This is the strongest attack classification. A key management scheme that withstands this attack is referred to be collusion-resilient.

4.4 Traditional Key Management Schemes

Since a description of all yet published key management schemes would go beyond the scope of this work, this section will present a selection of relevant key management schemes, addressing the access control problem in hierarchies. Undoubtedly, the one with the most impact was the first scheme of this type, which was published in 1983 by Akl and Taylor. Although their approach, which is based on number theory, is not very practical, it has become the classic and possibly best

4.4 Traditional Key Management Schemes

known scheme that is referenced by many subsequently developed schemes in this context. Sandhu contributes some solutions to this problem based on hash functions. A very flexible, and at the same time efficient (in terms of space complexity) solution is proposed by Atallah. Tzeng takes the time factor into consideration and suggests a time-bound key management scheme.

4.4.1 Akl and Taylor's Scheme

Akl and Taylor proposed at first a cryptographic solution for solving the hierarchical access control problem [AkTa83]. Therein, methods to derive keys for hierarchical structured security classes are suggested. The main idea is based on number theory that uses exponentiation in $\mathbb{Z}_n$ (where n is a RSA modulus) to derive subsequent keys. Hereby the public exponents are chosen such that direct and indirect key derivations for descendant nodes are possible.

Totally ordered sets: For a totally ordered set C with $C_n \leq C_{n-1} \leq \ldots \leq C_1$, the following key assignment scheme is proposed, that assigns the key k_i to security class C_i, using a publicly known one-way function f:

$$k_i = f(k_{i-1}), \quad \text{for } 2 \leq i \leq n$$

For the root class C_1 a random key k_1 is selected. Each key for a security class different from C_1 is generated from the key of its immediate predecessor class. The authors suggest using an encryption function (e.g. DES) as a one-way function (with trapdoor): $k_i = E_{k_{i-1}}(k_{i-1})$. To increase the effort for a brute force attack on the key significantly, the usage of two secret keys k_i and k_i' for each security class is discussed. For this purpose, the keys are generated as follows: $k_i = E_{k_{i-1}}(k_{i-1}')$, $k_i' = E_{k_{i-1}'}(k_{i-1})$.

Arbitrary partially ordered sets: To solve the hierarchical access control problem for an arbitrary poset, the authors give the following solution: assign a public integer t_i to each security class C_i, such that t_i divides all values assigned to its descendant security classes. This is performed by first assigning a distinct prime number p_i to each security class C_i. Then, t_i is calculated by:

$$t_i = \prod_{C_k \not\leq C_i} p_k \tag{4.1}$$

By convention, if $|\{p_k\,|\,C_k \not\leq C_i\}| = 0$, then $t_i = 1$. This is the case for a security class with no predecessors. It follows that t_j MOD $t_i = 0$ if and only if $C_j \leq C_i$. Starting with a randomly chosen k_0 as the secret key of the central authority, each further secret key k_i assigned to security class C_i is computed by a public one-way function f_t with t as an integer:

$$k_i = f_{t_i}(k_0)$$

For a practical realization of f_t, the following exponentiation in $\mathbb{Z}_n$ is suggested, where n is the product of two strong prime numbers of sufficient bit length:

$$k_i = k_0^{t_i} \text{ MOD } n$$

Figure 4.1 illustrates an example for the assignment of distinct primes (left Hasse diagram) with their public parameters (right Hasse diagram) to hierarchically ordered security classes. The nodes represent the security classes in the poset.

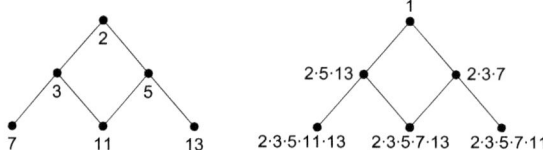

Fig. 4.1: Hierarchy of security classes with their public parameters

For example, if the security class C_i with the prime number 3 is taken, its public parameter consists of all prime factors p_k in each security class $C_k \notin DoS(C_i)$. These are the security classes with the assigned prime numbers 2, 5, and 13. Hence, $t_i = 2 \cdot 5 \cdot 13 = 130$.

Theorem 4.1: The key assignment scheme is complete.

Proof. Let $C_i, C_j \in C$ with $C_j \in Des(C_i)$. From the definition of the public parameters (Equation 4.1), it follows that all prime factors of t_i are also prime factors of t_j. Thus, t_i divides t_j and, therefore, the key k_j can be calculated in polynomial time: $k_j \equiv k_0^{t_j} \equiv k_0^{t_j \cdot t_i / t_i} \equiv (k_0^{t_i})^{t_j/t_i} \equiv k_i^{t_j/t_i} \pmod{n}$. This enables a key derivation from a key in a security class $C_i \in C$ to the key assigned to a security class $C_j \in Des(C_i)$. □

4.4 Traditional Key Management Schemes

Contrarily, if $C_j \not\subseteq C_i$ then, by the definition of the public parameter, $\frac{t_i}{t_j} \notin \mathbb{Z}$. In such case the computation of k_i from k_j is considered to be infeasible, provided that n cannot be factored. This leads to the following corollary:

Corollary 4.2: The key assignment scheme is sound.

Consider a group of users, each of which is assigned to a security class. Suppose these users collaborate in order to compute further keys, to which none of them has access.

Let $G \subset C$ be the union of all security classes the users are assigned to. We declare $G^* = \bigcup_{c \in G} DoS(c)$ and denote T as the set of the public parameters from each security class in G^*.

Lemma 4.3: A group of users who share a set of keys $K_G = \bigcup_{c \in G^*} \kappa(c)$ can feasibly compute a key $k_i \notin K_G$ iff $\gcd(T)$ divides t_i (for a proof cf. [AkTa83]).

Theorem 4.4: The key assignment scheme is collusion-resilient.

Proof. Suppose a group of collaborators, which shares T and the corresponding keys K_G, wants to compute k_i of a class C_i with $C_i \notin G^*$. Note that any class $C_j \in G^*$ has the property $C_j \not\supseteq C_i$. Since p_i is a factor of t_j for each class $C_j \not\supseteq C_i$, p_i divides $\gcd(T)$. From the definition of the public parameter (Equation 4.1) it follows that p_i does not divide t_i. Thus $\gcd(T)$ does not divide t_i. From the Lemma above it follows that computation of k_i from K_G is intractable. □

Evaluation: For m security classes, the public parameter t_i grows exponentially. The largest public parameter is bound by $O(m \cdot log(m)^m)$. To compute k_j from k_i, $O(log(t_j/t_i))$ operations, in particular squaring, multiplying, and reducing to $\mathbb{Z}_n$, are necessary. Since t_j/t_i is less than n, the computation that is necessary for a key derivation is bound by $O(log(n))$ multiplication operations modulo n.

Drawbacks: Since the size of t_i grows dramatically with an increasing number of classes, a huge storage space is necessary, making it less suitable for practical usage. Furthermore if a new security class C_j is inserted, every public parameter from the security classes $C - Anc(C_j)$ has to be updated. Because the public parameter of a security class is used to compute its secret key, this also leads to an update of the corresponding secret keys.

MacKinnon, Taylor, Meijer, and Akl's Improvements: In [MTMA85] methods are discussed for generating the smallest possible values of the public parameters. The main idea is to decompose the hierarchy into disjointed chains and assign a distinct prime to each chain, instead of to each security class. To produce the smallest possible values for the public parameters, they propose the following rules for selecting the primes:

1. If $C_j \not\leq C_i$ and $C_i \not\leq C_j$ then $p_i \neq p_j$
2. If $C_j \leq C_i$, $p_i = p_j$ where this does not conflict with rule 1
3. p_i is the smallest allowable prime.

Crampton, Martin, and Wild's Improvements: In [CrMW06] an efficient representation of the public parameters is proposed that simplifies the storage complexity and the calculation effort for the key derivation. In particular, an isomorphic representation for the public parameters t_i of class C_i is suggested. In case of a key derivation for k_j, this allows to reduce the division t_i/t_j for computing the exponent to a single XOR operation: $k_i^{\theta^{-1}(\theta(t_i) \oplus \theta(t_j))}$ MOD n. Here $\theta : P \to \{0,1\}^\ell$ denotes a function that maps a public parameter t_i (P is the finite set of all assigned prime numbers) to a bit sequence of length $\ell = |C|$, where the bit position s is 1, if the s-th least prime number, which is assigned to a security class, is a factor of t_i; otherwise it is 0. The factors of t_i are given by the following set: $\{p_j \in P \mid p_j$ is assigned to C_j and $C_j \in (C - DoS(C_i))\}$.

For example, referring to Figure 4.1, let C_i be the class with the prime 3 and let $t_i = 2 \cdot 5 \cdot 13$. Let C_j be the class with the prime 11 and $t_j = 2 \cdot 3 \cdot 5 \cdot 7 \cdot 13$. Then $\theta(t_i) = 101001$, because the first (2), the third (5), and the sixth (13) least prime numbers are factors of t_i. Analogously, we have $\theta(t_j) = 111101$. The result of the operation $\theta(t_i) \oplus \theta(t_j)$ is 010100, which corresponds to the primes 3 and 7. By multiplying the primes, we get 21 for the exponent, which is taken to compute $k_j = k_i^{21}$ MOD n.

Due to the fact that each class has a public parameter, which is represented by a bit sequence of length $\ell = |C|$, there are ℓ^2 bits necessary for storing the public parameters $t_1, \ldots, t_\ell$. The costs for the division, which is necessary in case of a key derivation, are replaced by the costs of an XOR operation, of an inverted mapping from the binary representation to its public parameters, and at most n multiplications, where n is the number of security classes.

4.4 Traditional Key Management Schemes

The authors also remark that the argument after which key updates are kept locally is misleading, because in case of a key update for class C_i, also each key $k_j \in Des(C_i)$ has to be updated. The reason for this is that normally a key update is performed after a key was compromised or a user was removed from a class. Since it has to be assumed that k_j was derived from k_i, k_j should also be considered to be compromised.

Furthermore they notice that in order to change all keys in $DoS(C_i)$, it is sufficient to change a single prime for an arbitrary class $C_k \in (C - DoS(C_i))$. But this affects not only the keys in $DoS(C_i)$: since $t_i = \prod_{C_k \in (C-DoS(C_i))} p_k$ MOD n, generally this causes a key change of all classes in $(C - AoS(C_k))$.

Remarks: Sandhu [Sand87] describes approaches based on one-way functions and sealed keys (see Section 4.4.2). In [ZhHS93] the authors investigate one-way functions and, therein, distinguish between direct derivation from the root node and indirect derivation from parent nodes. Recent approaches in that context particularly address the flexibility to change user keys, while trying to keep the cost for maintenance low [CLTW04, ChCT04, Zhon02].

4.4.2 Sandhu's Scheme

In [Sand87] Sandhu elaborates a key management scheme, where hierarchies are organized as trees with the most privileged security class at the root. Hereby two variants are proposed, one with one-way functions and another one based on sealed keys.

One-way functions: For the key derivation, a publicly known one-way function (eventually with trapdoor) f_k is selected. The following steps are performed:

1. Assign a randomly chosen key k_0 for the security class at the root node.

2. For each $C_j \in Chd(C_i)$, the key k_j of class C_j is computed by:

$$k_j = f_{k_i}(id_j)$$

With this derivation scheme, all keys in a tree can be computed. For a practical realization of $f_{k_i}(id_j)$, an encryption function $E_{k_i}(id_j)$ is proposed.

Theorem 4.5: The key assignment scheme is complete.

Proof. Let $C_i, C_j \in C$ with $C_j \in Des(C_i)$. Given the secret key k_i assigned to C_i, the secret key k_j assigned to C_j can be computed in polynomial time. Since the partially ordered set $(C, \leq)$ is a tree, there exists a path p from C_i to C_j in $(C, \leq)$. Proceeding the path top down (from parent to child node), k_j can be calculated in $|p|$ derivation steps. □

Theorem 4.6: The key assignment scheme is sound.

Proof. Let $C_i, C_j \in C$ with $C_j \in Des(C_i)$. Because an inversion of a one-way functions is practically infeasible, from k_j it is intractable to compute k_i. □

A disadvantage of this variant is that, if a new security class C_i is inserted, all keys in $Des(C_i)$ have to be updated. Figure 4.2 shows the tree before (left tree) and after (right tree) an insertion of a new security class.

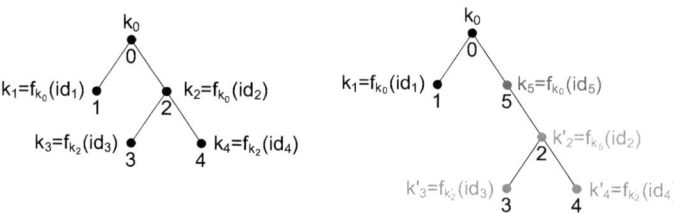

Fig. 4.2: Effects when a new node is inserted

Hereby the inserted node (node 5) causes updates in the subtree rooted at the inserted node (affected nodes: 2, 3 and 4). Also, if a security class C_i is removed, all keys assigned to $Des(C_i)$ has to be updated. This means that all users in the corresponding security classes need to refresh their keys. An advantage of this variant is that no further keys (like sealed keys described below) must be stored.

Sealed keys: For each security class C_i, select a distinct random number k_i. Let C_i, C_j be two elements from C with C_i as the parent from C_j. Then, the sealed key of C_j is computed by $E_{k_i}(k_j)$ and stored at node C_j. Note that the root node has no sealed key. The possession of a secret key of a security class enables to decrypt the sealed keys belonging to any of its successors. This in turn allows to access the data that is associated with these security classes. Repeatedly applied on successor nodes, each key can be computed with this scheme.

4.4 Traditional Key Management Schemes

Theorem 4.7: The key assignment scheme is complete.

Proof. Let $C_i, C_j \in C$ with $C_j \in Des(C_i)$, then there is a path p from C_i down to C_j in the hierarchy. Starting with C_i and processing each edge (v_x, v_y) in p, the subsequent key k_y can be computed by decrypting the sealed key in node v_y with k_x. The key k_j is computed after performing $|p|$ decryption operations. □

The security of this variant is based on the strength of the encryption function. In order to insert a new security class C_i, only the sealed key of its successor has to be updated. Figure 4.3 shows the tree before and after an insertion of a new security class. A drawback of this variant is the additional storage of the sealed keys. Assuming to have n security classes, $(n-1) \cdot b$ bits are necessary to store the sealed keys whereas b is the output bit size of the used encryption function.

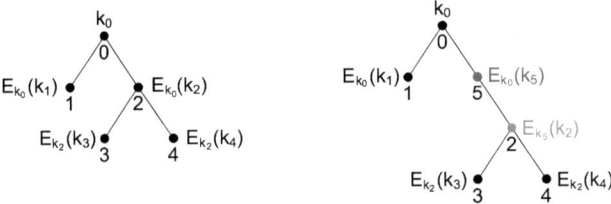

Fig. 4.3: Effects when a new node with its sealed key is inserted

Analogously, when a node has to be deleted, then only the sealed keys of the child nodes have to be recalculated.

Remarks: It should be noted that the considerations in this scheme are restricted to trees. Regarding the space complexity, the one-way variant of this scheme is very efficient.

4.4.3 Chen, Chung, and Tian's Scheme

The scheme described in [ChCT04] takes advantages from direct derivations. In a direct key derivation scheme, the key of each security class can be computed from any of its ancestor security classes directly. Figure 4.4 illustrates the direct derivation in an example poset.

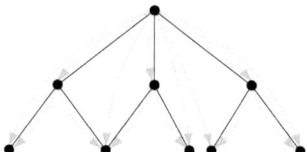

Fig. 4.4: Direct key derivation

The proposed scheme requires that the key of each node is directly computable from any of its ascendants. Chen, Chung, and Tian suggest to extend the key derivation graph such that each node is directly connected with all of its ascendant nodes. Therefore, edges might be inserted into the key derivation graph such that this requirement is met. Referring to Figure 4.4, for each leaf an edge from the root needs to be inserted. Public values are assigned to the edges so that computing the key of a class $C_j \in Des(C_i)$ from the key of the class C_i is possible.

Chen, Chung, and Tian propose the following key management scheme. The central authority chooses an appropriate hash function h and performs as follows:

1. For each $C_i \in C$, select a public identifier id_i and a random secret key k_i.

2. For each pair $C_i, C_j \in C$ with $C_j \in Des(C_i)$ compute the public parameter $r_{i,j} = E_{k_{i,j}}(k_j)$ with $k_{i,j} = h(id_j \oplus k_i)$ and make $r_{i,j}$ publicly available.

Theorem 4.8: The key assignment scheme is complete.

Proof. Let $C_i, C_j \in C$ with $C_j \in Des(C_i)$. From the requirement of the graph, C_i is connected with C_j by an edge $e_{i,j}$. The key k_j is computed by decrypting the public parameter $r_{i,j}$ of edge $e_{i,j}$ with the key $k_{i,j} = h(id_j \oplus k_i)$. □

Theorem 4.9: The key assignment scheme is sound.

Proof. The key of each class $C_i \in C$ is randomly selected, sufficiently large to withstand a brute force attack, which aims at guessing the right keys. The edge values represent the encrypted keys, whose keys are encrypted by the keys that are produced by the hash function upon two inputs: the key of the starting node and the identifier of the ending node of each edge. Assuming that the hash function is appropriately chosen, the security of the presented scheme is given by the strength of the used encryption function. When, additionally, an adequate encryption function is used, the proposed scheme provides computational security. □

4.4 Traditional Key Management Schemes

Remarks: For a modification of any secret key or a structural modification in the hierarchy, all public parameters between the affected node and its ascendant, as well as descendant nodes in the hierarchy, have to be updated. Furthermore, the integration of direct edges highly influences the storage capacity: for each pair C_i, C_j with $C_j \in Des(C_i)$ an edge with a public parameter is required, which has to be stored. In practice, it should be evaluated, whether or not an indirect derivation approach is more suitable.

4.4.4 Atallah, Frikken, and Blanton's Scheme

A very flexible and efficient scheme is contributed by Atallah et al. [AtFB05]. It supports any hierarchical structures. Since some ideas of this scheme are used as components of the subscription models, we describe this scheme in more detail.

1. For each class $C_i \in C$, choose a public unique identifier id_i and randomly select a secret bit sequence k'_i, both of bit length ℓ.

2. Compute the secret key as $k_i = h_{k'_i}(id_i)$ where h_k denotes an appropriate cryptographic keyed hash function (with key k).

3. For each edge (C_i, C_j), publish the value $r_{i,j} = (k_j - h_{k_i}(id_j))$ MOD 2^ℓ.

Here the dynamic scheme (extended version of the base scheme) is described. In the base scheme the secret keys of the nodes are randomly selected (not produced by a keyed hash function), i.e. $k_i = k'_i$ and Step 2 is left out. Figure 4.5 illustrates an example poset with its public and secret parameters. Suppose a user who is given the key k_2 of the security class id_2. From the key k_2 and the public identifier id_3, the user can compute $h_{k_2}(id_3)$. Adding the result to the edge value $r_{2,3}$ (modulo 2^ℓ) yields to the key k_3 of class id_3. Generally, let C_i be the parent node of C_j and let k_i be the secret key of C_i. Then, from k_i and the public parameter $r_{i,j}$, one can compute k_j.

Theorem 4.10: The key assignment scheme is complete.

Proof. Let $C_i, C_j \in C$ with $C_j \in Des(C_i)$. Then there is a path from C_i to C_j. Suppose to have the key k_i of the class C_i. Starting at C_i with $C_x := C_i$ and processing each edge (C_x, C_y) in the path from C_i to C_j, each subsequent key k_y, and thus finally k_j, can be computed by taking the $\ell - 1$ lower bits from the result of the addition of $h_{k_x}(id_y)$ with the public parameter $r_{x,y}$. □

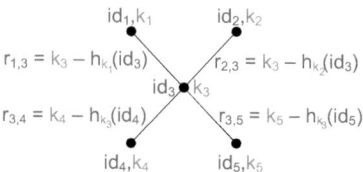

Fig. 4.5: Example poset: keys (private), identifier, and edge values (public)

Theorem 4.11: The key assignment scheme is sound.

Proof. Let $C_i, C_j \in C$ with $C_j \notin AoS(C_i)$. Here two possibilities arise: either $C_j \in Des(C_i)$ or $C_j \notin Des(C_i)$. In the first case, one might try to attack the public edge $r_{x,j}$, which belongs to the path from C_i to C_j. In this case the attacker knows the key k_j and hence a component of $r_{x,j}$ is known so that the attacker can get the hash value $h_{k_x}(id_j)$, when k_j is added to $r_{x,j}$ modulo 2^ℓ. Retrieving the key of a keyed hash function from a hash value and a known argument is considered as intractable. In the other case the ciphertexts (public edge values) may be a target of desire. From any edge value $r_{x,y}$ neither k_x nor k_y is known. The values cannot be gainfully combined so that some keys are revealed. Consider attacking the secret key k_i, which is produced by a keyed hash function. Hereby the attacker does neither know the used key for the keyed hash function nor its output. When sufficiently large keys and appropriate keyed hash functions are used, revealing the secret keys from these ciphertexts is intractable. □

Modifying edges: When a new edge from C_i to C_j has to be inserted, the edge value $r_{i,j} = k_j - h_{k_i}(id_j)$ MOD 2^ℓ is computed. The edge value is made publicly available. To delete the mentioned edge, $r_{i,j}$ needs be removed.

Modifying classes: When a class has to be inserted, a new secret bit sequence (resulting in a new secret key) and a new public node identifier are selected. To delete a class, its identifier, its secret key, and all edges from respectively to that node are removed. When a key needs to be updated, the edge value of each edge that starts or ends at the relevant class is updated.

It should be remarked that, in case of removing an edge or a class, users associated with relevant classes might have computed all keys of descendant classes before

4.4 Traditional Key Management Schemes

and they might have stored them locally. Excluding such users from relevant classes requires refreshing all keys of these classes, distributing the refreshed keys to designated users, and updating corresponding public edge values.

Inheritance: Let $G = (V, E)$ be the graph representation of the hierarchy C. Then, the reversed graph $G^R = (V, E^R)$ supports reversed inheritance, where for each edge $(v_i, v_j) \in E$, the reversed edge (v_j, v_i) is in E^R. Users with downward respectively upward inheritance are supplied with keys associated with nodes in G respectively in G^R.

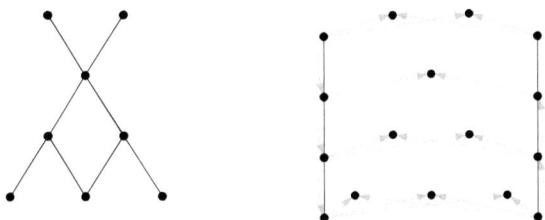

Fig. 4.6: Original hierarchy (left) with inheritance limits (right)

Suppose that the inheritance should be limited to a given length. Figure 4.6 illustrates an example where upward inheritance is bound. To disable inheritance, any edge values in the hierarchy are deleted. The limited inheritance is created as follows. For each layer in the hierarchy a node is created, which is connected with its parent node by an edge. Additionally, from the created nodes, edges are inserted to the classes in the corresponding layers. For the newly constructed edges public values are created according to the described scheme. Hence, the downward inheritance list (left list) is constructed. Analogously the upward inheritance list (right list) is created. In the given example the upward inheritance is limited: from keys assigned to lower nodes in the upward inheritance list, it is not possible to compute keys for the highest node in the hierarchy. According to the access rights of users (full or limited downward/upward inheritance), they are supplied with keys from the downward inheritance list respectively upward inheritance list.

Figure 4.7 shows how restrictions for both, downward and upward inheritance, can be combined. In the left example, the access condition for nodes lower or equal than v_a and higher or equal than v_b is shown. To restrict inheritance in such a way, users get the key k_a of node v_a and k_b of node v_b. The upward and downward inheritance lists in the right half of the picture show an example of restricting inheritance between two nodes only. According to the required direction, users get the key k_a, respectively k_b. The possession of both keys grants access to all security classes between v_a and v_b.

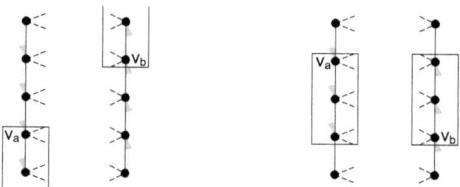

Fig. 4.7: Inheritance below k_a and above k_b respectively between k_a and k_b

Improvements for trees: A centroid of a tree $T = (V, E)$ with n nodes is a node, which – if removed from T – leaves no connected component of size greater than $n/2$ with $n = |V|$. In each tree there is either one or there are two centroids. In the latter case they are adjacent. Figure 4.8 illustrates such centroids on two example trees.

Fig. 4.8: Left tree with one centroid and right tree with two centroids

Especially in the case where the trees are unbalanced and deep, a derivation from the root to a leaf in the unbalanced subtree could require many derivation steps and thus it may be inefficient. To reduce the path length between any two nodes in each path of the tree, shortcut edges are added as follows. For every node v in T do the following:

1. Let T_v be the subtree rooted at v. Compute the centroid v_c of T_v. If there are two centroids, v_c is the parent among the two.

2. Add a shortcut edge from v to v_c, unless it already exists or $v = v_c$.

4.4 Traditional Key Management Schemes

3. Remove the subtree rooted at v_c from T.

4. Repeat until T_v is empty.

The algorithm calculates a set of shortcut edges such that there is a path with a length less than $log\, n$ between any ancestor-descendant pair. Since in each iteration the size of T_v is halved, the total number of such edges is less than or equal to $n \cdot log\, n$. To improve the efficiency the recursion is terminated, if the size of the tree has reached $\sqrt{n}$ or it is less than that. Listing 1 shows the algorithm for adding such shortcut pathes.

Algorithm 1 AddShortcuts(T=(V,E)):

1: **if** $n = |E| \leq 4$ **then**
2:     **return** $\emptyset$
3: **else**
4:     $S := \emptyset, C := \emptyset, T'=(V',E'):=T$
5:     **while** $size(T') > \sqrt{n}$ **do**
6:        compute centroid v_c of T'
7:        $C := C \cup \{v_c\}$
8:        $T' := T' - DoS(v_c)$ (removing relevant edges and nodes)
9:     **end while**
10:     **for all** $v_j \in (Des(v_i) - Chd(v_i))$ with $v_i, v_j \in C$ **do**
11:        $S := S \cup \{(v_i, v_j)\}$
12:     **end for**
13:     **for all** connected component T_i with root v_i in $(T-C)$ **do**
14:        **for all** $v_j \in (Des(v_i) - Chd(v_i))$ **do**
15:           $S := S \cup \{(v_i, v_j)\}$
16:        **end for**
17:        $S := S \cup$ AddShortcuts(T_i)
18:     **end for**
19:     **return** S
20: **end if**

The number of shortcut edges are given by the following recurrence:

$$f(n) = \begin{cases} 0 & \text{if } n \leq 4 \\ f(n) \leq \sum_{i=1}^{k} f(\sqrt{n}) + c \cdot n & \text{if } n > 4, k \text{ as number of residual trees} \end{cases}$$

Here n is the number of nodes, $T_i \leq \sqrt{n}$, c and k are constants. According to [AtFB05], this recurrence is bound by $O(n \cdot log(log(n)))$.

Since a tree with n nodes has $n-1$ edges, the number of edges in a tree is limited to $O(n)$. The shortcut edges ensure that for each ancestor-descendant pair there is a path with a length that is limited by $O(log(log(n)))$. The overall storage effort for public parameters in this scheme is bound by $O(n \cdot log(log(n))))$.

The efforts for storing the public information are covered by the same complexity class as necessary for storing the whole graph. Updates are handled locally.

4.5 Time-Bound Key Management Schemes

In the key management schemes presented in previous sections, secret keys are assigned to security classes. Depending on the scheme, key updates cause more or less consequences. Recently, some key management schemes have been developed that change the secret keys periodically. They inherently support key updates by time-bound keys. Some of them are described in the following sections.

4.5.1 Tzeng's Scheme

In [Tzen02] a key management scheme is presented that takes temporal aspects into consideration. This means that for each security class C_i there is a key for a given time period: data that is put into a security class in a given period t is encrypted with that key.

Definition 4.2: Let n be the product of two distinct strong primes p and q of appropriate bit length. For $i \geq 2$, the *Lucas function* for a value $m \in \mathbb{N}$ is defined as $V_i(m) = (m \cdot V_{i-1}(m) - V_{i-2}(m))$ MOD n. The initial values are defined as $V_0(m) = 2$ and $V_1(m) = m$. The sequence $\langle V_i(m) \rangle_{i=0}^{\infty}$ is called the *Lucas sequence* over m.

If α is a root of the characteristic polynomial $f(x) = (x^2 - mx + 1)$ MOD n, then each term from $V_a(m)$ with $a \geq 0$ can be computed directly by

$$V_a(m) = (\alpha^a + \alpha^{-a}) \text{ MOD } n \qquad (4.2)$$

For any $a, b \in \mathbb{N}$ the following properties are true:

- $V_a(V_b(m)) = V_b(V_a(m)) = V_{ab}(m)$
- $V_{a+b}(m) = V_a(m)V_b(m) - V_{a-b}(m)$ MOD n

If e is greater than 2, having $\gcd(e, (p^2 - 1)(q^2 - 1)) = 1$, and if d is chosen such that $e \cdot d \equiv 1 \pmod{(p^2 - 1)(q^2 - 1)}$ then the following facts are true:

4.5 Time-Bound Key Management Schemes

- $V_e(V_d(m)) = 1$

- To compute $V_a(m)$, first $V_{2r}(m) = (V_r^2(m) - 2) \text{ MOD } n$ is calculated. The next value is given by $V_{2r+1}(m) = (V_{r+1}(m)V_r(m) - m) \text{ MOD } n$. Applied recursively, $V_a(m)$ is computed in $2 \cdot \lfloor log_2(a) \rfloor + 2$ modular multiplications.

- From a, n, and $V_a(m)$, m cannot be computed efficiently.

Initializing: The central authority CA chooses four large primes p_1, p_2, q_1, and q_2 and calculates $n_1 = p_1 \cdot q_1$ and $n_2 = p_2 \cdot q_2$. The CA also chooses two random numbers a and b with $1 < a < n_1$ and $1 < b < n_2$. Let there be m security classes $C_1, C_2, \ldots, C_m$. Then $e_1, \ldots, e_m$ each relatively prime to $\phi(n_1)$ and $d_1, \ldots, d_m$ are chosen such that $e_i \cdot d_i = 1 \text{ MOD } \phi(n_1)$ for $1 \leq i \leq m$. For each security class C_i, CA computes the secret key:

$$k_i = a^{\prod_{C_k \leq C_i} d_k} \text{ MOD } n_1$$

This can also be formulated as $(a^{d_1 d_2 \cdots d_m})^{\prod_{C_j \not\leq C_i}(e_j)} MOD\, n_1$, since each d_j having $C_j \not\leq C_i$ is neutralized. For the time period the CA selects two appropriate public integers f_1 and f_2 and computes the value w_t of the Lucas function modulo n_2:

$$w_t = V_{f_1^{z-t} f_2^t}(b)$$

The system starts at time period 0 and it ends at a predefined integer z. The actual time period t is between 0 and z.

Key assignment: The CA chooses g_1, g_2, both relatively prime to $\phi(n_1)$, and calculates h_1 and h_2 such that $g_1 \cdot h_1 \equiv g_2 \cdot h_2 \equiv 1 \pmod{\phi(n_1)}$. Then, the following key is assigned to security class C_i for time period t:

$$k_{i,t} = h(k_i^{h_1^t \cdot h_2^{z-t}} \text{ MOD } n_1, w_t)$$

Parameters: The parameters $g_1, g_2, f_1, f_2, e_1, e_2, \ldots, e_m, n_1, n_2$ are made publicly available, all others are kept secretly. For a user in security class C_i the following secret data is necessary:

$$I(i, t_1, t_2) = (k_i^{h_1^{t_2} \cdot h_2^{z-t_1}} \text{ MOD } n_1, V_{f_1^{z-t_2} \cdot f_2^{t_1}}(b))$$

Key derivation: Suppose a user holds the secret $I(i, t_1, t_2)$ which should enable to access C_i between t_1 and t_2. To get $k_{j,t}$ for a class $C_j \in Des(C_i)$ at time t with $t_1 \leq t \leq t_2$, the user computes $(k_i^{h_1^{t_2} \cdot h_2^{z-t_1}})^{g_1^{t_2-t} \cdot g_2^{t-t_1} \cdot \prod_{C_k \leq C_i, C_k \not\leq C_j} e_k}$ MOD n_1. This can also be written as $((a^{\prod_{C_\ell \leq C_i} d_\ell})^{h_1^{t_2} \cdot h_2^{z-t_1}})^{g_1^{t_2-t} \cdot g_2^{t-t_1} \cdot \prod_{C_k \leq C_i, C_k \not\leq C_j} e_k}$ MOD n_1, which is $a^{g_1^{t_2-t} \cdot h_1^{t_2} \cdot g_2^{t-t_1} \cdot h_2^{z-t_1} \cdot \prod_{C_\ell \leq C_j} d_\ell \cdot \prod_{C_k \leq C_i, C_k \not\leq C_j} e_k \cdot d_k} \equiv a^{g_1^{t_2-t} \cdot g_2^t \cdot h_2^z \cdot \prod_{C_\ell \leq C_j} d_\ell}$ (mod n_1). This finally gives $k_j^{h_1^t \cdot h_2^{z-t}}$ MOD n_1. For the temporal weight the following has to be computed (modulo n_2): $V_{f_1^{t_2-t} \cdot f_2^{t-t_1}}(V_{f_1^{z-t_2} \cdot f_2^{t_1}}(b)) = V_{f_1^{t_2-t} \cdot f_2^{t-t_1} \cdot f_1^{z-t_2} \cdot f_2^{t_1}}(b)$, which can be transformed into $V_{f_1^{z-t} \cdot f_2^{t}}(b)$, which is w_t. Thus, the associated key $k_{j,t}$ of class C_j at time t can be computed as $k_{j,t} = h(k_j^{h_1^t \cdot h_2^{z-t}}$ MOD $n_1, w_t)$. This leads to the following corollary:

Corollary 4.12: The key assignment scheme is complete.

Performance: For a key derivation from a key to security class C_i to the key of a descendant class C_j there are $t_2 - t_1 + r$ modular exponentiations and $t_2 - t_1$ Lucas operations necessary, whereas r denotes the number of classes that satisfies the conditions $C_k \leq C_i$ and $C_k \not\leq C_j$. Note that a single operation for the Lucas function is roughly equivalent to a modular exponentiation. Additionally a single hash operation is necessary.

Security: First a children's attack on Tzeng's scheme is investigated. Let C_i and C_j be two security classes with $C_j < C_i$. Suppose a user has only the key k_j that enables to access security class C_j. To compute the key k_i of security class C_i, the user must be able to compute k_i from k_j whereas $k_j = k_i^{e_1 \cdots e_m}$ MOD (n_1). This is equivalent to breaking the RSA cryptosystem.

However, Tzeng's scheme is insecure against the collaborative attack. In [YiYe03] such an attack on Tzeng's scheme is presented. In particular the authors have shown how three users $a \in C_a, b \in C_b$, and $c \in C_c$ with $C_a \leq C_b \leq C_c$ having the access information $I(i, t_1, t_2), I(j, t_3, t_4)$, and $I(k, t_5, t_6)$ can collaborate to compute $k_{j,t}$ such that $t_2 < t < t_3$.

4.5.2 Yeh's Scheme

Yeh [Yeh05] uses Tzeng's idea to build a key assignment scheme that is based on the RSA cryptosystem. In contrast to Tzeng's scheme, also for the time-bound

4.5 Time-Bound Key Management Schemes

keys the RSA cryptosystem (instead of the Lucas function) is applied. In [Yeh07] the case for an unlimited time (without an expiration date) is considered.

Initialization:

1. The CA selects two distinct large primes p and q and computes the public value $n = p \cdot q$.

2. The CA chooses a random number a less than n.

3. For each class $C_i \in C$, the CA selects a distinct public prime e_i, relatively prime to $\phi(n)$ and computes the secret d_i such that $e_i \cdot d_i \equiv 1 \pmod{\phi(n)}$.

The public parameters $e_1, \ldots, e_m$, and modulus n are made publicly available; the secret parameters $d_1, \ldots, d_m$ are stored secretly.

Key assignment: At the beginning of a time period t, the CA selects a distinct public prime e_t, relatively prime to $\phi(n)$ and computes the corresponding secret d_t such that $e_t \cdot d_t \equiv 1 \pmod{\phi(n)}$. The secret key $k_{i,t}$ for class C_i at time period t is computed by:

$$k_{i,t} = a^{(\prod_{C_j \leq C_i} d_j) d_t} \text{ MOD } n$$

A user, who should be able to access C_i for a set of time periods T, confidentially gets the following key:

$$k_{i,T} = a^{(\prod_{C_j \leq C_i} d_j) \prod_{t_s \in T} d_{t_s}} \text{ MOD } n$$

Key derivation: For deriving the key of a class $C_\ell \in Des(C_i)$, the public RSA parameters are selected so that exponents, not used in $k_{\ell,t}$, are neutralized:

$$k_{i,T}^{(\prod_{C_j \leq C_i, C_j \not\leq C_\ell} e_j) \cdot \prod_{t_r \in (T-\{t\})} e_{t_r}} \equiv$$

$$a^{((\prod_{C_j \leq C_i} d_j) \prod_{t_s \in T} d_{t_s})(\prod_{C_j \leq C_i, C_j \not\leq C_\ell} e_j) \prod_{t_r \in (T-\{t\})} e_{t_r}} \equiv$$

$$a^{(\prod_{C_j \leq C_i} d_j)(\prod_{C_j \leq C_i, C_j \not\leq C_\ell} e_j)(\prod_{t_s \in T} d_{t_s})(\prod_{t_r \in (T-\{t\})} e_{t_r})} \equiv$$

$$a^{((\prod_{C_j \leq C_\ell} d_j) d_t)} \equiv k_{\ell,t} \pmod{n}$$

This leads to the following corollary:

Corollary 4.13: The key assignment scheme is complete.

Security: Yeh's Scheme was shown to fail a collaborative attack [ASFM06].

4.5.3 Chien's Scheme

In [Chie04] a time-bound hierarchical key assignment scheme is presented that is based on hash functions and uses tamper-resistant devices. Analogously to Tzeng's Scheme, the time is divided into z periods, where the system starts at time period 0 and ends at time period z.

Initialization: A trusted agent selects two random values a and b and for each security class C_i a secret key k_i. For each directed edge $C_j \leq C_i$ it publishes the public parameter $r_{i,j} = h(x \,||\, id_i \,||\, id_j \,||\, k_i) \oplus k_j$ on an authenticated public board, whereas h is a hash function, x is the trusted agent's secret key, and id_i denotes the identity of C_i. Here $h^m(x)$ denotes $h(...h(h(x))...)$ where h is applied m times.

User Registration: To assign a user to C_i, the user gets a tamper-resistant device from the trusted agency. In the device, the following parameters are stored: $x, id_i, h^{t_1}(a), h^{z-t_2}(b)$. Additionally the user confidentially gets k_i.

Encryption: The data in the security class C_i is encrypted with the key $k_{i,t}$, whereby $k_{i,t} = h(k_i \oplus h^t(a) \oplus h^{z-t}(b))$.

Decryption: Consider a user who has access to C_i from time period t_1 to t_2. For decrypting the encrypted data in C_i at time period t, with $t_1 \leq t \leq t_2$, the user enters k_i into his tamper-resistant device. The device is then able to compute $k_{i,t} = h(k_i \oplus h^t(a) \oplus h^{z-t}(b))$.

If the user wants to decrypt the encrypted data in C_j at time period t, whereby $C_j \leq C_i$ and $t_1 \leq t \leq t_2$, his or her tamper resistant device computes $k_{j,t}$ as follows: let $C_{\ell_1}, C_{\ell_2}, \ldots, C_{\ell_m}$ be the path from C_i to C_j with $C_i = C_{\ell_1}$ and $C_j = C_{\ell_m}$. The user enters k_i into the device and all public parameters along the path one after the other, which are $r_{\ell_1,\ell_2}, \ldots r_{\ell_{m-1},\ell_m}$ and $id_{\ell_1}, \ldots, id_{\ell_m}$. The device performs the following steps, whereas $k_{\ell_m} = k_j$:

$$k_{\ell_2} = r_{\ell_1,\ell_2} \oplus h(x \,||\, id_{\ell_1} \,||\, id_{\ell_2} \,||\, k_i)$$
$$k_{\ell_3} = r_{\ell_2,\ell_3} \oplus h(x \,||\, id_{\ell_2} \,||\, id_{\ell_3} \,||\, k_{\ell_2})$$
$$\vdots$$
$$k_{\ell_m} = r_{\ell_{m-1},\ell_m} \oplus h(x \,||\, id_{\ell_{m-1}} \,||\, id_{\ell_m} \,||\, k_{\ell_{m-1}})$$

To compute the key for the given time period, the hash values $h^t(a)$ and $h^{z-t}(b)$ are needed. These terms can be represented as $h^t(a) = h^{t-t_1}(h^{t_1}(a))$ respectively $h^{z-t}(b) = h^{t_2-t}(h^{z-t_2}(b))$. Finally the key $k_{j,t} = h(k_j \oplus h^t(a) \oplus h^{z-t}(b))$ is computed by the device, in which the values $h^{t_1}(a)$ and $h^{z-t_2}(b)$ are stored. This leads to the following corollary.

Corollary 4.14: The key assignment scheme is complete.

Security: Chien's Scheme was shown to fail a collaborative attack [Yi05].

4.6 Comparison of the Schemes

In this section the presented schemes are compared with each other concerning the necessary operations when keys are derived, consequences for key updates, and the required public storage. The schemes are listed in Table 4.1 whereby n denotes the number of nodes (respectively security classes) in the hierarchy. Note that the last three schemes are time-bound key management schemes, whereby keys are periodically refreshed by the scheme.

Akl Taylor's scheme provides direct key derivations. A serious disadvantage of their scheme is the exponential increase of the public parameters. For assigning prime numbers to the n classes, the smallest n prime numbers are taken. The size of the n-th prime is limited by $O(n \log(n))$. Because each public parameter in that scheme consists of at most $n-1$ prime factors – which is the case for leaf nodes – the largest t_i in the scheme is bound by $O((n \log(n))^n)$. Also, the scheme is very inefficient when keys are updated. In particular, if a security class C_i is inserted, then all public parameters and, more drastically, all secret keys from $C - Anc(C_i)$ have to be updated. Akl-Taylor's scheme requires n multiplications with reductions to $\mathbb{Z}_m$ (where m is the RSA modulus) and additionally n exponentiations for a key update. Computing keys from others takes at most

Tab. 4.1: Complexity comparison

Scheme	Key Derivation	Key Update	Public Storage
Akl Taylor	$O(log(m))$ M	$C - Anc(C_i)$ k,P	$O(n)$* P
Sandhu OWF	$O(n)$ H	$Des(C_i)$ k	$O(n)$ I
Sandhu SK	$O(n)$ D	$Chd(C_i)$ P	$O(n)$ E
Chen	$O(1)$ D,H	$Anc(C_i)+Des(C_i)$ P	$O(n^2)$ E
Atallah	$O(n)^\dagger$ X,H	$Par(C_i)+Chd(C_i)$ P	$O(n^2)^\ddagger$ E
Tzeng	$O(t_2 - t_1 + n)$ Exp + $O(1)$ H	periodically	$O(n)$ P
Chien	$O(t_2 - t_1 + n)$ H + $O(n)$ X	periodically	$O(n^2)$ E
Yeh	$O(n + |T| + log(m))$ M	periodically	$O(n + |T|)$ P
Legend M	Multiplication in Z_m	E	Encrypted data
H	Hash operation		(fixed size)
D	Decryption	k	Key
X	XOR	P	Public data
Exp	Exponentiation in Z_m	I	Id (fixed size)

* The public parameters grow rapidly with n: $O((n \, log(n))^n)$
† Could be reduced to $O(1)$
‡ For trees it is bound by $O(n)$

$2 \cdot log_2(t_j/t_i)$ multiplications (with reductions to $\mathbb{Z}_m$). For any node, its key can be directly derived from the key of any ancestor node. Since t_j/t_i is less than m, this is bound by $O(log(m))$ multiplications modulo m.

In Sandhu's scheme, which is based on one-way functions, n public identifiers (with a fixed bit length) have to be stored. If a key in a security class C_i is updated, all keys in descendant classes have to be revised. In the worst case scenario (key of the root is changed) all nodes are affected. For a balanced tree, a key derivation according to Sandhu's scheme would take $log(n)$ hash operations. In the worst case the hierarchy is represented by a list, in which a derivation from the root node to the leaf takes $n - 1$ derivation steps. In Sandhu's sealed key variant, a modification of secret keys only affects the sealed keys (public) of the child nodes. A key derivation requires performing a decryption operation instead of a hash operation. There, only the sealed keys need to be stored publicly.

4.6 Comparison of the Schemes

Chen's scheme requires at most $n(n-1)/2$ edges (due to the direct derivations). Public parameters are assigned to the edges. Hence the public storage is limited to $O(n^2)$. A key derivation only requires one decryption and one hash operation, because every security class C_i is directly connected with a node in $Anc(C_i)$. However, a key update can cause a complete revision of the public parameters in the hierarchy. In particular the public parameters, which are assigned to the edges from the affected node to all its ancestor nodes and additionally to all its descendants, have to be recalculated.

Referring to Atallah's scheme, $n(n-1)/2$ edges emerge in the worst case. Since each edge has a public parameter, the worst case requires storing $n(n-1)/2$ public parameters. Nevertheless, efficient extensions of the base scheme are proposed. In case of a key derivation for child nodes, a single XOR-operation and a hash operation are necessary. For a path with length p, this results in p such operations. Key updates affect the edge weights for the parent and child nodes only. Notice that in case of $n(n-1)/2$ edges (each class is connected with any other class in the hierachy), the costs for the key derivation are reduced to $O(1)$ hash operations and $O(1)$ XOR operations.

Tzeng's scheme requires publishing $n+6$ public parameters. The bit length of these parameters are less than or equal to the size of the selected RSA modulus (e.g. 1024 bit). A key derivation from C_i to $C_j \in Des(C_i)$ requires $t_2 - t_1 + r$ modular exponentiation operations, where t_1 and t_2 denote the time limits for the time-bound access control, and r is the number of classes satisfying $C_k \leq C_i$ and $C_k \not\leq C_j$. Additionally, $t_2 - t_1$ Lucas operations and a hash operation are necessary. Since the costs of a Lucas operation are roughly the same as required by a modular exponentiation operation, the efforts for a key derivation can be bound by $O(t_2 - t_1 + n)$ modular exponentiation operations plus $O(1)$ hash operation.

Yeh's scheme has to manage $O(n + |T|)$ public parameters (less than $\phi(n)$) where T denotes the set of the time periods. To derive key k_ℓ from k_i in Yeh's scheme, $DoS(C_i) - DoS(C_\ell)$ plus $|T|$ multiplications with reductions to $\phi(m)$ are necessary for computing the correct exponent. Additionally the exponentiation requires less than $2 \cdot log_2(m)$ multiplications (with reductions to $\mathbb{Z}_m$). Hence, the key derivation is bound by $O(n + |T| + log(m))$ multiplication operations modulo $\phi(m)$.

In Chien's scheme there are as many public parameters as there are edges in the hierarchy. In the worst case we have $n(n-1)/2$ edges and public parameters. For a key derivation in a path with length p, one has to be perform p hash operations and p XOR operations. To generate the key in a given time period, there are additionally $t_2 - t_1$ hash operations and two XOR necessary. In the worst case, in which the hierarchy is a list, there has to be accomplished $(n-1) + (t_2 - t_1)$ hash operations plus $(n-1) + 2$ XOR operations. Thus, the complexity is given by $O(t_2 - t_1 + n)$ hash operations and $O(n)$ XOR operations. It should be noted that in case of $n(n-1)/2$ edges (each class C_i has an edge to all nodes in $Anc(C_i)$), the costs for the key derivation are reduced to $O(t_2 - t_1)$ hash operations and $O(1)$ XOR operations.

5 Broadcast Encryption

> *Three may keep a secret,*
> *if two of them are dead.*
>
> B. Franklin

Broadcast encryption encompasses a broadcast center that transmits encrypted contents over an insecure broadcast channel such that only a privileged subset of users can decrypt them. An obvious approach is to supply every privileged user with the same decryption key. However, a vital requirement of such applications is that users should be able to dynamically join, but also leave a target group. High flexibility can be achieved by providing each user with an individual key and encrypting the contents for each user separately. Dependent on the number of users, this naive approach can have drastic consequences on the bandwidth and also on the efforts for the center, which encrypts the data individually. In particular, in case of live transmissions with many receivers this approach is probably be infeasible. Therefore, efficient schemes should offer high flexibility and high security while still keeping the bandwidth and efforts low. The security of such schemes should not unconditionally rely on tamper-resistant devices, because attackers have been making progress in tampering such devices and it has to be expected that this trend will carry on. In this section related work on broadcast encryption is presented.

5.1 Contribution and Structure

The following section summarizes the literature on broadcast schemes. Some examples are given in more detail and several proofs are demonstrated, which are omitted in the original text.

The next section deals with the question of how broadcast schemes can be designed such that individually composed user sets can be addressed in the broadcast scenario. Therein security issues like the resistance against a collaboration of excluded users are reflected. This section starts with the fundamental work of Fiat and Naor who contributed several schemes in this context. Aside the

k-resilient base scheme, two 1-resilient approaches are presented that aim at reducing the amount of keys per user. Then a method is described that allows to convert 1-resilient schemes into k-resilient ones. Section 5.3 outlines the Logical Key Hierarchy (LKH) scheme, which is a broadcast scheme that is specified as RFC 2627. Section 5.5 presents the Subset-Cover framework introduced by Naor et al., firstly facing the problem of stateless receivers, where users are supplied with a fixed number of keys that can neither be changed nor extended. In practice the requirement for stateless receivers is desired in several scenarios, especially when receivers cannot be expected to be continuously online (e.g. CD/DVD players, smart cards, GPS receivers). Additionally two implementations of the mentioned framework called Complete Subtree and Subset Difference schemes are presented. It should be remarked that the latter one is deployed for device revocation of Blueray discs [AAC06a, AAC06b]. Section 5.7 briefly describes some further schemes. Finally, in Section 5.8 the schemes are compared in context of the necessary key storage per user, header length of broadcasted messages, resiliency, and security.

5.2 Fiat and Naor's Scheme

Fiat and Naor [FiNa94] propose several broadcasting techniques, which ensure that only authorized users are served with contents. The schemes are designed such that they withstand a coalition of up to a certain number of corruptive users.

Definition 5.1: Resiliency

- Let U be the set of the users. A scheme is called *resilient* to a set $S \subset U$, if the members of S cannot obtain knowledge about the secret key of any set $T \subset U$ with $T \cap S = \emptyset$.

- A scheme is *k-resilient*, if it is resilient to any set $S \subset U$ with $|S| \leq k$.

- A scheme is *(k,p)-random-resilient*, if the scheme is resilient to a randomly chosen set $S \subset U$ of size k with probability of at least $1 - p$.

Consider the case where secret keys are stored in tamper-proof devices. According to the random-resiliency property, an attacker, who randomly captures devices from users, must collect and break a significant amount of devices to break the scheme. For many applications the random-resiliency is sufficient.

5.2 Fiat and Naor's Scheme

5.2.1 Basic Scheme

For every subset of at most k users the broadcast center randomly selects a key. The key of each subset B is confidentially transmitted to every user except to the members of B. Selected keys are combined by an XOR operation such that only members of the the target group T can compute the associated group key k_T. The scheme is initialized by the following steps.

1. For every set $B \subset U$ with $|B| \leq k$ a key k_B is randomly selected.

2. k_B is confidentially delivered to each user in the set $(U - B)$.

3. The secret key k_T of a set T is given by

$$k_T = \bigoplus_{B \subset (U-T)} k_B$$

Theorem 5.1: The converted scheme is k-resilient.

Proof. Let S be a coalition of users with $|S| \leq k$ and $S \cap T = \emptyset$. Since every subset less than or equal to k is given a key, also S gets a key k_S assigned. The key of subset T is calculated such that the key of every group of at most k members, who are not members of T, is added by an XOR operation. Therefore, also k_S is used in this computation. Since the group members do not know their group key, they cannot compute k_T. A single argument (randomly chosen group key) changes each output bit in the XOR operation equally likely. Sincde random keys are used, the members of S do not have any information about the key k_T. □

Tab. 5.1: Example with $U = \{1, 2, 3, 4, 5\}$ and $T = \{4, 5\}$

Subsets $B_i \subset (U - T)$ with $|B_i| \leq 2$ and their assigned users			
$B_0 = \emptyset$,	$B_4 = \{u_4\}$,	$B_8 = \{u_1, u_4\}$,	$B_{12} = \{u_2, u_5\}$,
$B_1 = \{u_1\}$,	$B_5 = \{u_5\}$,	$B_9 = \{u_1, u_5\}$,	$B_{13} = \{u_3, u_4\}$,
$B_2 = \{u_2\}$,	$B_6 = \{u_1, u_2\}$,	$B_{10} = \{u_2, u_3\}$,	$B_{14} = \{u_3, u_5\}$,
$B_3 = \{u_3\}$,	$B_7 = \{u_1, u_3\}$,	$B_{11} = \{u_2, u_4\}$,	$B_{15} = \{u_4, u_5\}$

Example 5.1: Table 5.1 shows an example with five users where no two users from the set $(U - T) = \{u_1, u_2, u_3\}$ can collaborate to obtain any information about the secret key of $T = \{u_4, u_5\}$.

The key k_T is computed as $k_T = \bigoplus_{B \subset (U-T)} k_B = k_{B_1} \oplus k_{B_2} \oplus k_{B_3} \oplus k_{B_6} \oplus k_{B_7} \oplus k_{B_{10}}$. User u_1 and user u_2 do not share k_{B_6}, user u_1 and user u_3 do not have k_{B_7} in common, and u_2 and u_3 do not have $k_{B_{10}}$. Since the keys are randomly chosen, the listed users do not have any information about k_T. Table 5.2 shows the keys that each user holds where $K = \{k_{B_0}, k_{B_1}, \ldots, k_{B_{15}}\}$ denotes the set of all keys.

Tab. 5.2: Example with $U = \{u_1, u_2, u_3, u_4, u_5\}$ and $T = \{u_4, u_5\}$

Users	Assigned keys
u_1:	$K - \{k_{B_1}, k_{B_6}, k_{B_7}, k_{B_8}, k_{B_9}\}$
u_2:	$K - \{k_{B_2}, k_{B_6}, k_{B_{10}}, k_{B_{11}}, k_{B_{12}}\}$
u_3:	$K - \{k_{B_3}, k_{B_7}, k_{B_{10}}, k_{B_{13}}, k_{B_{14}}\}$
u_4:	$K - \{k_{B_4}, k_{B_8}, k_{B_{11}}, k_{B_{13}}, k_{B_{15}}\}$
u_5:	$K - \{k_{B_5}, k_{B_9}, k_{B_{12}}, k_{B_{14}}, k_{B_{15}}\}$

In this example 2-resiliency is realized. Surely, if all three users are collaborating then k_T can be computed. This scheme requires $\sum_{i=0}^{k} \binom{n}{k}$ keys in total.

5.2.2 1-resilient Scheme based on One-way Functions

Suppose that the a 1-resilient broadcast scheme is sufficient. According to the k-resilient basic scheme (with $k = 1$), a user has to store $O(n)$ different keys. Provided that one-way functions exist, it is possible to reduce the number of keys per user to $O(log(n))$. If one-way functions exist, then a pseudo-random bit generator can be constructed, which passes all probabilistic polynomial time statistical tests [Håst90]. Fiat and Naor suggest building a binary key derivation tree as described below. Hereby the keys of the users are allocated to the leaf nodes of the tree. The idea of this approach is that a user only needs a fraction of keys, rather than all other keys as described in the basic scheme. From this fraction of keys users can derive other user keys by applying a pseudo-random number generator. Let $f : \{0,1\}^\ell \to \{0,1\}^{2\ell}$ be a pseudo-random number generator. The tree with the assignment of the keys to its nodes is constructed as follows.

5.2 Fiat and Naor's Scheme

1. Assign a seed $s \in \{0,1\}^\ell$ to the root node.

2. Apply f to the root node (seed s) and create two successor nodes. Assign the left half (ℓ bits) of the output as key to the left successor node and the right half (ℓ bits) as key to the right successor node.

3. Repeatedly apply f level by level on successor nodes until the number of leaves is equal to or greater than n.

4. Assign each user uniquely to a leaf.

Similar to the basic scheme, a user u_i should have all keys except his or her own keys. Instead of supplying the user with n keys the idea would be the following: delete the path from the root node to the leaf node u_i from the tree. This leads to $\lceil log(n) \rceil$ (respectively $\lfloor log(n) \rfloor$) separated trees. Provide a user with the keys, which belong to the root nodes of the resulting trees. The user is then able to compute the keys of the leaves, which are assigned to other users. This scheme is only 1-resilient: already two users can compute all user keys.

5.2.3 1-resilient Scheme based on the RSA Problem

The necessary key storage of $O(log(n))$ keys per user as described in the previous scheme can be further reduced to one secret key, provided that extracting roots in an RSA modulus is intractable. The following 1-resilient broadcast scheme is based on the RSA problem [RiKa03, RiSA77]. The steps are the following:

1. Choose a secret integer $g \in_R \mathbb{Z}_m$ with m (RSA modulus) as the product of two appropriately chosen primes such that the order of g modulo m is sufficiently high (cf. [ACJT00, CaGe98]).

2. Assign a public number p_i to each user i such that $gcd(p_i, p_j) = 1$ holds for two different users i and j; p_i is published afterwards.

3. Assign a secret key $k_i = g^{p_i} \text{ MOD } m$ to each user i.

4. The common key k_T for a privileged target subset T is given by:
$k_T = g^{\prod_{i \in T} p_i} \text{ MOD } m$.

Each member i of the set T can compute k_T by using his or her own secret key:

$$k_i^{\prod_{j \in T-\{i\}} p_j} \equiv g^{\prod_{i \in T} p_i} \equiv k_T \pmod{m}$$

Let p_T be equal to $\prod_{i \in T} p_i$. Suppose a user $j \notin T$ has an algorithm that computes k_T efficiently. This implies that the user could also compute the center's secret g. Since $gcd(p_j, p_T) = 1$ holds, the user can compute $a, b \in \mathbb{Z}_m^*$ such that $ap_T + bp_j = 1$ by using the extended euclidian algorithm. If k_T is known, then the user can compute g as follows:

$$k_T^a k_j^b \equiv g^{ap_T} g^{bp_j} \equiv g^{ap_T + bp_j} \equiv g \pmod{m}$$

Computing roots modulo a RSA composite is considered to be intractable.

Corollary 5.2: This scheme is not 2-resilient, because any two users can efficiently reconstruct g.

Tab. 5.3: Comparison of Fiat Naor's schemes

Scheme	Keys per User	Resiliency	Security
Basic scheme	$O(2^n)$	k	perfect secrecy
Scheme based on OWF	$O(log(n))$	1	computationally
Scheme based on the RSA problem	$O(1)$ secret + $O(n)$ public	1	computationally

5.2.4 Converting 1-resilient into k-resilient Schemes

Fiat and Naor propose to use so-called *perfect hash functions* [CoLR90] to extend a 1-resilient scheme to a k-resilient one. Let $f_i : U \to \{1, \ldots, m\}$ be a function family, in which for every subset $S \subset U$ of size k there exist some integers $1 \leq i \leq \ell$ such that for all $x, y \in S$ the condition $f_i(x) \neq f_i(y)$ holds. These functions are used to convert a 1-resilient scheme into a k-resilient one as follows (cf. [FiNa94]).

1. For every $1 \leq i \leq \ell$, $1 \leq j \leq m$ use an independent 1-resilient scheme $R_{i,j}$.

2. Every user $x \in U$ gets the key associated with the schemes $R_{i,f_i(x)}$ for all $1 \leq i \leq \ell$.

3. To send a secret message M to a subset $T \subset U$, the center generates random bit strings $M_1, \ldots, M_\ell$ such that $M_1 \oplus M_2 \oplus \ldots \oplus M_\ell = M$ holds.

5.2 Fiat and Naor's Scheme

4. For all $1 \leq i \leq \ell$ and $1 \leq j \leq m$ the string M_i is transmitted to the privileged subset $\{x \in T \mid f_i(x) = j\}$ by using the scheme $R_{i,j}$.

Every user $x \in T$ can obtain M, because members of T receive each M_i through the scheme $R_{i,f_i(x)}$. By performing the XOR operation over all $M_i's$ the original message M is recovered.

Theorem 5.3: The scheme is k-resilient.

Proof. Let S be a coalition of users with $|S| \leq k$ and $S \cap T = \emptyset$. Then there exists an integer $1 \leq i \leq \ell$ such that f_i is one-to-one on S. In the schemes $R_{i,j}$ with $1 \leq j \leq m$ the coalition S has at most the keys of a single user $y \notin T$. Considering M_i in $R(i,j)$, S can get no information on M_i in the information-theoretic sense, respectively S is computationally bound. This depends on the property of the underlying 1-resilient scheme $R_{i,j}$. In the XOR operation, a randomly chosen argument influences each output bit such that 0 and 1 is equally likely. Thus, even if only a single M_i is unknown, no information about M is given (resp. revealing M is computationally bound in the computational security case). □

Comparing the resulting scheme with their underlying 1-resilient schemes, the number of keys per user is multiplied by ℓ. Moreover, the number of transmissions is multiplied by $\ell \cdot m$. Now consider the question of how to choose m and ℓ. It turns out (see below) that it is sufficient to set $m = 2k^2$ and $\ell = k\, log(n)$.

For any two users in S, the chance to have same values in f_i is $\binom{k}{2} \cdot \frac{1}{m}$. Hence, the probability that a random function f_i is one-to-one on S is at least $1 - \binom{k}{2} \cdot \frac{1}{m}$, which is $1 - \frac{k \cdot (k-1)}{2m}$. By setting $m = 2k^2$ we have $1 - \frac{k-1}{4k}$, which is greater than $1 - \frac{k}{4k} = \frac{3}{4}$. From the other point of view, the probability that a randomly chosen function is not one-to-one is less than $\frac{1}{4}$. Having ℓ such functions this probability is reduced to $(\frac{1}{4})^\ell$. For $\ell = k \cdot log(n)$ we have a probability of $\frac{1}{4^{k \cdot log(n)}} = \frac{1}{2^{2k \cdot log(n)}} = \frac{1}{(2^{log(n)})^{2k}}$, which is equivalent to $\frac{1}{n^{2k}}$. Thus, for all subsets $S \subset U$ of size k the probability that there is a one-to-one f_i is at least $1 - \binom{n}{k} \cdot \frac{1}{n^{2k}} \geq 1 - \frac{1}{n^k}$.

For the practice $F = \{f_p(x) = x \bmod p \mid p \in \mathbb{P},\, p \leq k^2 log(n)\}$ is suggested. Let a 1-resilient scheme be given. Then there exists a k-resilient scheme, including

i) A user stores $O(k\, log(n)\, w)$ keys (w as storage amount in the 1-resilient scheme)

ii) The center broadcasts $O(k^3\, log(n))$ messages

5.3 Logical Key Hierarchy

The Logical Key Hierarchy (LKH) scheme is a broadcast scheme that provides user revocation. It was specified by the NSA members Wallner, Hager, and Agee [WaHA98] (also described in [WoGL98]). Let n denote the maximum number of users in the system. When a single user is revoked, $log(n)$ keys are updated and broadcasted such that only authorized users can access them. The LKH scheme assumes that receivers are always online and can update their keys.

Setup: Create a full binary tree T such that the number of system users will not exceed the number of leaves at any time. Each user is assigned to a leaf in T and a unique key per user is negotiated with the server. Assign a randomly chosen key to each inner node in T. Then, the server transmits the keys of the inner nodes in T level by level as follows: starting from tree height minus one, the server encrypts the key assigned to each node v_i in that level with the key of each successor node. This task is continued until the key of the root is encrypted and transmitted. In the end each user u has the keys, which are assigned to the nodes along the path from the root to the leaf node that represents u. In particular the users share the root key, which is used for encrypting the data before it is broadcasted.

Rekeying: To revoke a user u, all keys, which are assigned to nodes on the path from the root to node u, have to be changed and distributed to affected users. The server chooses different keys for these nodes, encrypts and broadcasts them as described in the setup phase with the difference that in the first step the encryption for the revoked user is omitted. For a full binary tree with n leaves (users), this requires encrypting and broadcasting $2 \cdot log(n) - 1$ keys.

Example 5.2: Suppose user u_4 in Figure 5.1 is revoked. Then, all keys on the path, i.e. nodes 5, 2, and 1, have to be changed. The keys are sent to the users, who are covered by the subtree rooted at the relevant node. In the given case the refreshed key k'_5 has to be transferred to user u_3, the new key k'_2 needs to be sent to users u_1 and u_2, and the updated key k'_1 has to be handed over to every valid system user. Referring to Figure 5.1, the server encrypts the refreshed key k'_5 with k_{10}. Next the refreshed key k'_2 is encrypted with both, k_4 and the new key k'_5. Finally the newly chosen key k'_1 is encrypted with the updated key k'_2 as well as with k_3. The resulting ciphertexts (encrypted keys) are broadcasted.

5.4 Extended Header Scheme

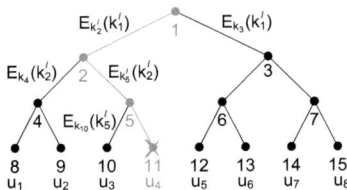

Fig. 5.1: Rekey process

Alternatively the center encrypts $E_{k_{10}}(\langle k'_1, k'_2, k'_5 \rangle)$, $E_{k_4}(\langle k'_1, k'_2 \rangle)$, and $E_{k_3}(k'_1)$ and broadcasts the encrypted data. This variant increases the size of the ciphertexts, but reduces the number of differently encrypted data packages to $log(n)$.

The keys are refreshed and distributed so that all affected users except the revoked user can access them. Any set of revoked users (non-registered users respectively) cannot access those keys and thus they cannot access further messages. This leads to the following corollary.

Corollary 5.4: The LKH scheme is collusion-resilient.

Encryption and Decryption: To send messages to users in $U - R$ the root key is used, which is refreshed when a user is revoked. Since the refreshed root key is transmitted such that revoked users cannot access it, messages encrypted with that key exclude revoked users from reading the messages. It should be noted that receivers need to be reachable from the center at any time otherwise they could miss broadcasted key updates and henceforth they would be disabled from further authorizations.

Remarks: Briscoe explains how LKH can be combined with binary hash trees such that the system is disburdened from the costs for preplanning leaves (cf. [Bris99]). This idea is readopted in [ZXHJ07] and is described in Section 5.7.2. McGrew et al. propose a bottom-up approach [McSh98].

5.4 Extended Header Scheme

The extended header scheme, which was first suggested by Wool [Wool00], is an approach that adds header information to the broadcasts. Programs are clustered to packages where each package is associated with a package key. The basic idea is to encrypt contents with a freshly chosen session key and encrypt the session key with each associated package key separately. Aside resulting ciphertexts, the indices of the used keys are included in the header so that users are able to find out whether their keys are supported or not. The header consists of two fields: the list of the supported identifiers and the field of encrypted keys.

Encryption: Let m be the plaintext of the offered program and let $k_{i_1}, \ldots, k_{i_n}$ be the package keys of the associated programs. Then the center broadcasts the sequence $\langle (i_1, E_{k_{i_1}}(k)), (i_2, E_{k_{i_2}}(k)), \ldots, (i_n, E_{k_{i_n}}(k)), E_k(m) \rangle$. Hence, access to contents is restricted to users that have an associated package key. It should be noted that the encryption function for encrypting the keys and the one for the programs may be chosen differently. For realtime transmissions the latter may perform more efficiently in terms of the decryption time. For the sensitive data (keys) Wool suggests to use an approved encryption scheme that may takes longer.

Decryption: A user needs to scan the header information to find out whether a package index i_j, for which the user has the key, is listed. If such an index is listed, then the user can extract $(i_j, E_{k_{i_j}}(k))$ and $E_k(m)$ from the header. Then the ciphertext $E_{k_{i_j}}(k)$ can be decrypted resulting in the session key k. With k the ciphertext that covers the relevant program can be decrypted.

Header Length: A shortcoming of this scheme is that it requires additional amount of data. Let b_i be the bit size of an identifier and b_k be the bit size of an encrypted session key. For a program m that belongs to t packages the scheme requires $t \cdot (b_i + b_k)$ bits among the encrypted data package $E_k(m)$. As it is pointed out in [Wool00], this information has to be sent frequently, because when a user switches to a program, the header information is required for decrypting the program contents. Thus, the STB needs to wait for the next header. Wool suggests installing a module in the STB that continuously receives the relevant header information and stores them in a low cost storage unit. Alternatively another channel can be considered coming up with the header information.

5.5 Subset-Cover Framework

In [NaNL01] a revocation framework called *Subset-Cover* is presented, which divides authorized users into groups such that the number of these groups is kept low. It is based on the extended header scheme, i.e. each program is encrypted with a session key. The session key is encrypted with each group key separately. The header message consists of the indices of the authorized user groups and the encrypted session keys. Together with the header message the resulting ciphertexts are broadcasted. The presented framework is resilient against an arbitrary number of collaborators. Additionally, it supports mechanisms to trace traitors.

Definition 5.2: Let U denote the set of n users and let $R \subseteq U$ be the set of r revoked users. A *subset-cover* is a collection of subsets $S_1, \ldots, S_w \subseteq U$ where a key k_{S_j} is assigned to each subset S_j with $1 \leq j \leq w$. Each member $u \in S_j$ should be able to compute k_{S_j}. The target set $S = U - R$ is divided into t disjoint subsets S_{i_j} with $1 \leq j \leq t$ so that, exclusively, all legitimate users are covered:

$$S = \bigcup_{j=1}^{t} S_{i_j}$$

Notice that the framework does not describe how these subsets are created. The concrete realization depends on the used implementation (see subsequent sections).

Encryption: The broadcast center performs the following steps:

1. Choose an encryption key k.

2. Find a partition of disjoint subsets $S_{i_1}, \ldots, S_{i_t} \subseteq S$ with their keys $k_{i_1}, \ldots, k_{i_t}$.

3. Broadcast $([i_1, \ldots, i_t, E_{k_{i_1}}(k), E_{k_{i_2}}(k), \ldots, E_{k_{i_t}}(k)], E_k(m))$ whereby m is the plaintext (offered program).

Decryption: From $([i_1, \ldots, i_t, E_{k_{i_1}}(k), E_{k_{i_2}}(k), \ldots, E_{k_{i_t}}(k)], E_k(m))$ a user u has to find an index i_j with $1 \leq j \leq t$ such that $u \in S_{i_j}$. Due to disjoint subsets, $u \in (U - R)$ is assigned to exactly one such a subset. Provided that i_j is listed in the header, the user can compute the key k_{i_j} from the user's secret information. With k_{i_j} the corresponding ciphertext $E_{k_{i_j}}(k)$ can be decrypted, which enables to decrypt $E_k(m)$. If $u \in R$ then there is no listed subset to which user u belongs to.

5.6 Subset-Cover Revocation Algorithms

Naor et al. propose two implementations (as described below) of the given framework. Both schemes assume that $|U| = n$ is a power of 2, making it possible to create a full rooted binary tree T with n leaves (T covers $2n - 1$ nodes in total) where the users are assigned to the leaves. For each node v_i in T a key k_i is chosen uniquely and randomly.

To partition $U - R$ into disjoint sets, the Steiner tree $ST(R)$ is used, which is the minimal subtree of the full tree that connects all the leaves that are to be revoked. For r revoked leaves, the Steiner tree consists of r leaves and incorporates at most $r \cdot log(n)$ nodes. Figure 5.2 illustrates two full binary trees with $n = 8$ nodes. In the left tree, two users are revoked; the right tree deals with four out of eight revoked users where the resulting Steiner trees are solid black. The examples explicitly show that the amount of subsets (connected components of the gray nodes) is given by the number of nodes that have only one child node in $ST(R)$.

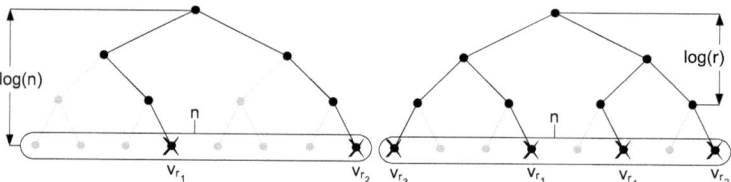

Fig. 5.2: Steiner tree (black) and resulting subsets (gray)

Theorem 5.5: For a $ST(R)$ with r leaves, $O(r \cdot log(\frac{n}{r}))$ subsets arise in T.

Proof. Let h denote the tree height of T. It is clear that for each node v_i there is exactly one subset if and only if $|Chd(v_i)| = 1$ in $ST(R)$. For a single leaf node v_r, which is revoked, $ST(R)$ is the path from the root node to v_r in T. In this case there are h nodes that have only a single successor node in $ST(R)$, i.e. h subsets arise. Consider the case when a further node $v_{\tilde{r}}$ is revoked. Then a new path p is added to $ST(R)$ starting at a node v_s in $ST(R)$ and ending at $v_{\tilde{r}}$. By adding a new path p, $|p| - 1$ nodes that have only one successor node in $ST(R)$ are added to $ST(R)$ and hence $|p| - 1$ subsets emerge. On the other hand v_s has now two child nodes in $ST(R)$, which diminishes the number of subsets by one. To add the highest possible number of subsets, p needs to have the maximum possible path

5.6 Subset-Cover Revocation Algorithms

length. The first two paths would have full path length, but they would disable the root node for further paths (since the root then has two child nodes in $ST(R)$). Each further revoked node disables the next node in the binary tree with the shortest distance to the root. Hence, revoking r nodes will affect $r-1$ nodes that have closest distance to the root node, which form a subtree T_D of $ST(R)$ that is a binary tree with a tree height of $log(r)$ (see right tree of Figure 5.2). In general, if we consider each path of full length from the root down to the leaf, there would be $r \cdot h$ nodes in total from which at least $r \cdot log(r)$ has to be subtracted, because they are covered by T_D. Then we have at most $r \cdot log(n) - \lceil r \cdot log(r) \rceil$ nodes that have only one child in $ST(R)$ and thus we have $O(r \cdot (log(n/r))$ subsets. □

5.6.1 Complete Subtree Method

In the Complete Subtree (CS) method, the subtrees $S_1, \ldots, S_w$ are considered as complete subtrees in the full binary tree T with n leaves. For each node $v_i \in T$ a randomly chosen key is assigned independently from each other. Each user $u \in U$ gets the keys associated with the nodes in the path from the root to the leaf u. Thus, every user gets $log(n) + 1$ keys. To obtain the subset-cover the Steiner tree $ST(R)$ is subtracted from T.

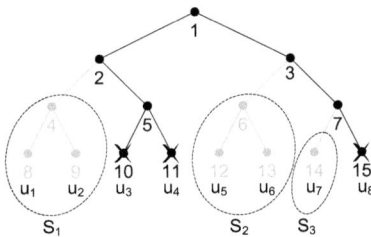

Fig. 5.3: Subset cover

Example 5.3: Figure 5.3 shows an example where users u_3, u_4, and u_8 are revoked. There remain three subsets S_1, S_2, and S_3 after extracting the Steiner tree $ST(R)$ (black tree) from the original binary tree.

Encryption: The center chooses a session key k and encrypts the plaintext m with it. Then k is encrypted with the key of each subset that remains when $ST(R)$

is subtracted from T. Together with the indices belonging to the root nodes of each remaining subset the ciphertexts are broadcasted. In the given example $\langle 4, 6, 14, E_{k_4}(k), E_{k_6}(k), E_{k_{14}}(k), E_k(m) \rangle$ is broadcasted.

Decryption: A user u has to find out whether an index is listed in the header that is part of the path from the root to u. If there exists such an index i, the user u can decrypt the corresponding ciphertext $E_{k_i}(k)$, which will reveal the session key k. With k the message can be decrypted.

Removing $ST(R)$ from T will leave $O(r \cdot log(\frac{n}{r}))$ subtrees (proof see above) whose union is the subset-cover. Therefore, the broadcast messages in this scheme cover $O(r \cdot log(\frac{n}{r}))$ indices and ciphertexts. The receiver has to store $log(n)$ keys and needs to perform $O(log(log(n)))$ comparison operations plus a single decryption.

5.6.2 Subset Difference Scheme

Naor et al. [NaNL01] suggest a method called *Subset Difference Method* which is an implementation of the subset-cover framework described above. To build the subset-cover, authorized users are represented as the differences of two subsets.

Definition 5.3: Given two nodes v_i and v_j with $v_j \in Des(v_i)$, then $S_{i,j}$ denotes the collection of users which is covered by the set difference $DoS(v_i) - DoS(v_j)$.

As in the previous scheme, the users are assigned to leaves in a complete binary tree where n is assumed to be a power of 2. Figure 5.4 illustrates a subset difference.

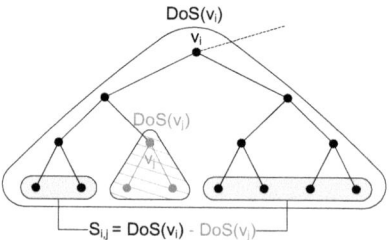

Fig. 5.4: Subset difference $S_{i,j}$

5.6 Subset-Cover Revocation Algorithms

Key assignment: To each inner node $v_p \in T$ a randomly chosen secret label $label_p$ is assigned. Additionally each subset $S_{i,j}$ is associated with a key $k_{i,j}$ that is derived from $label_i$ by the following procedure: for computing the key of the subset $S_{i,j}$, a pseudo-random sequence generator f similar to [GoGM86] is used that takes a secret label (seed) of b bits as its input and produces a $3b$-bit output. Given $label_i$ of the node v_i, $f(label_i)$ produces $label_\ell \,\|\, k_i \,\|\, label_r$ where $label_\ell$ and $label_r$ are the labels of the child nodes (left and right respectively) and k_i denotes the key of node v_i. The key $k_{i,j}$, which is assigned to the subset $S_{i,j}$, is the output k_j of f, which is the case when the function, started with the input $label_i$, is repeatedly applied and branches to the subtree in which v_j is located, finally reaches v_j after proceeding top down in the path from v_i to v_j. The function is called at most $log(n)$ times. Let $f_r(x)$ denote the right third, $f_\ell(x)$ the left third and $f_m(x)$ the middle third of the output bits of $f(x)$. Referring to Figure 5.5 the key $k_{1,5}$ assigned to $S_{1,5}$ is computed by $f_m(f_r(f_\ell(label_1)))$.

User u should be able to compute the keys of any subset $S_{i,j}$ such that $v_i \in AoS(u)$ and $v_j \notin AoS(u)$ holds. In particular if $v_j \in AoS(u)$, then the user u is revoked.

Example 5.4: Figure 5.5 illustrates an example. The path p from the root to user u_4 is blue colored. For user u_4 the nodes v_3, v_4, and v_{10} are those nodes that are adjacent to the nodes in p, but are not elements of p. The user is member of the following subsets: $S_{1,x}$, $S_{1,y}$, $S_{1,10}$, $S_{2,y}$, $S_{2,10}$, $S_{5,10}$, and the set without any revoked users, with $x \in DoS(v_3)$ and $y \in DoS(v_4)$.

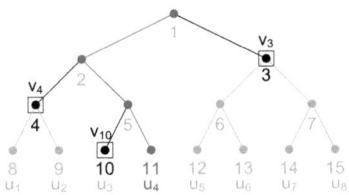

Fig. 5.5: The adjacent nodes of a user's path

The possession of the key $k_{i,j}$ that is assigned to a subset $S_{i,j}$ enables to compute any key $k_{i,s}$ of subset $S_{i,s}$ with $v_s \in Des(v_j)$. Therefore, it is not necessary for a user to store each key of a legitimate subset. It is sufficient that a user is supplied with keys of any subset $S_{i,j}$ where v_i is located on the path p from the root to the relevant user node and v_j is adjacent to that nodes, but no part of it. To be able to build subset differences $DoS(v_i) - DoS(v_j)$, v_j must be covered by $DoS(v_i)$. This reduces the number of possible pairs (v_i, v_j) to $log^2(n)$ (proof see below).

To partition $U - R$ into disjoint subsets, the following algorithm is performed. Initially set T to the Steiner tree: $T = ST(R)$. The following steps are repeated until T only consists of a single node.

1. Find two leaves v_i, v_j in T such that the least-common ancestor v of v_i and v_j does not contain any other leaf of T in its subtree.

2. Let v_ℓ and v_r be the children of v such that $v_i \in DoS(v_\ell)$ and $v_j \in DoS(v_r)$. If there is only one leaf left, then $v_i = v_j$ becomes that leaf and $v = v_\ell = v_r$ becomes the root of T.

3. If $v_\ell \neq v_i$ then add $S_{\ell,i}$ to the collection. If $v_r \neq v_j$ add $S_{r,j}$ to the collection.

4. Remove all $Des(v)$ from T, which makes v a leaf.

This algorithm removes nodes from T and adds subsets to the collection until there is only one node left.

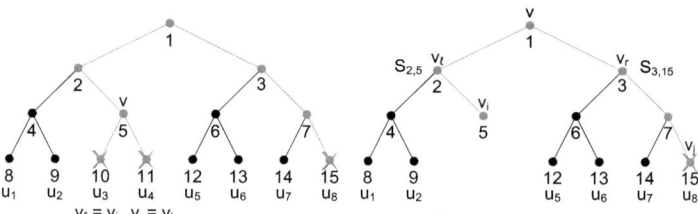

Fig. 5.6: Cover-finding algorithm

Example 5.5: Figure 5.6 illustrates how the presented algorithm works. In the first iteration the revoked users u_3 and u_4 are taken, which have the least-common ancestor node v_5. Since $v_r = v_i$ and $v_\ell = v_j$, no subtree is added to the collection. Afterwards the descendants of node v_5, which are the nodes of the revoked users u_3 and u_4, are removed. For the second iteration there are only the leaves v_5 and v_{15} left. Their least-common ancestor node is the root node. Then we have v_2 and v_3 as child nodes of the root, which are different from v_i and v_j, and hence $S_{2,5}$ and $S_{3,15}$ are added to the collection. The descendants of the root node are

5.6 Subset-Cover Revocation Algorithms

removed afterwards. Finally the exit condition of the algorithm is satisfied. Thus, the algorithm partitions $U - R$ into $S_{2,5} = \{v_8, v_9\}$ and $S_{3,15} = \{v_{12}, v_{13}, v_{14}\}$.

The algorithm partitions non-revoked receivers into at most $2r - 1$ subsets due to the addition of at most 2 subsets (at Step 3) in each iteration (cf. [NaNL01]).

Encryption: For each partitioned subset the contents are encrypted separately. This determines the header size: $O(r)$. In the example above, given a content m, the sequence $\langle (2,5), (3,15), E_{k_{2,5}}(k), E_{k_{3,15}}(k), E_k(m) \rangle$ is transmitted.

Decryption: Similar to the complete subtree scheme, a user u needs to find the subset $S_{i,j}$ in the header of the broadcasted message such that $u \in S_{i,j}$, which is bound by $O(log(log(n)))$ when data is accordingly preprocessed. If (i, j) is listed in the header, the key k is also encrypted with the key $k_{i,j}$. The user u computes the key $k_{i,j}$, decrypts $E_{k_{i,j}}(k)$, and decrypts the broadcasted ciphertext. When not listed, u cannot decrypt the broadcasted ciphertexts due to inadequate keys.

Theorem 5.6: The number of keys at user side is bound by $O(log^2(n))$.

Proof. Let the subset keys be the result of the pseudo-random function f after proceeding the path nodes, which define the subset difference, top down (see key assignment above). A user u is member of $S_{i,j}$ with $j \in Des(i)$ if and only if $u \in Des(i)$ and $u \notin DoS(j)$. This means that for a user u all combinations of i and j are taken into account where i is a node on the path p from the root to u and $j \in Des(i)$ is not an element of that path. Since the key of a subset $S_{i,j}$ is computable from the label associated with the node v_i, the choice for $j \in Des(i)$ can be restricted to such nodes that are adjacent to the path nodes without being a member of it (note that j cannot be a path node, because this would exclude user u). The number of combinations for each path element i with such an element j is given by the number of successor nodes on the path: each successor node adds an adjacent node, which is a descendant but not a path element. Notice that the last node in the path does not add such a node, but this can be counted as the adjacent node to the root. In a full binary tree with n leaves we have $log(n)$ such path nodes, which have an ancestor node in the path. Hence we have $\sum_{i=1}^{log(n)}(i)$ plus 1 (for no revocations) combinations, which is $1 + \frac{1}{2} \cdot (log(n))^2 + \frac{1}{2} \cdot log(n)$. □

5.6.3 Comparison

The question remains: Which broadcast scheme should be favored over the other one? Here we consider the expected number of revoked users. For the worst case we have a header length of $O(r \cdot log(\frac{n}{r}))$ in the Complete Subtree Method and $2r-1$ in the Subset Difference Scheme. Figure 5.7 illustrates the necessary header size of the schemes for an example with one million users. The left chart shows the number of ciphertexts (encrypted session keys) in thousands when the number of revoked users make up at most 5% of all users; the right chart illustrates the case for at most 50%. Additionally the average case of the Subset Difference Scheme, which is $1.38r$ (cf. [NaNL01]), is also taken into consideration.

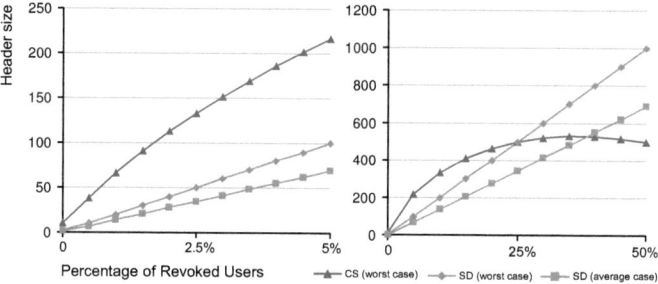

Fig. 5.7: Estimated header size of CS/SD schemes

If the ratio between revoked users and all users is expected to be low, then concerning the header size the Subset Difference Scheme is the better choice (see left chart). In the case of 25% the header size is approximately equal for both schemes reflecting the worst case. When it is expected that revoked users encompass 50% or more, the Complete Subtree Scheme needs less header size in the worst case.

One shortcoming of the Subset Difference Scheme in comparison to others, such as the Complete Subtree Scheme, is that a user has to manage $O((log(n))^2)$ keys. For some applications, in particular in environments with limited resources, this might be a serious knock-out criterion. Halevy and Shamir [HaSh02] propose the *Layered Subset Difference Scheme*, which is a modification of the Subset Difference Scheme. The idea is to carefully select the subsets such that redundant and never used subsets are excluded. In particular their method reduces the key storage at the user side to $O((log(n))^{\frac{3}{2}})$. However, the price for this is paid in the header length of the broadcasted messages. Because in the worst case the header size is doubled, which means that the header consists of $4r - 2$ encrypted session keys.

5.6.4 Extensions

In [NaNL01], Naor et. al also discuss strategies to marry the CS method, respectively the SD method, with public key cryptosystems. Notice that public key cryptography offers mechanisms that allow each participant to securely broadcast messages. Dodis and Fazio [DoFa02] applied public key cryptography to the SD scheme. However, conventional public key cryptosystems require a trusted instance that maintains the public keys. To remedy this shortcoming, identity-based encryption schemes [Sham84, BoFr03, BoBo04] could be taken into consideration.

5.7 Further Schemes

In this section we briefly summarize some further mechanisms in this context. The first approach treats the problem of how to organize programs in order to reduce the key storage for the broadcast encryption. This is different from the approaches given above, since the others address the user organization and their revocation. Afterwards some trivial schemes that are used in practice are sketched out briefly, which are practicable, but insecure. Details on these schemes can be found in the book of McCormac [McCo98]. A good summary can be found in [Wool00].

5.7.1 Tree Scheme

Wool presents a scheme that uses binary trees [Wool00]. The basic idea is that program encryption keys are identified by public binary strings that are generated, when a binary tree is "walked" top down. These strings indicate, which keys are taken for the package encryption. In contrast to other schemes described in previous sections, the leaves of the tree represent programs instead of users. Since user revocation is not addressed at all, this scheme is not comparable with others.

Setup: Assign an identifier *id* to each broadcasted program. Create a full binary tree T where the tree height is equal to the number of bits the identifier is intended to have. Edges from nodes to their left successor nodes are labeled 0 and those branching to right successors are labeled 1. Assign a master key k_0 to the root node of the tree. A user gets a secret information (by handing out a smart card), such that the STB can only compute keys for designated programs (see below).

Encryption: To calculate the keys for a given identifier, perform the following steps: starting from the root, visit the edges in T top down such that the visited labels yield the required identifier. In each step apply $h(x \,||\, 0)$ when branched to the left edge and $h(x \,||\, 1)$ when turned to the right edge. Here h denotes an appropriate hash function and x is the result of the last hash output, which is k_0 for the first round. This produces the key k with which a program p is encrypted: $E_k(p)$. The encrypted program is broadcasted together with its identifier. Figure 5.8 illustrates an example where the key k, assigned to $CID = 011$, is computed.

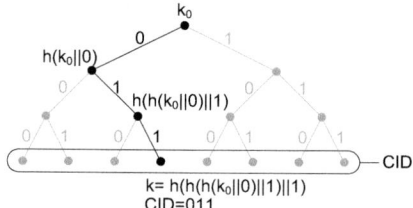

Fig. 5.8: Computation of program keys

Decryption: According to designated packages, the user is equipped with a smart card, which stores such keys securely. Here a key assigned to an inner node v_i means that all packages having an identifier, which matches the prefix of the visited edges on the way from the root to v_i, can be accessed. The reason for this is that from v_i all such identifiers can be computed by the concept given above. As described above, a user receives the id and the ciphertext $E_k(p)$ from the center. The user has to find out whether any of the identifiers, the user is equipped with, is equal to or is a prefix of the broadcasted identifiers. For the first case the user has already the right key and can decrypt the broadcasted ciphertext. In the other case, the user needs to derive the key from the key assigned to a prefix of the CID and can decrypt the ciphertext afterwards. In any other case the user is not authorized to decrypt the ciphertext.

5.7 Further Schemes

Let V be the set of all nodes in T, P be the programs represented as leaves in T, and S be a collection of programs that need to be packaged. The minimal set of tree nodes that covers S and nothing else is given by $C = Z \subseteq V$ such that $\bigcup_{v_i \in Z}(DoS(v_i)) \cap (V - P) = S$ with $|Z|$ is minimal. For the minimal cover set the number of nodes is bound by $O(n)$.

In [Wool00], Wool does not give a proof for this proposition. We motivate this claim by the following consideration.

Proof. Consider a user who wants to have access to the items associated with every second leaf in the tree (see Figure 5.9). It is obvious that in this case the worst case scenario is given: for any leaf node no parent node exists that encompass two excluded leaves, because one is taken and the other one is left out. Here a user needs $\frac{n}{2}$ keys to access the encrypted items. If any further leaf has to be excluded, we can combine the identifiers where both siblings are left out (see right tree). With respect to this situation, the identifier of their parent node can be used. □

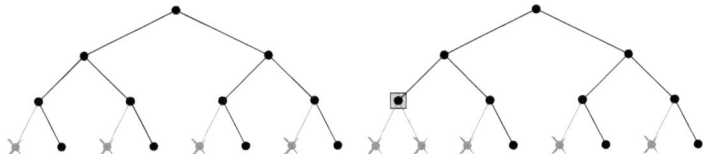

Fig. 5.9: $O(n)$ keys in the worst case

Remarks: Wool proposes a further scheme called *Vspace Scheme*. This scheme uses a secret matrix. To derive the according package keys, identifiers are multiplied with that matrix. The interested reader on this scheme is referred to [Wool00]. However, only collections of programs of size $2^n - 1$, for $n \in \mathbb{N}$, can be grouped to a package. Furthermore it suffers from the fact that a combination of keys would lead to further package keys.

5.7.2 Extended LKH

Recently, an improved scheme based on MARKS [Bris99] and LKH [WaHA98] was published as an internet draft [ZXHJ07]. It should be mentioned that Briscoe has already suggested the combination of these schemes in his paper [Bris99].

The basic ideas is to group members together according to their expected leave time. The encryption key for a data package is a combination of time-dependent key with a so-called *intermediate key* (IK). A user is revoked by updating the intermediate key to affected legitimate users. However, receivers are expected to be continuously online, otherwise users will miss update messages, which would disable them to decrypt further ciphertexts. Furthermore, the scheme assumes that receivers can store refreshed keys (non-stateless receivers). Aside, revoking a user causes a lot of updates.

Setup: The transmitted data is divided into data units of the same time length. The corresponding encryption keys, which are used to encrypt the data units in different time periods, are produced by so-called *Binary Hash Trees* (BHT) [Bris99]:

1. Create a binary tree such that the number of leaves is greater than or equal to the number of item units.

2. Assign a randomly chosen seed to the root node.

3. Exploit a circular left shift on the input and apply a hash function to generate the secret key of the left successor. Analogously, the original input data undergoes a circular right shift for the hash operation, which results in the secret key of the right successor.

Applied recursively all keys for the item units are produced. The keys, which are assigned to the leaves, are used for the encryption of data units in the corresponding time period (see left tree in Figure 5.10).

Additionally, the data structure *TR-LKH* based on the LKH concept is used. Note that in the LKH users cannot compute keys efficiently from parent to child node like in the BHT. TR-LKH is a tree that consists of two layers (see right tree in Figure 5.10), namely the *Time Logical Key Hierarchy* (T-LKH) and the *Receiver's Logical Key Hierarchy* (R-LKH). A leaf node in T-LKH is associated with a single time unit. All members, whose access authorization expires on the same date, are assigned to the same group. The groups represent a subtree of receivers (R-LKH) rooted at the expiration date in T-LKH. For each new member a further node is created in the related R-LKH. Thus, every node (also inner nodes) in R-LKH corresponds to a group member.

5.7 Further Schemes

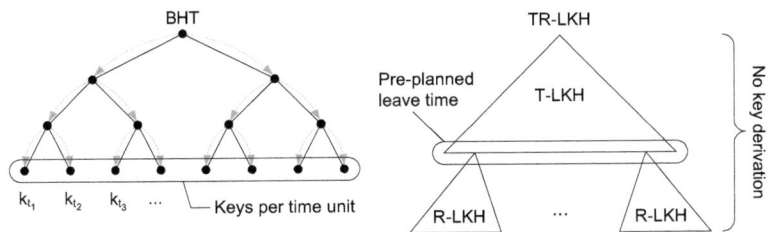

Fig. 5.10: BHT and TR-LKH

Adding a new member: When a new member has to be added, a new node is created in R-LKH rooted at the T-LKH's leaf, which is associated with the member's expected leaving time. Then the new member gets all keys on the path from the root to the new node in TR-LKH. Additionally the IK is sent to the new member. Note that the center shares an individual key with each user, so the keys can be transferred confidentially.

Encryption and decryption: First the data m is divided into blocks such that each block m_i belongs to a single time unit. Afterwards the key k_{t_i} associated with the leaf node v_i in the BHT is uniquely assigned to each block m_i. Next the center computes the corresponding encryption key as follows: $k_i = IK \oplus k_{t_i}$. Finally the center encrypts m_i with k_i and broadcasts the resulting ciphertext $E_{k_i}(m_i)$.

Revoking users: To revoke a user r having leaving time t_r, the center chooses a fresh intermediate key IK'. The revoking procedure requires that users are always online, because the refreshed key is transmitted to all other members. For members whose authorization expiration is after t_r, IK' is encrypted with the first key $k_{t_{r+1}}$ after t_r. To transmit the refreshed intermediate key to these users, the center broadcasts $E_{k_{t_{r+1}}}(IK')$. For users whose authorization expires before t_r the rekey process needs to be performed. Also affected nodes, i.e. common nodes between the path from root to that member and the path from the root to r, may be transmitted securely to these users.

Remarks: The scheme suffers from the assumption that all users are constantly online. In case of a revocation, many messages need to be sent (cf. [ZXHJ07]) where receivers are expected to save refreshed keys. Thus, stateless receivers are not supported. It should also be noted that if a single user is revoked, all members whose authorizations are active are involved by key updates, i.e. each member that uses the system needs to refresh at least one key.

5.7.3 The Biased Subset Scheme

In [AdGr05, Grev06] a broadcast encryption scheme is presented that does not strictly separate target set of receivers from others. This relaxation was first considered by Abdalla et al. [AbSW00]. Its idea is based on probabilities where designated receivers are expected to receive session keys more likely than others. Thus, a small number of so-called *free-riders*, which are users who are able to get contents they are not entitled to, are accepted. It focuses on the case where the designated receivers encompass approximately half of all users.

Setup: At the beginning users are grouped into t subsets $N_i \subset N$ such that $|N_i| = 0.5 \cdot |N|$. For each subset N_i a subset key k_{N_i} is generated. A user u stores the subset key k_{N_i} of a subset N_i if and only if u is a member of N_i. Thus, a user approximately stores $0.5\,t$ subset keys. When using PRNGs, this can be reduced.

Broadcast: Before programs are encrypted with a session key and are broadcasted afterwards, the user groups, which are established in the setup phase, are sorted according to their number of designated receivers. Then, the session key is transmitted bit-wise to the sorted groups as follows: let $k = k_1 k_2 \ldots k_\ell$ be the session key with $k_i \in \{0,1\}$. The single bit k_1 is encrypted with the key of the subset that is ranked in the first place of the sorted set (thus having the most legitimate users); k_2 is encrypted with the key of the subset that is ranked in second place and so forth. After that the encrypted bits are broadcasted. Then a certain number of users $\tilde{T} \subset T$ has received at least $d < \ell$ bits of the session key k. The authors suggest using a secret sharing scheme [Sham79] where the session key is distributed as $s_1, \ldots, s_\ell$ shares in a (d, ℓ)-threshold scheme. Then, instead of the single bits $k_1, \ldots, k_\ell$, the shares $s_1, \ldots, s_\ell$ are encrypted and broadcasted as described above. This allows to compute the session key k from d shares.

Additionally, each user shares a common key with the center. Legitimate users, who did not receive enough bits of the session key by the broadcast scheme given above, are served individually. For each such a user the center encrypts the session key individually (with the user key) and broadcasts the ciphertext afterwards.

5.7 Further Schemes

Remarks: As already pointed out by the authors, the scheme is highly vulnerable to a collaborative attack. They suggest applying the method described in Section 5.2.4 in order to achieve k-resiliency. However, the difficulty for a realization in practice and their increasing efforts are not mentioned.

In [AdGr05] it is claimed that the scheme is unconditionally secure due to the secret sharing scheme. However, the authors neglect the fact that the shares are transmitted conventionally, i.e. they are encrypted with symmetric group keys. Since the security of a system is always characterized by its weakest element, unconditional security is not guaranteed by the presented scheme.

5.7.4 The Bit-Vector Scheme

The bit-vector scheme is used by many analog European satellite TV systems. It is based on an obvious approach: all programs are encrypted with the same key, which is stored in every set-top box. For controlling access to the programs, the STB stores a bit vector indicating whether access to a program is granted or denied. The STB decrypts a program only if the corresponding bit in the vector is set to one. Hence, a package can be composed of any program subset, i.e. the highest possible flexibility is achieved. To prevent the vector from unauthorized manipulations, it needs to be stored in a tamper-proof memory. With increasing programs, the bit vector also augments. The security is not based on cryptographic mechanisms; it rather depends on the closure of the tamper-proof memory only. If an attacker is able to change the relevant zeros in the bit vector into ones, the STB would decrypt every program.

5.7.5 The Block-by-Block Scheme

In the block-by-block scheme, programs are split into n disjoint blocks. All programs assigned to a block are encrypted with the same key. Hence at most n keys are necessary. The STB stores the key a user buys. Since the access control depends on the user's secret key, it is more secure than the bit-vector approach. However, the flexibility of building packages from programs is reduced to the number of blocks. Assigning only a few programs to a block requires storing a huge number of keys for subscribers that may use programs from different blocks.

5.8 Comparison

Table 5.4 gives a comparison of the presented schemes. The comparison reflects header length in the broadcasted messages, keys that a user has to store, costs for a user revocation, resiliency and the strength of the security. In the column *Security*, information-theoretic security is denoted by *I*. All others refer to computational security. Hereby *OWF* denotes the security strength given by one-way functions, *RSA* refers to the security given by the RSA problem and *E* relates to the security of the underlying encryption function.

Tab. 5.4: Comparison of the schemes

Scheme	Header	Keys per user	Revoking	Resiliency	Security
Naor Basic	$0^\dagger$	$O(2^n)$	inherent	k	I
Naor OWF	$0^\dagger$	$O(log(n))$	inherent	1	OWF
Naor RSA	$0^\dagger$	$1^\ddagger$	inherent	1	RSA
LKH	0	$O(log(n))$	$2\,log(n)-1$	arbitrary	E
CS	$O(r\,log(\frac{n}{r}))$	$O(log(n))$	inherent	arbitrary	E
SD	$2r-1$	$O((log(n))^2)$	inherent	arbitrary	E
$\dagger$ requires a center that manages revoked users and that lists them on request					
$\ddagger$ requires a center that manages $O(n)$ public keys and delivers them on request					

The benefit of the Naor's Basic Scheme is that it is resistant against k collaborators in the information-theoretic sense. Furthermore the user revocation does not add data overhead for the broadcasted messages. However, it requires that non-revoked users have access to the revoked user list (where also measures need to be taken against manipulation), so that they can compute the currently used encryption key. Moreover a user has to manage $O(2^n)$ keys. This is far beyond the scope of devices with small resources (like smart cards). In particular, a user needs to hold all keys in the $\sum_{i=1}^{k} \binom{n}{i}$ subgroups of $U-T$. To compute the actual session key, $O(2^n)$ XOR operations are necessary at user side.

The OWF-based approach described by Naor et al. limits the key storage at user side to $O(log(n))$, because in this scheme a user only has to manage the keys of all nodes "hanging off" from the path. As in the scheme above, the access to the revoked user list has to be managed. Two users, where one is located in the left

5.8 Comparison

subtree of the root and the other is located in the right one, could reconstruct all user keys when they share their keys belonging to the right child of the root and to the left child respectively. With these keys any user key can be computed.

Naor et al. propose a further scheme, which uses the RSA encryption scheme. Apart from the resiliency and the maintenance of the revoked user list, this scheme seems to have idealistic complexity behavior, i.e. the scheme supports user revocation where no header information is necessary and a user only needs to store a single key. It has to be remarked that in this scheme users are assumed to access $O(n)$ public keys. Furthermore a user needs to execute costly $O(n)$ multiplications in $\mathbb{Z}_{\phi(m)}$ and an exponentiation in $\mathbb{Z}_m$. Hence a practical use of this scheme, especially when smart cards are used, is questionable.

The Logical Key Hierarchy scheme is resistant against an arbitrary number of collaborators from the revoked user set. In this scheme a user u has to store $log(n)$ keys due to the path length from the root to the leaf node u. No additional header information is required. In the case of a user revocation, the center broadcasts $2\,log(n) - 1$ ciphertexts. This scheme expects receivers with writable data storage. Moreover, the scheme assumes that the receivers are always online so that refreshed keys can be transferred. When it has to be expected that receivers may sometimes be powered off, these assumptions may disqualify this scheme.

The Complete Subtree method is more practical than the previous schemes, although $O(r\,log(\frac{n}{r}))$ additional header information is required. Here the tree is decomposed into at most $O(r \cdot log(\frac{n}{r}))$ subsets that incorporate all non-revoked users and none from the revoked users. A user needs to manage $O(log(n))$ keys. User revocation is implicitly realized by the header. The session keys are encrypted before their broadcast such that only non-revoked users are able to decrypt them.

The Subset Difference Method is similar to the Complete Subtree Method. The main difference between them is that the Subset Difference Scheme divides the non-revoked users in subsets whereby only the number of revoked users has a consequence on the header size. Notice that in the worst case $2r - 1$ encrypted session keys are necessary. However, this comes with an increase in the number of keys a user has to store: $O((log(n))^2)$. Both schemes are resilient against an arbitrary number of collaborators.

Key Derivation 6

> *The significant problems we face cannot be solved at the same level of thinking we were at when we created them.*
>
> ALBERT EINSTEIN

The past has showed us many examples, where attackers have succeeded in revealing secret information. Often the use of self-made algorithms was the main reason for its leakage. Sometimes, and not rarely, sudden disclosures are due to a careless key management. Bruce Schneier classifies key management as "the hardest part of cryptography" [Schn96]. Why attacking an encryption function, if the keys in a key storage can be much easier compromised? Securing a few keys is generally more feasible than protecting many keys. In particular, if the number of keys are expected to increase continuously or even exponentially, the key storage will exceed sooner or later the capacity of any storage component. Hence, the main aspect of this section focuses on a minimization of the amount of keys, such that the efforts for the key management are low. In particular, a key assignment scheme for posets is proposed that helps to reduce the key storage. This concept is used in the subscription models and key derivation schemes later.

6.1 Contribution and Structure

At the beginning a conceptual approach for a tree-based key derivation is defined. The main contribution of this section is an extension of the key assignment schemes for general posets, i.e. also non-trees are supported. Furthermore, an in-depth discussion on technical realization of the concept is given. Hereby implementation aspects of the key derivation function are considered; in particular when the HMAC, the AES, DLP-based one-way functions, and the RSA encryption scheme respectively is used as the derivation function.

This section is organized as follows: first, a motivation for a key derivation is given. Then, the key derivation function is defined conceptually. An easily applicable approach to cover also non-trees is described afterwards. The subsequent sections present some technical implementations. Finally, the last section compares the implementations reflecting performance and security concerns.

6.2 Motivation

Access control is a main topic in heterogenous environments. The question of how to efficiently control access to resources for different participants attracts many researchers. A popular strategy that reduces the effort for this task is the so-called *Role-Based Access Control* (cf. [SCFY96, SaSa96]). In this model rights are assigned to roles to which users are assigned. In particular operating systems have been taking advantage of this idea and in this context it has become common to declare roles like administrator, guest et cetera.

A possibility to enforce access rights on publicly accessible data is to encrypt it. Only those users who have the corresponding keys can decrypt the ciphertexts and thus can access the data. According to the security level, data is organized in different security classes. Dependencies between security classes are the basis for modelling them as hierarchical graphs. For the access control used in this work secret keys are assigned to security classes. Security classes may encompass classes with lower security levels. Granting access to all nodes based on this approach implies the possession of all associated keys. This means that one has to store as many keys as there are nodes in the hierarchy. A possibility to reduce the key storage is to use one-way key derivation functions, which make keys computable from keys assigned to higher security classes. Let us first consider the case when hierarchies are modelled as trees. Suppose that all keys are computable from the key of the root node (see left tree in Figure 6.1). For a special user group, in analogy to the operating systems this could be the administrators' group, members are supplied with the key of the root node. The key of the root allows to compute all other keys in the hierarchy. To endow someone with full access, only the key of the root is necessary. Hence, when each key is computable from the key of the root node, an administrator only needs to store the key of the root.

In the case that access is granted either to all nodes or to a single node, this mechanism would be fine. However, when a fine-granular access control is desired, a scalable mechanism is needed. If each key is derived from its parent node (see right tree in Figure 6.1), a key to a node that is different from the root node can be computed from the key of any of its predecessors.

Fig. 6.1: Direct and indirect derivation trees

This approach enables inheritance of access rights. The key of the root node is derived from a master key. Issues on generating, installing, and distributing master keys are addressed in [Meye82]; an interesting comparison with physical master keys is drawn in [Blaz03].

6.3 Conceptual Design

In this section we define the key derivation mechanism, which is used throughout this work. Given a hierarchy $G = (V, E)$, keys are assigned to nodes such that they are computable from keys of their ancestor nodes. Hereby $\kappa : V \to K$ is the key allocation function, which maps a node to a key from key space K. Similar to [Sand87], a key derivation scheme based on one-way functions is given. Extensions to cover posets that are non-trees are given in Section 6.4. The key assignment process for trees is performed by the following steps:

1. Assign a unique public node identifier id_i to each node v_i.

2. Let $f_k(m)$ be a publicly known one-way function which produces outputs of an appropriate fixed bit length from an input m and a key k. The secret key of a node $v_j \in Chd(v_i)$ in G with identifier id_j is defined by:

$$\kappa(v_j) := f_{\kappa(v_i)}(id_j)$$

The key k_0 of the root node v_0, which has identifier id_0, can either be randomly chosen or it is derived from a randomly chosen master key $k_{mk} : \kappa(v_0) := f_{k_{mk}}(id_0)$. Starting at the root node and repeatedly applying step 2 to subsequent nodes, a secret key to each node is assigned. To use these keys for encrypting contents by a symmetric encryption scheme like the AES [Rijm04], f_k must be selected such that it produces outputs in an appropriate fixed bit length. In case of the AES, this could be 128, 192 or 256. For an example implementation, the described key derivation function can be realized by an HMAC [KrBC97]. Details on this issue as well as alternative implementations are described in the subsequent sections.

6.4 Extensions for Non-Trees

This section specifies the key derivation mechanism for general hierarchies. Let $G = (V, E)$ be a non-tree-structured poset. As above, $\kappa : V \to K$ denotes the key allocation function and f_k is an appropriate publicly known one-way function. The keys are assigned as follows:

1. Assign a unique public node identifier id_i to each node $v_i \in V$.

2. For each node v_r (with identifier id_r) that has no parent node, assign a secret key by deriving it from a randomly chosen master key k_{km} as follows:
$$\kappa(v_r) := f_{k_{mk}}(id_r)$$

3. For each node v_j (with identifier id_j) that only has one parent v_i, assign a secret key as follows:
$$\kappa(v_j) := f_{\kappa(v_i)}(id_j)$$

4. For each node v_ℓ (with identifier id_ℓ) that has more than one parent node, perform the following two steps:

    a) Classify the parent node v_i, which will be mostly used. If this is not determinable, select one randomly. Assign a secret key to the node v_ℓ by $\kappa(v_\ell) := f_{\kappa(v_i)}(id_\ell)$.

    b) For each other parent node $v_p \neq v_i$, an edge-oriented key derivation approach (as proposed in [AtFB05]) is applied: for the edge (v_p, v_ℓ) the public parameter $r_{p,\ell} = k_\ell \oplus f_{k_p}(id_\ell)$ is stored and made publicly available. Thus, with the key of the parent node and the public information, the key of the child node can be computed efficiently by $k_\ell = r_{p,\ell} \oplus f_{k_p}(id_\ell)$.

In Figure 6.2 an example is illustrated where the items $i_1, \ldots, i_4$ are arranged in groups g_1, g_2 and g_3. Additionally, these groups are assigned to packages $p'_{2/3}, p''_{2/3}$, and $p'''_{2/3}$ so that each package encompasses two out of three groups. In this example it is assumed that g_1 is the mostly used group followed by g_2. Furthermore $p'_{2/3}$ is supposed to be the mostly used package followed by $p''_{2/3}$. The items in g_1 have the highest precedence and, according to the rules given above, their keys are directly derived (thick edges) from the key of node g_1. Analogously the keys for the nodes g_1 and g_2 are derived from the key of node $p'_{2/3}$. The key for the node g_2 is derived

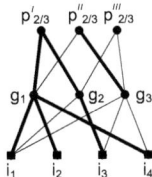

Fig. 6.2: Classifying the main parents

by its parent with the highest precedence, which is $p''_{2/3}$. For example, the item i_1 belongs to g_1 but also to g_2 and g_3. A computation of the key for item i_1 from g_2 or g_3 requires additional information as described in Step 4b).

In contrast to existing key assignment schemes as proposed in [AtFB05, ASFM06], additional data has to be stored only for those edges that are rarely used in the key derivation process. For frequently used edges no public edge information has to be stored. In each node a single bit could be used to decide whether the node or the edge derivation approach has to be applied.

6.5 Applying Keyed Hash Functions

When HMAC is used as the key derivation function, the key k_j of a node with identifier id_j is computed from the key k_i assigned to its parent node as follows:

$$k_j = \text{HMAC}_{k_i}(id_j) = h(k_i \oplus opad \,\|\, h(k_i \oplus ipad \,\|\, id_j))$$

To simplify discussions we choose RIPEMD-256, which is an extended version of RIPEMD-160 that produces 256 bit hash values, as an appropriate candidate for the applied hash function h. The parameters $opad$ and $ipad$ are two constants. Details on constructing keyed hash functions are given in Section 2.4.3.

For message authentication codes, the public identifier (as described above) does not need to be unique. In this case the strict uniqueness can be weakened to the following guideline: assign a public node identifier id_i to each node v_i, such that sibling nodes, i.e. nodes with the same parents, must have distinct identifiers; nodes with different parent nodes may have the same identifier. If there exist further hierarchies, the identifiers of the roots differ from each other.

For computing the key k_0 of the root, the master key k_{mk} (e.g. 256 bit) serves as the input key for the HMAC. From k_0 the key belonging to each child node of the root can be calculated by that function. Repeatedly applied to subsequent nodes, this function generates all keys in the corresponding subtree. Because all structural elements (node identifiers), constants (*ipad* and *opad*) and the presented derivation algorithm are publicly known by a system user, someone who has a key of a node can derive all keys in the subtree rooted at that node.

In fact, some attacks that can weaken MD5, RIPEMD-160, and recently also SHA1 [WaYY05, Lens05] are reported. Note that these attacks are mainly focused on breaking the collision resistance property of such hash functions and derive benefit from the birthday paradox. For a collision resistant hash function h the following must be practically intractable: find two different inputs x_1 and x_2 such that $h(x_1) = h(x_2)$. However, the problem in the context of key derivation functions using HMAC is a different one: having n HMAC outputs $y_1, \ldots, y_n$ denoting the secret keys of n sibling nodes $id_1, \ldots, id_n$ find $k \in \{0,1\}^c$ with constant c (here $c = 256$) such that for all i with $1 \leq i \leq n$ the following holds:

$$\text{HMAC}_k(id_i) = y_i$$

In other words, the goal of this attack is to compute the keys of parent nodes from those assigned to child nodes. In practice a user has one or only a few such outputs, depending on the structure of the hierarchy and the assigned permissions a user has. Even if such a k is found, for case $n = 1$ it is still not guaranteed that this would be the desired key, because a further key $k' \neq k$ might exist that yields to the same output. Since an attacker is interested in the original key of the parent node id_i, the birthday paradox emerging on collisions is not applicable in this context, i.e. the birthday paradox does not effectively reduce the efforts for the mentioned attack. Generally, message authentication codes fulfill the preimage resistant and second preimage criterion so that they withstand mentioned attacks.

The performances of the hash functions MD5, SHA-1, SHA-256, SHA-512, RIPEMD-160, RIPEMD-256, RIPEMD-320 are compared in [Dai07]. Table 6.1 shows the throughput results of these hash functions as software programs and hardware modules. The software is provided by the Crypto++ library proceeded by an AMD 64-bit Opteron 2.4 GHz processor running on Linux 2.6.18. One might observe that SHA-512 achieves a higher throughput than SHA-256. The reason for this is that SHA-512 processes 1024-bit block and operates with 64-bit operations whereas the other variants work with 512-bit blocks and 32-bit operations.

Tab. 6.1: Throughput (in Mbit/s) of hash functions

Algorithm	Software [Dai07]	Hardware [Sain05]
MD5	376	2091
SHA-1	216	2006
SHA-256	106	2370
SHA-512	178	2909
RIPEMD-160	178	1442
RIPEMD-256	263	—
RIPEMD-320	174	—

Benchmarks on some hash functions can also be found in [BoGV96]. Some hardware optimization techniques are investigated in [MCMM06]. The paper [TLYL04] shows how the throughput can be improved by using network processors.

6.6 Applying the AES

This section shows how the key derivation function can be realized by a symmetric encryption scheme. We specify the implementation such that a key k_j of a node with identifier id_j is computed by the key k_i of its parent node as follows:

$$k_j = E_{k_i}(id_j)$$

As in the HMAC variant, the strict uniqueness of identifiers is not necessary. Only the identifiers of root nodes and those of sibling nodes need to differ from each other. Due to the one-to-one mapping property of symmetric encryption schemes upon the same key k_{mk}, unique root keys are produced when such schemes are taken for embodying the specified key derivation function. It should be noted that bits are stuffed according to a predefined padding scheme unless the bit length of the identifiers is a multiple of the block length of the applied encryption scheme. Given a plaintext of 128-bit length, the AES produces a ciphertext of the same length. This is already an adequate bit size, because 128-bit keys are supported by the AES. In this case the output of the key derivation can be taken as the input key for data encryption. The AES does not produce unique keys when it is chosen as the derivation function for the key assignment scheme: both arguments (node identifier and keys) are refreshed when a key is derived from one level to another in the key derivation graph. Thus, the outputs might be equal; they are only different between sibling nodes, because the encryption function produces different outputs, provided that different inputs (identifiers of child nodes) are taken but the same key is used.

6.7 Applying the Discrete Logarithm Problem

In this section we use the Discrete Logarithm Problem (DLP) [McCu90, Odly00] as the building block for the one-way functionality of the key derivation function.

Choose a safe prime number p of an appropriate bit length. Select each node identifier id_ℓ such that it is a generator of $\mathbb{Z}_p^*$ (cf. [MeOV96]). Let id_i be a parent node of id_j and let k_i be the key of the node id_i. We define the key derivation function $f_{k_i}(id_j)$ that computes k_j from k_i as follows:

$$k_j = id_j^{k_i} \text{ MOD } p$$

As required by the key derivation concept, this construction provides a mechanism for computing the secret key of a node from the secret key of its parent node. The security is based on the DLP: given k_j, id_j, and p, find k_i, which is the discrete logarithm (to base id_j) of k_j in $\mathbb{Z}_p$.

In the context of key derivation schemes the main goal is to produce secret keys that are generally used for symmetric schemes. For instance, the AES is designed so that it operates with a key size of either 128 bit, 192 bit or 256 bit. However, the prime p must be selected sufficiently large. Factoring an n-bit integer takes roughly the same time than computing discrete logarithms in n-bit fields (cf. [LeVe00, LaOd91]). Lenstra suggests lower bounds on the bit sizes for finite fields in order to avoid being considered as insecure. In particular, he proposes the following minimal bit sizes for the applied prime p: 1279-bit for the year 2008, 1613 bit for 2015, and 1881 bit for 2020. Hence, if the key derivation in the DLP-variant is planned to be used until 2020, the prime p should have a bit length of at least 1881. By defining p of such a bit size, the key derivation function produces keys of the same bit size. Therefore, keys generated in this way need to be reduced accordingly such that they can be used as keys for the applied symmetric encryption scheme. This in turn means that two different kind of keys appear: one for the key derivation, and the other for the symmetric encryption scheme.

To generate AES keys of an appropriate key length, we deploy an adequate hash function h that produces the desired output length. Thus, the secret key k_i' for encrypting contents of node id_i is defined by $k_i' = h(k_i)$.

6.8 Applying the RSA Encryption Scheme

An application of the RSA encryption scheme [RiSA77] as key derivation function requires some adaptations. For the key derivation function a one-way derivation mechanism is needed. Given the RSA public key, the RSA encryption scheme provides a one-way mechanism. Additionally, it supports a way back facility provided that one knows the secret key. Here we show how to use the inverted function in the setup phase such that a derivation from several parents to a single child node is possible (see below). However, for the purpose in this work an inversion of the key derivation function should not be possible. It needs to be investigated where such an inversion does make sense. This might be a topic of an ongoing study.

For the RSA encryption scheme some preconditions must be fulfilled. To initialize the RSA encryption scheme, the following steps should be performed in advance:

1. Assign a unique $id_j \in \mathbb{Z}_{\phi(n)}^*$ to each node in the tree. Trivial values like 1, $\phi(n)-1$, and others are excluded.

2. Choose two safe primes p and q each greater than 2^{640}.

3. Compute the RSA modulus $n = p \cdot q$.

Note that only in the bottom-up key derivation variant the unique identifier must be coprime to $\phi(n)$, because only there the inverse element of the unique identifier modulo $\phi(n)$ is needed. In the top-down variant the public identifier can be randomly selected from $\mathbb{Z}_{\phi(n)}$, apart from trivial values as described above.

An implementation of the derivation function can be realized by the RSA encryption or decryption function, where e and n represent the RSA public key components and d is the RSA private key component:

$$E(m, e) = m^e \text{ MOD } n = c, \text{ respectively}$$
$$D(c, d) = c^d \text{ MOD } n = m, \text{ with } m \in \mathbb{Z}_n \text{ as plaintext}$$

The left tree of Figure 6.3 shows a top-down key derivation starting at the root node. In the top-down approach the unique identifiers can be generated and assigned either in advance or during the key derivation process. With the RSA decryption function a bottom-up variant of the key generation can be realized (see right tree of the Figure 6.3). The key derivation starts from the bottom (second left leaf node from left). After generating the key to its parent node and further the key to the root node, the others can be computed in top-down manner.

Fig. 6.3: Top-down and bottom-up derivation trees

6.8.1 Top-Down Key Generation

Let k_j be the key of a node id_j and k_i be the key of its parent node. We define the RSA-based top-down key derivation function as follows:

$$k_j = k_i^{id_j} \text{ MOD } n$$

The security of this variant is based on the RSA problem: given k_j, id_j, and n, find k_i, which is the id_j-th root of k_j in $\mathbb{Z}_n$. If $gcd(id_j, \phi(n)) > 1$, then there does not exist a d satisfying $id_j \cdot d \equiv 1 \pmod{\phi(n)}$. To make the RSA decryption function applicable, id_j has to be chosen such that it is relatively prime to $\phi(n)$.

Similar to the DLP-based variant, the output of this key derivation variant is too large as it could serve as a key in a symmetric scheme such as the AES. If n is a 1280-bit number, then a key derivation with the RSA encryption scheme produces 1280-bit keys. We reduce the key size by applying a hash function h that generates the appropriate output size. As in the DLP-based variant, the secret key k_i' for encrypting contents associated with the node id_i is specified as $k_i' = h(k_i)$.

While it is possible to compute each key from its parent key (see left tree of Figure 6.4), the top-down approach also allows a key derivation from any ascendant node (see middle and right tree in Figure 6.4) on basis of some pre-computations. Since $k_b = E(k_a, b) \equiv k_a^b \pmod{n}$ and $k_c = E(k_b, c) \equiv k_b^c \pmod{n}$, k_c can be calculated from k_a as follows: $k_c \equiv (k_a^b)^c \equiv k_a^{b \cdot c} \pmod{n}$. Hence k_e can also be computed by multiplying the exponents first and reducing the result accordingly: $k_e \equiv k_a^{exp} \pmod{n}$ with $exp = (b \cdot c \cdot d \cdot e) \text{ MOD } \phi(n)$. For installing shortcut edges,

6.8 Applying the RSA Encryption Scheme

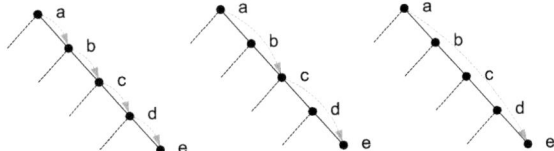

Fig. 6.4: Possible key derivation strategies

the relevant exponents might be pre-computed and stored accordingly. Then, a derivation from the corresponding node only requires one exponentiation in $\mathbb{Z}_n$.

6.8.2 Bottom-Up Key Generation

Suppose node id_j has two parent nodes (see Figure 6.5) whereby k_{i_1} is the key of the one and k_{i_2} is the key of the other parent. In the top-down approach producing a single key k_j from these parents would require satisfying the conditions $k_j = E(k_{i_1}, id_j)$ and $k_j = E(k_{i_2}, id_j)$. Assuming that different nodes have different keys, this requirement cannot be fulfilled by the top-down approach.

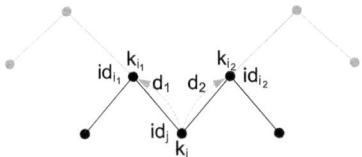

Fig. 6.5: Derivation trees

However, this requirement can be met by a bottom-up approach, whereas id_j is composed of two different RSA public parameters id_{j_1} and id_{j_2}. As mentioned above, in the bottom-up key derivation method relevant public parameters must be coprime to $\phi(n)$, because both mappings are needed: from the child node to the parent node during the key generation process by the system and vice versa during the key derivation by the users. A realization of the bottom-up key derivation variant that also supports a key derivation from multiple parents (here exemplarily shown with two parents) is given by the following steps.

1. Choose $k_j \in_R \mathbb{Z}_n^*$ as key for the child node id_j (trivial values excluded).

2. Select id_j as $id_j = id_{j_1} \| id_{j_2}$ such that id_{j_1} and id_{j_2} represent two different non-trivial RSA exponents that are relatively prime to $\phi(n)$.

3. Compute d_1 such that $id_{j_1} \cdot d_1 \equiv 1 \pmod{\phi(n)}$ and compute d_2 such that $id_{j_2} \cdot d_2 \equiv 1 \pmod{\phi(n)}$.

4. The keys of the parent nodes are computed as

$$k_{i_1} = D(k_j, d_1) \equiv k_j^{d_1} \pmod{n} \text{ and}$$
$$k_{i_2} = D(k_j, d_2) \equiv k_j^{d_2} \pmod{n} \text{ respectively}$$

Once the keys are computed, the two RSA secret parameters d_1 and d_2 are deleted. The key k_j can be computed from both, from k_{i_1} and also from k_{i_2}: $k_j = E(k_{i_1}, id_{j_1}) = E(k_{i_2}, id_{j_2})$. Hence, this approach enables key derivations from different parent nodes. This concept can be enhanced such that several parents are supported. As mentioned in the top-down approach, two types of keys per node emerge: one for the key derivation and the other serves as key for the symmetric encryption scheme. As above, the latter one is produced by applying an appropriate hash function on the key, which is generated by the key derivation.

6.9 Comparison

Table 6.2 shows the necessary time for a single, three, twenty, and one hundred key derivation/s per second when the HMAC, the AES or the RSA implementation is used. The time values are given in milliseconds. The test suites are carried out for several repetitions (three, twenty, and one hundred times as well as a single execution). All tests are performed on a Dell Latitude D800 notebook, with a Pentium M 1600 MHz processor, 512 MB RAM, java version 1.5.0_06-b05 and the IAIK crypto library jce_se_eval version 3.14.

Concerning the AES, performance results do not remarkably differ from each other when different key sizes (128,192, and 256 bit) are used. Comparing the variants in terms of performance, the AES achieves best results, imperceptibly quicker than HMAC. As one might expect, the RSA variant requires the longest computation time of these three variants. The careful reader might observe that the test suite for the DLP variant is left out. Similar to the RSA variant, an exponentiation followed by remainder computations is necessary. The speed of the computation is

6.9 Comparison

Tab. 6.2: Performance comparison

Mechanism	1x	3x	20x	100x
HMAC	0	0	10	20
AES	0	0	0	10
RSA	20	42	301	1466

weighty influenced by the size of the exponent. In the RSA variant, the public node identifier is taken for the exponentiation. Apart from fulfilling some properties, it is assumed that these values appear randomly. Therefore, it can be expected that the performance results for the DLP variant are close to those of the RSA variant.

6.9.1 Remarks

RSA variant: A serious security concern, which favors other variants over the RSA variant, is that all key derivations are calculated in the same modulus. If, in the RSA variant, $\phi(n)$ respectively p or q is revealed somehow, any other key (also the master key of the system) can be computed efficiently, provided that the unique identifiers are chosen coprime to $\mathbb{Z}^*_{\phi(n)}$ and the attacker knows at least one derived key. Under these assumptions it is possible to compute the key of any node in the system.

Furthermore in the RSA public key cryptosystem with the modulus $n = p \cdot q$ there exist $(1 + gcd(e-1, p-1)) \cdot (1 + gcd(e-1, q-1))$ so-called unconcealed plaintexts with the property $E(m, e) = m$ (e.g.: $m = 0$, $m = 1$ or $m = n - 1$). During the key generation, generated keys have to be tested on this criterion. If the described property is applicable, another id has to be chosen.

Derivation from multiple parents: Provided that each parent node identifier is selected appropriately, the RSA-based key derivation variant could be used to compute a single key from keys assigned to different parent nodes (see above). It should be noted that key derivations from multiple parents can also be realized by the AES or the HMAC. However, this requires that additional data has to be stored in the relevant nodes. The basic idea is to encrypt the key k_j of a node v_j (that has multiple parents) with each parent key separately. This concept is illustrated in the left key derivation graph of Figure 6.6. Alternatively to the

AES, the HMAC can be used. In this variant edge values are computed (similar to Attalah's scheme [AtFB05]) so that one with the secret key of the parent can compute the key of the child. The HMAC variant is illustrated in the right part of Figure 6.6.

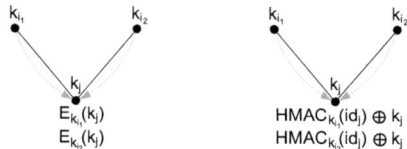

Fig. 6.6: Key derivation with multiple parent nodes

The ciphertexts, which are constructed in this manner, are attached to the node of the derived key. Someone with the key of a parent can decrypt the corresponding ciphertext in order to get the secret key of the child node.

Shortcuts: The concept of attaching ciphertexts for activating a derivation from multiple parents can also be used to install shortcut edges as illustrated in Figure 6.4. In particular when hierarchies are expected to be deep, it may help to reduce computation costs caused by the key derivation. Shortcut edges may contribute a crucial support for devices with small resources like smart cards.

Some applications require that keys are derived from the root key directly. When inheritance of rights is not desired, a simple derivation from the root node may be sufficient. The recursive approach enables inheritance of rights (see Chapter 11).

Concrete Implementation: Unless otherwise remarked, it is assumed that the key derivation functions in subsequent key management schemes are implemented as HMACs with SHA-256 [NIST02] as their applied hash function:

$$\kappa(v_j) := \mathrm{HMAC}_{\kappa(v_i)}(id_j)$$

The hash function within HMAC ensures that the output always has a fixed bit length. HMAC is designed such that it withstands a length extension attack. Furthermore, all contents, for which subscriptions should be defined, are symmetrically encrypted with the AES by keys of 256 bit.

6.9.2 Summary

There are several ways to realize a key derivation concept for hierarchies. In this section four types of implementations are investigated. An obvious implementation is given by MACs. Especially when pseudo-random keys are required, they are usually the first choice. If a symmetric encryption function is used for the key derivation, we have the assurance that sibling nodes are assigned with different keys. It should be mentioned that in a symmetric encryption scheme the number of output blocks depends on the input size. When the input is expected to be variable, the output needs to be reduced accordingly (here 256 bit). The performance of these implementations depends on what algorithms are used. Generally both variants (MACs and symmetric encryption schemes) are very suitable in practice and require unnoticeable time delays for small input values.

A different approach is followed by the DLP variant. However, it turns out to be less suitable for our purposes. A serious disadvantages over MACs and symmetric encryption schemes is that ensuring the security of the DLP requires large bit sizes. This drawback is two-fold. First, the operation of huge numbers leads to bad performance results, when compared with others. Second, two secret keys per node arise, one for the key derivation process and the other for the symmetric encryption scheme. Nevertheless the latter argument could also be an advantage, since per node two differently powerful keys are generated: one allows inheritance of access rights for descendant nodes and the other only allows local access. Some aspects on this issue are discussed in Section 8.5.

Asymmetric encryption schemes provide a further alternative for implementing the key derivation function. For instance, the RSA variant offers a top-down and also a bottom-up derivation. We have used the bottom-up facility to allow a key derivation from different parents. However, it must be further investigated, where such a "secret way back" (trapdoor in RSA) would make sense. This might be a topic for ongoing research. The disadvantages are analog to those described in the DLP-based variant. For the purposes described in this work, key derivations based on the DLP or the RSA-Problem are not recommended.

7. Subscription Models

> *Habe Mut, dich deines eigenen Verstandes zu bedienen.*
>
> IMANUEL KANT

Subscriptions are characterized by a privileged use of services whose validity is generally restricted. The following constructions receive their motivation from broadcast encryption (Chapter 5) and key assignment schemes (Chapter 4).

7.1 Contribution and Structure

This section contributes electronic subscription models. Subscriptions are introduced as authorizations to access contents in predefined time periods whereas different rights are represented by differently powerful keys. First, the *Tailored Subscription Model* (TSM) is presented, which suits to special situations in practice. We prove that subscription schemes of this type are resilient (based on computational security) against an arbitrary number of collaborators. Then, a general subscription model is proposed. After showing a weak construction, a secure variant is elaborated, which is referred to as the *Flexible Subscription Model* (FSM). This model is also proven to withstand any number of collaborators. In contrast to the TSM, it requires additional data to be sent. However, the FSM offers a combination technique that provides flexibility for creating subscriptions.

Some parts of this section are published at pertinent conferences. The ideas concerning derivation strategies are outlined in [Koll06]. Tailored subscription models are published in [Koll07a] and a preliminary version of the Flexible Subscription Model is published in [Koll07b].

After a motivation for subscriptions, this section raises questions concerning requirements. Then, a definition of subscriptions is given followed by a structural representation for contents (items) and time classes. Next both subscription models (TSM and FSM) are specified. A comparison of the models with other time-bound key assignment schemes follows afterwards. Finally security aspects of the presented schemes are discussed.

7.2 Motivation

Generally broadcast schemes assume to serve a large number of receivers. In times of globalization, service providers are often faced with a worldwide audience. The soccer world championship, the super bowl final or the Olympic Games are typical examples of global interest. For such global dimensioned events the live characteristic of the transmission is usually decisive, i.e. it is crucial that contents arrive at the receivers without noticeable time delay. Thus, potential bottlenecks, such as simultaneous user authentication of countless users, will possibly knock down the service provider. Hence, the traditional process, where users first log in and authenticate themselves in order to use services, may be inadequate.

Among audio and video broadcasts, there are further broadcast services of global scope. A prominent worldwide broadcasting service used today is the Global Positioning System (GPS cf. [gps]). It consists of at least 24 satellites, which orbit around the earth. They continuously transmit information that contains the satellite's identifier, the precise time, and the satellite's position. From the transmitted information of several GPS satellites, a GPS receiver is able to compute its position on earth. The GPS offers a more precise mode, the Precise Positioning Service, which is reserved for the US military merely. The exclusive usage of the more precise variant for reserved users is enforced by data encryption. Such applications could be taken into consideration for subscription systems: a privileged subgroup from all receivers should be able to use advanced services.

Another method that leads to an exact location determination is Differential GPS (DGPS) This is a service that supports GPS receivers with additional information such that they can react against faulty information transmitted by satellites. Basically stationary GPS receivers collect data from GPS satellites and compute divergences. The error reports are bundled and broadcasted either by geostationary satellites, which is called *Satellite-Based Augmentation Systems* (SBAS) or by local transmissions called *Ground-Based Augmentation Systems* (GBAS). Modern GPS receivers are capable of evaluating such reports.

These are just a few examples that give a vague idea of the potential when broadcast services for reserved user groups are desired. The careful reader may arouse the suspicion that belated changes of worldwide establishments can be very expensive. Therefore, before constructing such schemes, their requirements and functionalities need to be well considered. Possible extensions for the future might be carefully evaluated whether they should be (partially) integrated.

7.3 General Requirements

Dependent on practical use, requirements may differ. Criterions that the system has to fulfill should be considered well in advance. Hereby, designers are mostly afflicted with a trade-off between flexibility and practicability. Generally, the more features the scheme should support the more complex it will be, which makes it difficult for a realization in practice. It should be remarked that highly flexible schemes may need more payload than schemes that provide basic functionalities. On the other hand, inflexible schemes may need to be rebuilt from the scratch when additional features are to be supplemented later. Hence requirements should be well considered when such schemes are planned. Canetti et al. [CGI+99] raise some questions concerning broadcast security. Some of the described requirements are also reflected in this work and described below.

Group size: The number of participants can reach from small groups up to a world audience. While small groups may be handled by traditional concepts, the situation for a huge number of users can be a challenge. Bottlenecks could arise such that the availability of services is in danger. For instance, a simultaneous user authentication of numerous participants might cause a denial of service.

Computer power: What resources are expected? Do all members have similar resources or are there discrepancies? In the pay TV scenario there may be devices with limited resources. Nevertheless, alternatives need to be evaluated: are there possibilities for pre-computation that could be done by devices with more resources? When we refer to the pay TV example, is it possible to use the decoder box in order to assist the smart card with extensive computations?

Membership dynamics: Should users be able to join groups? Is it desired that members can leave groups at any time or are predefined leave times sufficient? How frequently are changes to be expected? How fast should they become effective? Is there a control center? What are the expected life times of such groups? In this work several types of user dynamics are investigated. Primarily time-bound memberships with a special emphasis on anonymity but also the revocation of single subscriptions are of main interest.

Sender: Which subjects should be able to send? Is there a single transmitter or are there several senders? Should all members be endowed to send messages? What about non-members? Conference systems usually expect that all group members are able to broadcast messages to the group members. The classic broadcast scenario assumes to have a single sender. Investigations in this work focus on the single transmitter scenario.

Payload: Is heavy payload expected? What is the maximum allowed latency? What type of data is transmitted (text, pictures, audio, video etc.)? Are real-time transmissions necessary? The following subscription models are capable of real-time transmissions with many receivers.

When contents are confidential and reserved for group members, security issues arise. Hereby, one might consider the following security concerns:

- Access control: How can it be ensured that only legitimate users are able to use services? Access control mechanisms need to be well considered and are crucial when a subscription scheme needs to be created.

- Secrecy: Is short-term secrecy or long-term secrecy required? For example news lose their attraction even after a short period of time. Thus, it may not be a main concern to encrypt this type of data by strong encryption schemes. However, in this work computational security is required.

- Availability: Are solutions considered for counteracting potential denial of services? What consequences are to be expected when a service breakdown occurs or when connections fail? In this work broadcast scenarios (without user interaction) but also protocols with user interaction are considered.

- Anonymity: Is it required that users remain anonymously? Should the broadcast sender be anonymous (cf. [DoOs97])? In this work approaches that preserve the users' anonymity are discussed.

In [BlMS96] three general strategies are classified so that a common key between privileged users is arranged. These are predistribution schemes, broadcast encryption schemes, and interactive key distribution schemes. Ensuring confidential communications between several participants, as it is required in confidential conferences (cf. for instance [BuDe94, BSH$^+$93]), is a related research topic. Although not exclusively, this work mainly focuses on broadcast communication.

7.3 General Requirements

Further requirements and security goals can be found in [CGI+99]. Note that some requirements may be contradictory. For instance, the need for anonymity and the need for restricting access to legitimate users may be conflicting requirements. We give a solution that meets both demands at the same time. However, a single solution satisfying all mentioned requirements is illusive. Nevertheless, we propose solutions for some practical scenarios and discuss several extensions.

Generally, the focus of an electronic subscription system is to deliver contents to privileged users within a set of receivers. An approach to ensure that only legitimate users will be able to access contents, is to encrypt the contents. Assuming that a privileged group has an adequate secret key, the decryption of broadcasted ciphertexts is possible. But such keys can be easily distributed to others, unless measures are taken against it. Often smart cards are used for protecting keys from unauthorized reading, copying, and distributing. For satellite television, *Set-Top Box* (STB), also called *Set-Top Terminals* (STT), are used that are able to read smart cards. It has to be evaluated whether it is sufficient to have a one-way communication channel or a bidirectional communication is favorable. In some applications reverse channels (uplinks) exist. For the subscription models we assume that there is no such reverse channel.

Dynamic group sizes: Subscription schemes should be aware of receivers that may tune in or tune out at any time. When a user joins a privileged receiver group, the key needs to be changed, because the joining user could have collected broadcasted ciphertexts before. If the same key is still used, the user is able to decrypt the collected ciphertexts. The prohibition of accessing previously sent data is referred to as *backward security*. For a similar reason the keys also need to be changed when a user leaves such a group (*forward security* see [McSh98]). Many approaches are based on the obvious idea to broadcast refreshed keys when keys are changed. However, this technique assumes that all receivers are able to store refreshed keys and are continuously listening for updates.

User revocation: For many commercial applications it is sufficient to have preplanned expiration dates of membership. Members may decide in advance how long they want to use services. Consider for instance traditional subscriptions for newspapers and magazines. Hereby subscriptions are typically defined over fixed time periods (e.g. month, quarters etc). In such scenarios installing strong user revocation mechanisms is usually exaggerated and may be out of scope.

Suppose that authorized users (e.g. users who pay for their subscriptions) are supplied with keys, which are valid for a certain time period only. A simple approach to revoke subscribers is to stop supplying them with any further keys. Then users are automatically revoked at the end of a key's lifetime. This approach is easy to implement and other users are not affected when the membership of users expires. Ad hoc revocation is not supported by this concept.

However, there occur situations in which mechanisms for an unplanned user exclusion is required. In literature approaches are proposed that realize immediate revocation of subscribers (see Chapter 5). Extensions for ad hoc subscription revocation are investigated in Chapter 8. To compare schemes with each other, performance results need to be evaluated. In this context especially the following questions are of main interest:

- How many keys have to be stored secretly by a user?
- How much data overhead is expected for the broadcast center?
- Which features are supported?
- How secure is the scheme against non-members (resp. revoked users)?

7.4 Assumptions

For the following subscription models we assume that there is a single broadcast center that serves a huge number of receivers. We take the infrastructure of the broadcast transmission for granted. Furthermore we suppose that receiver devices are generally affordable. Contents that are to be transmitted are encrypted and the resulting ciphertexts are broadcasted afterwards. We assume that in principle any receiver can capture the transmitted ciphertexts. The secret information, which is necessary for the decryption of the delivered ciphertexts, is protected by tamper-proof devices like smart cards. Only a privileged subset, e.g. paying customers, called *subscribers* are supplied with such devices. This ensures that the plaintexts are reserved for privileged users. Furthermore, the issued smart cards should prevent privileged users from distributing their keys to non-privileged users.

Since attackers have been making progress to enfeeble the security of tamper-resistant hardware, reliable subscription schemes should not unconditionally trust tamper-resistant devices if possible. Suppose one has managed to reveal the secret

7.4 Assumptions

information from the smart card. Then, the attacker should ideally not gain more information than the smart card is entitled to (cf. [Wool00]). Upgrades from a less privileged to a more privileged package should be prevented. Hence, no other secret except the subscription information should be stored in the smart card.

However, problems arise when the data, which is sent from the smart card to the decoder box, is tapped. Usually sensitive data like the Control Word (CW) that enables to decrypt the scrambled data is transmitted. The interception and distribution of this information is known as the McCormac Hack [McCo98]. This attack is usually easy to carry out in practice. Some countermeasures are described in Section 3. For now we assume that the connections between smart card and the STB, respectively between the STB and the output device are sufficiently secured by some standard technologies.

We require that the subscription models are able to handle dynamic user behavior. This means that users may join or leave at any time. Additionally we require considering measures for protecting the anonymity of users.

The data transmissions for the subscriptions are expected to be heavy, as it is the case for video broadcasts. We assume that delivered contents (items) are divided into groups, which for instance are offered by further packages. A package could for example consist of two item groups out of three, which is illustrated by the left poset in Figure 7.1. Often products can be uniquely assigned to groups that can be further uniquely arranged to other groups. This would form a tree structure as illustrated in the right tree in Figure 7.1. Note that in both cases the items are represented as leaves, while non-leaves represent groups of items.

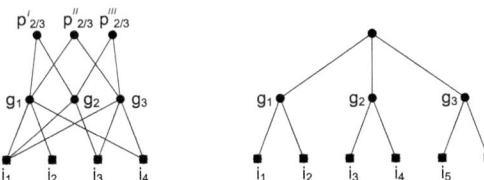

Fig. 7.1: DAGs and trees

In the following sections the proposed concepts are mostly based on trees, because trees are very likely to appear in practice. However, it should be remarked that the functionality of the described variants are not limited to trees: in Section 6.4 an approach is given that allows to extend the proposed variants for non-trees.

7.5 Definitions

Let $G_P = (V_P, E_P)$ be a graph that covers the items (products), to which a subscription can be assigned, with the relationships to their groups. Leaf nodes represent items and a node $v_p \in V_P$ covers the elements of $DoS(v_p)$.

Let $G_T = (V_T, E_T)$ be a graph that represents the time intervals with the relationships to their time categories, whereby the shortest specified time periods are leaf nodes and a node $v_t \in V_T$ covers the time intervals of $DoS(v_t)$.

Figure 7.2 illustrates a tree-based representation of G_T, where subscriptions can be uniquely assigned to the classes in $T_C = \{\text{unlimited}, \text{year}, \text{month}, \text{day}\}$. It is clear that the time intervals could be easily structured in more detail, for instance quarters, several years or hours of a day. Generally the time intervals can be arbitrarily refined.

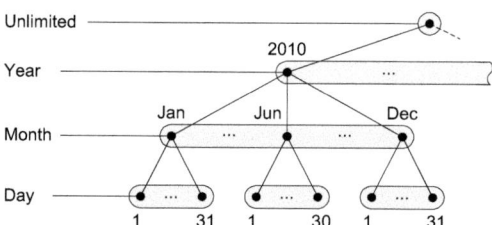

Fig. 7.2: Time interval classes

Let $\kappa : V \to K$ denote the *key allocation function*, which maps each node to a key from key space K.

Subsequent sections show several subscription models, which are based on a *key derivation graph* $G = (V, E)$ whose keys are computable from associated keys of their parent nodes in G. Now we specify what we mean by a subscription.

7.6 Tailored Subscription Models   109

A *subscription* $s \in \kappa(V)$ is a secret information, which is associated with a node in the key derivation graph $G = (V, E)$. According to the position in G, it enables to derive keys for the corresponding contents within corresponding time periods. Thus, it represents a time-bound authorization to access a certain item, a selected group of items or all items of offered digital contents.

It is assumed that G_T, G_P, and G are publicly available. Apart from a single exception, a subscription described in this section represents a single secret key that is assigned to a node in the key derivation graph G. Therefore, a user only needs to store a single key per subscription.

7.6 Tailored Subscription Models

This section describes Tailored Subscription Models, referred to as *TSM*. They offer solutions that are well applicable for many needs in practice. A key derivation graph based on TSM is easy to implement, keeps the storage costs low, and it provides resiliency against an arbitrary number of collaborators. However, a disadvantage of the TSM is that belated changes in the derivation tree can cause high efforts, since the tree is tailored for special needs at the beginning.

We start with simple subscriptions that often appear in practice. In particular, key derivations are investigated that are limited to either G_P or G_T. The first case allows to construct key derivation graphs for subscriptions that have no predefined expiration dates. In the second case subscriptions with full access to offered electronic goods are supported. Afterwards we present combination techniques that enable the integration of temporal and structural components into the subscriptions. For a subscription described in this section, a user only needs to store a single secret key that is assigned to a node in the key derivation tree G.

7.6.1 Subscriptions without Time Limitations

Consider the case for which it is not possible or not wanted that the time periods of subscriptions are limited in advance. Hereby the time limits for associated keys are indefinite. To realize subscriptions for an indefinite time period, it is sufficient to reflect G_P only, i.e. here the key derivation is restricted to G_P. Therefore, we define the key derivation graph G as $G := G_P$ where subscriptions are elements from $\kappa(V_P)$. A realization of such a concept is given by the following two steps.

1. Apply the key derivation process to G_P as described in Chapter 6.

2. Each assigned key is used for encrypting the contents, which are associated with the corresponding structural level.

A subscription $s \in \kappa(V_P)$ is the secret key of a node in V_P. The power of the subscription depends on the associated node. Provided that the key derivation graph is a tree, the subscription associated with the root node provides full access to all contents. Aside key derivation, each subscription serves as key for encrypting the contents that are associated with that node as well as for the decryption of their ciphertexts. The presented approach is time independent. But this does not necessarily mean that these subscriptions last endless: for instance, a change of the secret key on the root node can make all subscriptions invalid for further use.

7.6.2 Subscriptions without Access Limitations

In some cases only subscriptions with full access to contents are of interest. For such scenarios it is not necessary to divide subscriptions into separate structural divisions. Therefore, we specify the key derivation graph G as $G := G_T$ where a subscription s is an element in $\kappa(V_T)$. Subscriptions without structural limitations are realized by the following steps.

1. Apply the key derivation process to G_T as described in Chapter 6.

2. Each assigned key is used for encrypting the contents, which are associated with the corresponding structural level.

The associated node in V_T determines the validity of the subscription. In particular a subscription for a node v_t covers the time periods of $DoS(v_t)$ in G_T.

7.6.3 Hybrid Key Derivation Trees

For subscriptions that should be temporally and structurally scalable, both aspects have to be considered. Figure 7.3 shows two possibilities to combine G_P with G_T.

Structure extended by time: Consider the case where the structural tree is extended by the temporal tree (left variant of Figure 7.3). Let I_P be the non-leaves (inner nodes) and L_P be the leaves in G_P. We define $G = (V, E)$ as the key

7.6 Tailored Subscription Models

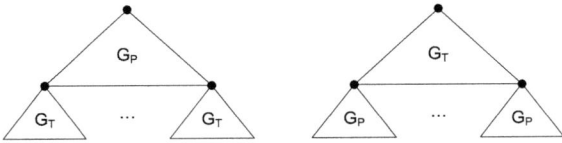

Fig. 7.3: Hybrid variants

derivation graph by taking G_P and replacing each leaf in G_P with a copy of G_T. Hence the set of vertices is given by $V = I_P \cup (L_P \times V_T)$. As before, a subscription $s \in \kappa(V)$ is the secret key of a single node in V. To extend the structural graph G_P with the temporal graph G_T, we apply the following algorithm:

Algorithm 2 AddTrees($G_1 = (V_1, E_1)$, $G_2 = (V_2, E_2)$):

$G = (V := V_1, E := E_1)$
L$:= Leaves(G)$
for all $v_j \in L$ with v_i as its parent node **do**
  $G'_2 = (V'_2, E'_2) := G_2$ with uniquely renamed nodes and v'_{02} as the root of G'_2
  $V := V \cup V'_2$
  $E := E \cup E'_2 \cup \{(v_i, v'_{02})\}$
  $E := E - \{(v_i, v_j)\}$
  $V := V - \{v_j\}$
end for
return G

The basic idea is the following: all leaf nodes in G_P are replaced by a copy of the graph G_T. The nodes in the temporal subtrees are renamed accordingly so that the identifiers are unique. AddTrees(G_P, G_T) returns the result, which is illustrated in the left tree of Figure 7.3. Concerning the temporal validity, subscriptions associated with non-leaves in G_P are indefinite, while subscriptions related to leaves are temporally customizable. Depending on the time period, the relevant contents are encrypted with the key of the associated leaf (in G). According to the key derivation concept, keys assigned to inner nodes represent subscription keys from which the keys of the leaf nodes can be iteratively computed (see Section 6.3). This approach is suitable when subscriptions defined on item groups should always be indefinite or unlimited, while a subscription on a single item should be scalable. With this concept, it is possible to generate $|I_P| + |L_P| \cdot |V_T|$ different keys. All possible combinations would require supporting $|I_P| \cdot |V_T| + |L_P| \cdot |V_T|$ different subscription variants, which is equal to $|V_P| \cdot |V_T|$.

Time extended by structure: Another possibility of combining G_P with G_T is to extend G_T by G_P. Analogously to the previous variant, we define the key derivation graph $G = (V, E)$ as G_T and replace each leaf in G_T with a copy of G_P: $\text{AddTrees}(G_T, G_P)$. This variant could be interesting when the structure of G_P has to be changed very often. In case of a structural change in G_P, the subscription keys are not affected in G_T. Let I_T be the non-leaves in G_T and let L_T be the leaves. A subscription is a secret key, which is associated with a node $v \in V$. It allows to derive keys for nodes in $DoS(v)$. This variant offers $|I_T| + |L_T| \cdot |V_P|$ different subscriptions.

Mixture of time and structure: Further special cases can be realized, when structural and temporal aspects are mixed in the derivation graph. In Figure 7.4 the items are embedded between the temporal classes year and month. Thereby different types of several subscription classes are covered: a subscription for a year can either be defined on a single item (e.g. node i_1) or on all items (node 2010).

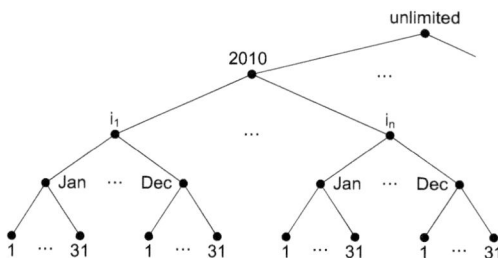

Fig. 7.4: Mixture of structure and time

A mixture of time and structure supports customized cases, i.e. the set of possible subscriptions is a selected subset of $\kappa(V_P \times V_T)$. It suits many needs in practice.

7.6.4 Security

In the schemes described above, a subscription consists of a single secret key. More precisely, it represents the secret key of a node in the corresponding derivation tree. By applying the derivation function, the secret key enables to compute the key for each descendant node in the key derivation tree. Since any subscription enables to derive keys for descendants nodes, we get the following corollary.

7.7 The Flexible Subscription Model

Corollary 7.1: The proposed schemes are complete.

The question, which has to be clarified, is whether or not it is feasible to create a new valid key for a node v_i from keys assigned to nodes that are not members of $AoS(v_i)$. We denote collaborators as a group of users, who share their keys and work together aiming to obtain keys they do not possess. Suppose that they try to obtain a key assigned to a node in $AoS(v_i)$, to which none of them has access.

Theorem 7.2: The presented scheme is resilient (based on hash functions) against an arbitrary number of collaborators.

Proof. Let $G = (V, E)$ be the key derivation graph. In the proposed schemes a subscription $s \in \kappa(V)$ is represented by the key of a single node $v_i \in V$. According to the derivation concept, s entitles access to $DoS(v_i)$. Computing a key of a node from a key of its descendant node is infeasible, i.e. the security is given by the strength of the underlying one-way function (here HMAC). Discussions on this issue are covered in Chapter 6. Also, keys from the collaborators cannot be profitably combined so that a key is created to which the collaborating actors are not entitled. The reason for this is that the key k_i assigned to node v_i undertakes a unique derivation path from the root to v_i, i.e. the only objects that affect k_i are the keys assigned to nodes on that path. These nodes are covered by $AoS(v_i)$, whose keys the collaborators do not share. □

7.7 The Flexible Subscription Model

In this section the question of how to build subscription schemes that cover all tuple combinations of $(V_P \times V_T)$ is investigated. This section presents two solutions to this problem. In the first approach we show how to combine two secret keys to achieve full flexibility. However, the high level on flexibility comes with a drawback: the security of this variant is based on the difficulty to break tamper-proof devices. After that we present a second approach that is resilient against an arbitrary number of collaborators. We denote this model as the Flexible Subscription Model (FSM). Due to security restrictions, the first approach is referred to as FSM^-. For the FSM (second approach), the broadcast center needs to transmit additional information. However, the broadcast center only needs to store a single key and also per subscription only a single key is necessary. Aside low storage costs, the highest possible flexibility is achieved, which makes it very interesting for practical use. Section 7.8 discusses security issues of the presented schemes. In Section 6.4 an extension to support posets that are non-trees is given.

7.7.1 FSM$^-$

In this section a solution is given that achieves the full range of $|V_P \times V_T|$ combinations for building subscriptions. The basic idea is to assign secret keys to both graphs, G_P and G_T. According to the key derivation concept, these keys enable to derive the keys for subsequent nodes. The encryption (resp. decryption) key is created from the keys of the leaves from both graphs. Hence, in this approach, a subscription consists of two secret keys: one is associated with a node in G_P and the other is associated with a node in G_T. Exclusively for this approach, we redefine the subscription s as $s \in (\kappa(V_P) \times \kappa(V_T))$; the other subscription models use the definition ($s \in \kappa(V)$) as given above. The FSM$^-$ is defined as follows.

1. Apply the key derivation process to G_P as described in Section 6.3.

2. Apply the key derivation process to G_T as described in Section 6.3.

3. An item $v_x \in Leaves(G_P)$ at time $v_y \in Leaves(G_T)$ is encrypted with the key $k_{x,y} = \text{HMAC}_{\kappa(v_y)}(\kappa(v_x))$.

With only two secret keys, subscriptions for all combinations of $(V_P \times V_T)$ can be realized (see proof below).

Theorem 7.3: The proposed scheme is complete.

Proof. Let $G_P = (V_P, E_P)$ be the graph that represents the items with their associated groups; let $G_T = (V_T, E_T)$ be the graph that represents the time classifications. Let further $s = (k_p, k_t)$ be a subscription with k_p as the secret key of an arbitrary node $v_p \in V_P$ and k_t as the secret key of an arbitrary node $v_t \in V_T$. Then, for each $v_x \in DoS(v_p)$ with $k_x := \kappa(v_x)$, there exists a path w_p from v_p to v_x in G_P. Given the secret key k_p and proceeding the path top down (from parent to child node) according to the derivation concept, k_x can be calculated in $|w_p|$ derivation steps. Analogously for each $v_y \in DoS(v_t)$ with $k_y := \kappa(v_y)$, there exists a path w_t from v_t to v_y in G_T and hence k_y can be computed in $|w_t|$ derivation steps. The corresponding encryption key $k_{x,y}$ is produced by applying HMAC on k_x and k_y (see Step 3). Thus, from the keys of any pair $(v_p \in V_P, v_t \in V_T)$ corresponding encryption keys in $(DoS(v_p) \times DoS(v_t))$ can be computed. □

7.7 The Flexible Subscription Model

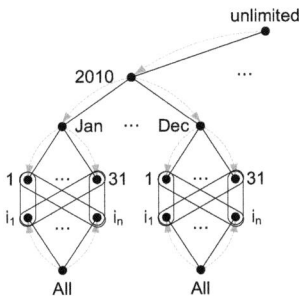

Fig. 7.5: Key derivation example according to FSM$^-$

Example 7.1: Figure 7.5 illustrates an example. The structural tree is flipped vertically so that one can easily observe that the leaves of both key derivation trees determine the corresponding encryption keys. The one-way derivation directions are marked by broken lined arrows. To realize a subscription for a year on all items, the key of node *2010* and the key of node *All* is necessary. Consider, for instance, a user wants to decrypt the encrypted item i_1, which is delivered on 31st December 2010. Then, with the subscription key of node *2010*, the key assigned to node *Dec* is derived. Subsequently the key k_y for 31st is computed from the key of node *Dec*. Analogously, from the subscription key of node *All*, the key k_x assigned to the item i_1 is derived. The decryption key is computed by $\text{HMAC}_{k_y}(k_x)$.

Security: The security of FSM$^-$ is based on the reliance of tamper-proof devices. Suppose two cardholders i and j have managed to undermine the security of their tamper-proof devices. Then, they can share their subscription information (k_{p_i}, k_{t_i}) and (k_{p_j}, k_{t_j}). If $k_{p_i} \neq k_{p_j}$ and $k_{t_i} \neq k_{t_j}$, then they could produce two further valid subscriptions (k_{p_i}, k_{t_j}) and (k_{p_j}, k_{t_i}). Generally, having n disclosed smart cards with empty intersections on items and time intervals, then $n \cdot (n-1)$ new subscriptions arise: n subscriptions refer to n items, which can be combined with the time intervals of the other $n-1$ subscriptions. Provided that a smart card only holds one subscription, at least two hacked cards with different subscriptions are necessary to exploit the described attack: breaking a single device would reveal only the information that the cardholder is already entitled to use. To prevent this attack, subscription information has to be stored in a "real" tamper-proof device. It should be noted that the confidentiality of data in tamper-proof devices serves as the basis of many applications (e.g. private keys for digital signatures) where cards are utilized for protecting secret keys against reading, copying, and distributing. Even though some cardholders could break their cards and share their keys, superior keys (and also the system's master key) could not be computed: this would require breaking the derivation function.

7.7.2 FSM

Ideally a subscription model offers maximum flexibility while being resistant against an arbitrary number of collaborators. In this section a model is proposed that meets these requirements. In contrast to the FSM$^-$, the broadcast center needs to transmit additional information. Let $G_P = (V_P, E_P)$ be the tree, which represents the product hierarchy, and let $G_T = (V_T, E_T)$ be the tree, which covers the time intervals for the subscriptions. Extensions for non-trees are described in Section 6.4. We define $G = (V, E)$ as the key derivation graph with $V = V_P \times V_T$ where each node $v_i \in V$ gets a unique identifier id_i. The FSM proceeds as follows.

1. For the root node of G_T, set $G = G_P$ and apply the key derivation process to G as described in Section 6.3.

2. While not already selected, choose a node v_{t_j} with shortest distance to the root in G_T. Let v_{t_i} be the parent of the selected node. Create a copy $G'_P = (V'_P, E'_P)$ of G_P, rename identifiers accordingly, and add V'_P to V: $V = V \cup V_P'$. For each node $v'_\ell \in V'_P$, derive its key k'_ℓ from the key $\widetilde{k_\ell}$ of the corresponding "mirror node" $\tilde{v}_\ell$ in the node set $\widetilde{V_P}$, which has been created for v_{t_i}. The mirror node $\tilde{v}_\ell$ has the same position (in $\widetilde{G_P}$) as v'_ℓ has in G'_P. The key k'_ℓ is computed as $k'_\ell = \text{HMAC}_{\widetilde{k_\ell}}(id'_\ell)$ with id'_ℓ as the public identifier of node v'_ℓ. Each derivation adds a further edge to E: $E = E \cup \{(\tilde{v}_\ell, v'_\ell)\}$.

This approach creates the key derivation graph G such that for each node $v_t \in V_T$ the set of nodes V_P is duplicated. The copied nodes are connected in such a way that for each node an incoming edge is built starting from its "mirror node" in the duplicated node set, which is associated with the parent in V_T.

Example 7.2: Suppose that unlimited subscriptions as well as subscriptions for years, months, and days should be supported. The right tree in Figure 7.6 represents the time hierarchy, whose nodes cause copies of V_P in the key derivation graph (left graph). The key derivation graph illustrates the derivation hierarchy

7.7 The Flexible Subscription Model

between the created copies of G_P. As illustrated, the keys for the copied nodes are derived from those, which are created for the parent node in V_T. Since for each node in V_T, all nodes of V_P are duplicated, $|V_P \times V_T|$ different nodes are created.

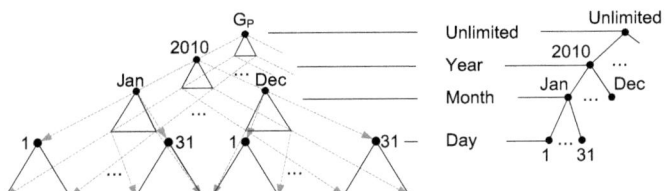

Fig. 7.6: Key derivation example according to FSM

Encryption: Before the contents are delivered, they are encrypted with corresponding keys. The key derivation graph prescribes the keys that are used for encrypting the contents (and decrypting the transmitted ciphertexts respectively): according to structural assignments, delivered contents correspond to leaf nodes in G_P. Remember that inner nodes represent sets of items, which allow to define subscriptions that refer to different items. Starting with the keys of these leaves, the key derivation process passes through the temporal hierarchy levels and finally reaches the lowest temporal level. Consider the encryption of contents associated with $v_p \in Leaves(G_P)$ for the 1st of January 2010 in the example above. Parameterized with the key of node v_p and the identifier of the corresponding node in V'_P of 2010, the key derivation function produces the key of the latter node. Analogously the corresponding key in the hierarchy that represents January and finally the corresponding key for the 1st January is produced. The latter key is used to encrypt the contents of v_p at the given date.

Additional data: Except for the nodes in the highest temporal level (see Figure 7.7), a key of a node in the key derivation graph does not support key derivation for descendants in the structural graph. In order to support also structural derivations, the broadcast center transmits the following additional data: for each edge (v_i, v_j) in the duplicated structural graph of the lowest temporal level with $k_i := \kappa(v_i)$ and $k_j := \kappa(v_j)$, the edge information $r_{i,j} = k_j \oplus h_{k_i}(id_j)$ is broadcast. Here id_j is the identifier of node v_j and h_k is an appropriate keyed hash function.

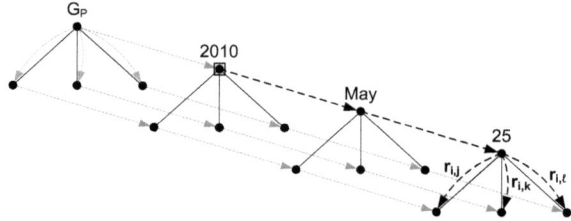

Fig. 7.7: Additional data to enable structural derivations

Subscription: A subscription represents the key of any node in the key derivation graph $G = (V, E)$. Since $V = V_P \times V_T$, a subscriber can be endowed with a subscription of any possible structural and temporal combination. The subscription enables the derivation of the corresponding keys of the associated contents for the intended time periods. According to the key derivation graph, temporal derivations are possible. As described in the previous paragraph, additional data is necessary for structural derivations in the lowest temporal level. In Figure 7.7 an example for a full year's subscription is given. The subscriber has the key of the root node of G'_P, which is associated with the year 2010. This key allows to derive the key of the root node in the lowest temporal dimension (here day). From additional data, which refers to the edges of the structural graph in the lowest temporal dimension, the relevant key of any descendant in G_P can be computed.

Theorem 7.4: The proposed scheme is complete.

Proof. A subscription represents a key of a node in the key derivation graph, so that it is associated with a structural node v_{p_i} in G_P and a temporal node v_{t_j} in G_T. The key derivation graph enables to derive the keys of the node v_{p_i} for any subsequent temporal level in $DoS(v_{t_j})$. Let w be the path from v_{t_j} to its leaf that represent the relevant time period (which is covered by v_{t_j}). Then, the key derivation process takes $|w|$ steps to compute the corresponding key for the lowest temporal level. From the additional data, the key of any structural node in $DoS(v_{p_i})$ can be computed for the relevant time period. Hence from a subscription associated with v_{t_j} and v_{p_i}, the key of any temporal and structural descendant node can be computed. □

Theorem 7.5: The presented scheme is resilient (based on hash functions) against an arbitrary number of collaborators.

7.7 The Flexible Subscription Model

Proof. In the proposed schemes a subscription s represents the key of a single node v_i in the derivation graph G. Suppose to have a set of collaborators where none of them has the key of any node in $AoS(v_i)$ in G. Their goal is to compute the key k_a of a node $v_a \in AoS(v_i)$. When none of the collaborators has a key of a node in $Des(v_i)$, they might try to guess such a key. Provided that the key size is sufficiently large and an adequate key derivation function is used, which produces appropriate pseudo-random keys, the chance for a successful guess is negligible. Consider the case that at least one of the collaborators has a key k_j of a node in $Des(v_i)$. If one member knows such a key, all of them know them, because we assume that collaborators share their keys. For each node in $v_t \in V_T$, G_P is copied whereby – except in the highest temporal level – each key is derived from the corresponding key (at the same hierarchy level) in the duplicated graph G'_P that is associated with the parent node of v_t in G_T. Thus, computing a time-bound key from a key with a shorter validity is intractable, provided that inverting keyed hash functions is intractable. As far as the structural hierarchy is concerned, the FSM supports key derivations from parents to child nodes only in the copied graph G'_P of the highest temporal level and that of the lowest temporal level (the latter is provided by additional data). In both cases keyed hash functions are used. Hence the security of the key derivation concept presented in this section is given by the strength of the keyed hash functions. $\square$

7.7.3 Evaluation

The derivation steps of the FSM⁻ and the FSM are bound by the longest path length in G_P plus that in G_T. For instance, referring to Example 7.2 the longest path length in G_T is 3. In practice the number of key derivations are typically bound by $O(1)$. To compute the decryption key, FSM⁻ requires an additional HMAC operation. Concerning the data complexity, the derivation concept, covering G_P and G_T, is made publicly available. All keys in the system can be derived from the master key, which is a random secret number of 256 bit. The service provider only needs to store the master key secretly.

At the user side, for a subscription two keys of 256 bit each are necessary when the FSM⁻ is used. The FSM requires only a single key (256 bit) per subscription. After the assigned time period has expired, the subscription cannot be applied to produce any further valid keys; the subscription becomes invalid. It is clear that in case of possessing multiple subscriptions where one is more powerful than the others a user only needs to store the most powerful one. For instance, a year's subscription covers a subscription of the same item for a month within that year.

For the FSM, the issuer has to publish additional information, which consists of the edge values in the lowest temporal hierarchy. This information can either be published in advance or the corresponding edge values can be sent with the associated contents by each broadcast. If we have by example 30 structural nodes in V_P, then 29 edge values are to be transmitted. Provided that for producing the edge information a keyed hash function is selected that produces 256 bit values, this would result in additional 0.91 kB data, which needs to be sent.

For a comparison of published time-bound schemes in literature with the FSM and FSM$^-$, an overview of the space and time complexity is listed in Table 7.1. Here m denotes the RSA modulus and t_1 and t_2 represent dates ("time points").

Tab. 7.1: Comparison with other schemes

Scheme	Key Derivation	Public Storage
Tzeng	$O(t_2 - t_1 + |V_P|)$ Exp + $O(1)$ H	$O(|V_P|)$ P
Chien	$O(t_2 - t_1 + |V_P|)$ H + $O(n)$ X	$O(|V_P|^2)$ E
Yeh	$O(|V_P| + |V_T| + log(m))$ M	$O(|V_P| + |V_T|)$ P
FSM$^-$	$O(|V|)^\dagger$ H	$O(|V|)$ Id
FSM	$O(|V|)^\dagger$ H	$O(|V|)$ Id + $O(|E_P|)$ P
Legend	<u>E</u>xponentiations in $\mathbb{Z}_m$	<u>E</u>ncrypted data (fixed size)
	<u>M</u>ultiplications in $\mathbb{Z}_{\phi(m)}$	<u>P</u>ublic values
	<u>H</u>ash operations	<u>Id</u>entifier (fixed size)
	<u>X</u>OR	
† This is typically $O(1)$ in practice		

For Tzeng's scheme [Tzen02], there are $|V_P| + 6$ public parameters necessary (each less or equal than the size of the selected RSA modulus). A key derivation in Tzeng's scheme requires $t_2 - t_1 + r$ modular exponentiation operations, where t_1 and t_2 denote the time limits for the time-bound access control, and r is the number of nodes, which satisfy $v_k \leq v_i$ and $v_k \leq v_i$. Additionally, $t_2 - t_1$ Lucas operations and a hash operation are necessary. The key derivation is bound by $O(t_2 - t_1 + |V_P|)$ modular exponentiation operations plus $O(1)$ hash operations.

In Chien's scheme [Chie04] the number of public parameters depends on the number of edges in the hierarchy. In the worst case there are $|V_P| \cdot (|V_P| - 1)/2$ edges and public parameters. For a key derivation in a path with length p, p hash operations and p XOR operations have to be performed. To generate the key in a given time period, there are additionally $t_2 - t_1$ hash operations and two XOR operations necessary. For the worst case, in which the hierarchy is a list, $(|V_P| - 1) + (t_2 - t_1)$ hash operations plus $(|V_P| - 1) + 2$ XOR operations have to be accomplished. Thus, the complexity is given by $O(t_2 - t_1 + |V_P|)$ hash operations and $O(|V_P|)$ XOR operations.

Yeh's scheme [Yeh07] has to manage $O(|V_P| + |T|)$ public parameters (each less than $\phi(m)$) where T denotes the set of the time periods. To derive a key k_ℓ from a key k_i, $|DoS(v_i)| - |DoS(v_\ell)|$ plus $|T|$ multiplications modulo $\phi(n)$ are necessary for computing the desired exponent. Additionally the exponentiation requires less than $2 \cdot log_2(m)$ multiplications (with reductions to $\mathbb{Z}_m$). Hence the key derivation is bound by $O(|V_P| + |T| + log(m))$ modular exponentiation.

It should be remarked that, according to Tzeng's and Yeh's schemes, the computations are each performed in the same RSA modulus. Besides, the models presented in this work do not assume to have a limited life time of the system like Tzeng's and Chien's scheme do.

7.8 Further Security Notes

When we investigate security features, we are interested in the question of what collaborators can attack. Indeed, one might transmit secret keys to non-legitimate users once they are disclosed. The key transmission is a serious problem in the DRM leadership. One counter-measure is to include techniques for user revocation, which we want to discuss in the subsequent chapter. We assume that keys are secretly stored in tamper-resistant devices. Even though we must strive for damage limitation, in case that the security of such devices is undermined. Therefore, a secure key management scheme disallows the ability of creating new subscriptions from existing ones. As already shown, the FSM$^-$ does not meet this requirement: already two legitimate subscribers can create two further subscriptions (see above).

For the TSM and the FSM, compromised subscriptions of broken tamper-proof devices cannot be combined such that new subscriptions arise. We motivate this in the following argumentation. A key management scheme is collusion-resilient if it withstands the collaborative attack. Assume that some attackers have managed to reveal the secrets in their tamper-proof devices, which they exchange with each other. Suppose that they have keys for different nodes in the hierarchy, but no key of any node in $AoS(C_j)$. Their goal is to get the plaintext of the encrypted items where none of them is entitled to use or to reveal a key, to which none of them has access. For this attack, among public parameters, they have the secret keys from all collaborators. Choosing HMAC with SHA-256 as its hash function produces 256 bit keys, which are supported by the AES. The security of the encrypted contents is thus guaranteed by the AES with the highest possible key length. To recover a key to which the collaborative attackers do not have access, it is necessary to invert the used key derivation function. The difficulty to reveal the key k_i of a node $v_i \in AoS(C_j)$ is given by the strength of the one-way function. In the given case HMAC is used as key derivation function. Alternative implementations and further details are given in Chapter 6 and in Section 2.4.3.

7.9 Comparison

The TSM almost offers perfect properties. In comparison to others, no additional header information for the users has to be sent and thus, it saves a lot of bandwidth. Furthermore a subscription requires storing a single key only. Additionally, schemes based on this model are computationally secure against an arbitrary number of collaborators. They are also resistant against a collusion of legitimate users that collaborate to create new subscriptions. During initialization, TSM-based schemes are adapted to meet specific requirements. A disadvantage of the TSM is that it allows to create less subscription variants in comparison to the FSM. When a great variety on subscriptions is required the FSM will probably be unfavorable.

Schemes based on the FSM^- provide the full range of possible subscriptions. However, a drawback of such schemes is that they only support 1-resiliency (based on keyed hash functions): the secret keys from already two different subscriptions can be gainful combined to build a new subscription provided that the secret keys of smart cards are revealed. For FSM-based schemes, the broadcast center does not need to send header information. Per subscription two secret keys are necessary.

The FSM provides both, full flexibility for subscriptions and resiliency (based on keyed hash functions) against an arbitrary number of collaborators. In contrast to the others, additional data needs to be sent. The amount of the additional data

7.9 Comparison

depends on the number of edges in G_P. However, the broadcast center only needs to store a single key. Also per subscription only a single key is necessary.

Tab. 7.2: Comparison of the subscription models

Scheme	Additional Data	Keys/Subscription	Revocation	Resiliency	Security
TSM	0	1	time-out	∞	E/HMAC
FSM$^-$	0	2	time-out	1	E/HMAC
FSM	$O(|E_P|)$	1	time-out	∞	E/HMAC

The presented subscription models are compared in Table 7.2. The security of all schemes is based on the applied encryption function and the applied key derivation function, which is HMAC. All three schemes offer subscription expiry by time-out, i.e. the subscriptions become invalid after their pre-planned time has passed by. Further extensions on these models are investigated in subsequent sections. Possible extensions reflecting revoking mechanisms are discussed in Section 8.3.5.

8 Extended Features

*Don't find a fault,
find a remedy.*

HENRY FORD

This section proposes possible extensions for the described subscription models. Plain subscriptions might need some adjustments to meet further requirements. The presented features are suitable for special cases that may occur in practice.

8.1 Contribution and Structure

In this section some extended features for the subscription models are described. In particular, we show how to support extraordinary subscriptions that are valid for non-continuous time intervals. Subsequently, it is investigated how revocation subscription can be supplemented. Hereby a framework is proposed that allows to integrate revoking mechanisms into the subscription models. Then, a strategy for upgrading existing subscription entitlements is presented. Finally, we show how to enable and also disable inheritance of rights. This in turn gives a transition for the final sections of this work, where rights on documents are studied.

8.2 Non-continuous Time Intervalls

In previous schemes it is assumed that a subscription is defined over consecutive time periods (e.g. subscription for a whole year). Sometimes only special parts within a time period are eligible. For instance, a subscriber for a newspaper could be only interested in Friday issues because on Friday the newspaper is shipped with an extended financial part. When using the described subscription models, special suited subscriptions require several keys; e.g. for each Friday issue a separate key is necessary. Henceforth, we classify subscriptions with consecutive time intervals as *standard subscriptions* and others as *special subscriptions*. To reduce the amount of keys for special subscriptions, we suggest the subscription issuer to create a further key derivation graph as follows.

1. For each special subscription, create a tree of height 1 such that each leaf is assigned to a separated time unit. If several special subscriptions can be interlaced, the tree height can also be extended (see example below).

2. Uniquely assign a public identifier id_j to each node v_j.

3. Choose a random number k_r and assign it to the root node.

4. Apply the key derivation concept on the special subscription tree such that a key k_j is assigned to each node v_j (different from the root): $k_j = f_{k_r}(id_j)$.

Let $k_{p,t}$ be the key with which the item p is encrypted at time period t. Suppose that the time period t corresponds with the leaf node v_j in the tree of the special subscription. To support special subscriptions, the service provider (issuer) delivers the additional information $c = E_{k_j}(k_{p,t})$ together with the encrypted contents. From c the user with the corresponding special subscription can compute the utilized decryption key: $k_{p,t} = D_{k_j}(c)$. The key $k_{p,t}$ enables to decrypt the transmitted ciphertexts belonging to p at time t.

A user needs to store only a single key per special subscription. The broadcast center needs to transmit additional information. If it is possible to combine some special subscriptions, then the derivation tree for the special subscription is adjusted such that several special subscriptions are addressed. The following example illustrates a realization of this idea.

Example 8.1: Consider a newspaper agency that offers among standard subscriptions also special subscriptions for workdays, weekdays, and for a single weekday within a year. Figure 8.1 illustrates a derivation tree that combines all such special subscription variants in a single derivation tree: those who subscribe for workdays get the secret keys of the corresponding workday nodes, weekend subscribers are supplied with the secret keys of the weekend nodes. Analogously subscribers of single weekdays get the secret keys of the corresponding weekdays. In this case the leaf nodes refer to calendar weeks. Their keys are used for encrypting the key $k_{p,t}$ with which the corresponding contents are encrypted.

This concept enables a coexistence of standard subscriptions and special subscriptions. The broadcast center encrypts the keys with those from the special subscription. Both ciphertexts, encrypted keys and encrypted contents, are broadcasted.

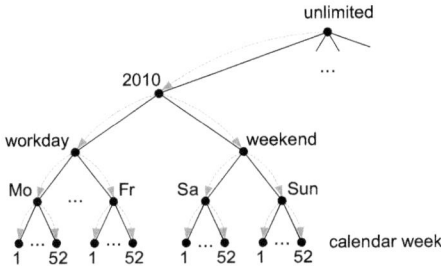

Fig. 8.1: Example for non-continuous time intervals (special subscriptions)

8.3 Revocation

In this section several proposals for integrating revocation mechanisms into the presented subscription schemes are contributed. Certain approaches ranging from simple precautions (causing no further efforts) to the integration of ad hoc revocation schemes (with additional efforts) are discussed. Also, a framework is given that conceptually specifies how subscription schemes can be extended by existing revocation schemes such that – among planned revocations – also unplanned revocations are provided. In context of storage complexity, the efforts of the resulting schemes are the same as they are necessary for the underlying revocation schemes.

8.3.1 Simple Precautions

Until now, ad hoc revocations of subscriptions are not considered in the presented subscription models. Excluding several subscriptions before they expire, requires that subscriptions can be uniquely distinguished. The broadcast center could send messages such that revoked subscriptions are set inactive for further use. Generally such an integration of revoking mechanisms will cause additional costs. In this section methods are discussed that aim at a trade-off between the integration of costly revoking schemes and schemes without revoking mechanisms.

Variant 1: Time Limits
The following idea could help to reduce the threat of compromised subscriptions and it may diminish the motivation for an attack. For subscriptions as described in this work, users can neither alter their content-specific assignments nor they

can change their designated validity time, even if the secret keys of the subscriptions are exposed. Hence subscriptions become worthless after their designated time period. The shorter the time period for a given key, the less powerful it is, since it will expire soon. When the broadcast center limits each subscription to a short time period, attackers may be discouraged from hacking smart cards and distributing compromised keys. In particular, unlimited subscriptions must not be issued. When only short-lived subscriptions are released, the consequences for a compromised subscription is less harmful as it would be the case for long-term subscriptions.

Variant 2: Key Update
Another possibility to avoid revoked subscriptions getting out of control is to unearth compromised keys, keep a record of them, and react as follows: when a specified number of compromised keys is exceeded, certain subscriptions are annulled. The easiest way to revoke and reset subscriptions is to install a new master key from which all other keys are generated. Then, all subscriptions lose their validity immediately. Valid smart card holders might be served with refreshed subscriptions and smart cards respectively. But the question remains: How do the system know when the number of compromised keys has evolved to such an extent? Here abnormal buying patterns of subscriptions, but also conclusions from news reports on the internet etc. can inform about such an incident. If fraud can be limited to a small set of subscriptions or to a few time periods, only their associated public identifiers need to be changed. Modifying the identifier of a node v_i in the key derivation graph will impact key updates of the nodes in $DoS(v_i)$. Therefore, the consequences of a key update are restricted to that node and its descendants.

Variant 3: Local Subscription Update
A key refreshment as described in the previous paragraph requires an update of all descendant keys. For a subscription revocation with local consequences, one might consider an edge-oriented approach as described in Section 4.4.4. Then, instead of deriving keys as described in Section 6, keys of appropriate bit length are randomly selected and assigned to the nodes in the key derivation graph $G = (V, E)$. For each edge $(v_i, v_j) \in E$, the edge information $r_{i,j} = k_j \oplus h_{k_i}(id_j)$ is made publicly available. Hereby id_j denotes the identifier of node v_j and k_j (resp. k_i) is the secret key of node v_j (resp. v_i). The advantage of this edge-oriented approach is that a modification of a single key for a node $v_i \in V$ evokes updates of the public information only for those edges, which start or end at node v_i (cf. Section 4.4.4) in

8.3 Revocation

G. However, due to the public information of the edges, the storage size increases by the number of edges in the key derivation graph.

8.3.2 1-resilient Revocation Scheme

For integrating an ad hoc revocation scheme while keeping the bandwidth low, this section suggests a 1-resilient scheme (the next section deals with stronger security requirements). Here an approach is presented that does not use the concept of header information as it is outlined in previous sections. The idea is that the encryption key is extended with a further component that only non-revoked users are able to compute. A technique which ensures computationally secure 1-resiliency is described in [FiNa94]. In particular this section shows an adaptation of this approach that allows to extend the presented subscription models of Chapter 7 so that ad hoc revocation of valid subscriptions is supported.

Setup:

1. TC chooses two different sufficiently large safe primes p and q and computes the RSA modulus $n = p \cdot q$.

2. TC randomly selects an integer $r \in \mathbb{Z}_n^*$ such that $gcd(r \pm 1, n) = 1$ and computes the secret value $g = r^2$ MOD n. This ensures that the order of g is high and has no small factors (cf. [ACJT00, CaGe98]).

3. For each subscription (resp. user) u an appropriate unique public RSA parameter e_i is chosen, such that $gcd(e_i, \phi(n)) = 1$ and $gcd(e_i, e_j) = 1$ for two different subscriptions (resp. users) i and j. TC computes d_i, such that $e_i \cdot d_i \equiv 1 \pmod{\phi(n)}$. TC publishes each e_i and keeps each d_i secretly.

4. For a subscription u, the corresponding secret subscription keys are stored together with the secret value $s_u = g^{e_u}$ MOD n in a smart card. The smart card might be offered to customers (e.g. for purchase) afterwards.

Let $k_{p,t}$ be the encryption key, which is produced according to the subscription model for encrypting content p at time t. Let $T \subseteq U$ be the target group within the user set U. Assume that users i and j are to be revoked, i.e. $T = U - \{i, j\}$. Then we define the new encryption key $k_{p,t,r}$ that also reflects revoked users r by using an appropriate hash function h as follows.

$$k_{p,t,r} = k_{p,t} \oplus k_r, \text{ with } k_r = h(g^{e_T} \text{ MOD } n), \text{ and } e_T = \prod_{i \in T} e_i \text{ MOD } \phi(n)$$

At time t the content p is encrypted with the key $k_{p,t,r}$ (instead of key $k_{p,t}$). Then, for the decryption one needs both, $k_{p,t}$ and k_r to compute the decryption key. Consider a single smart card holding a valid subscription u for item p. The smart card stores the key $k_{p,t}$ or it can compute this key according to the underlying subscription model. Among the valid subscription key also the secret s_u is stored in the smart card (see setup above). From s_u and the public exponents of the remaining non-revoked users the key k_r can be computed as follows.

Decryption:

1. TC announces the set of revoked subscriptions (resp. users) $R = U - T$. This information is made publicly accessible.

2. The smart card holding subscription u computes $h(s_u^{\prod_{i \in T - \{u\}} e_i} \text{ MOD } n)$. Provided that $u \notin R$, the result of this computation is k_r.

3. Now the smart card is able to compute the key $k_{p,t,r}$: $k_{p,t} \oplus k_r$.

Unless revoked, from s_u and the public exponents of the remaining non-revoked subscriptions, k_r can be computed. Suppose to have a subscription model where a valid subscription u enables to compute $k_{p,t}$. The definition of the encryption key $k_{p,t,r} = k_{p,t} \oplus k_r$ expands an existing subscription model by an ad hoc revocation mechanism. For every non-revoked valid subscription, the computation of the corresponding key is possible. This leads to the following corollary.

Corollary 8.1: This revoking scheme is complete.

Security: To compute the key $k_{p,t,r}$, the knowledge of $k_{p,t}$ and k_r is necessary. Assuming that both components are random numbers having the same bit length, a single component does not reveal any information about $k_{p,t,r}$. While the security of $k_{p,t}$ is given by the applied subscription model, the security of k_r is given by the problem of finding the e-th root (e as the public RSA key component) modulo a composite integer n, which is referred to as the RSA problem. Under the

8.3 Revocation

assumption that there does not exist an algorithm that efficiently computes roots modulo large composite integers, the presented scheme is 1-resilient (cf. [FiNa94]).

Suppose that a smart card, which holds a subscription u, is successfully attacked such that $s_u = (g^{e_u} \text{ MOD } n)$ is revealed. Knowing s_u does neither help to increase the designated subscription entitlements nor it empowers to annul revoked subscriptions. However, if a further secret revocation information, differently from s_u, is compromised, then both secret values can be used to compute g (see Section 5.2.3). As a consequence the subscription revocation can be cancelled. A disclosure of the generator g abrogates the revoking mechanism completely. Hence the mechanism does only guarantee 1-resiliency based on the RSA problem.

Performance: An advantage of the described revoking mechanism over header-based schemes is that the broadcast center is free from encrypting messages with several subgroup keys. In header-based schemes, broadcasting the numerous separately encrypted ciphertexts causes a lot of bandwidth waste. For the given concept the center only needs to broadcast a single ciphertext per plaintext. In the initializing process, the center computes $e_T = e_1 \cdot e_2 \cdots e_n$ MOD $\phi(n)$.

It is clear that when a huge number of subscriptions is expected, the computation given by step 2 cannot be performed by a smart card. The assistance of a powerful STB does not help here, because s_u should never leave the smart card. Even a pre-computation of the s_u's exponent by the STB is not a good idea, because, then, the STB needs to know the secret value $\phi(n)$.

To cope with this obstacle, a Trusted Third Party (TTP) can be taken into consideration that knows $\phi(n)$ and the secret key d_u of each subscription u. With this information it is able to compute the exponent for any subscription efficiently. The TTP computes $exp_u = e_T \cdot d_u$ MOD $\phi(n)$ for each subscription u. Provided that u is valid and not revoked, with s_u and exp_u the key $k_{p,t,r}$ can be computed.

Consider the case, when the broadcast center wants to revoke the subscriptions i and j. Changing the set of revoked subscriptions requires refresh e_T: TTP replaces e_T with the new value $e_T \cdot d_i \cdot d_j$ MOD n. As a consequence the current encryption key $k_{p,t,r} = k_{p,t} \oplus h(g^{e_T \cdot d_i \cdot d_j}$ MOD $n)$ for content p is refreshed.

The TTP manages the individual exponent of each user in a look-up table (see Figure 8.2). When a user r is revoked, the stored values are refreshed by multiplying each entry with the secret RSA component d_r of each revoked user r.

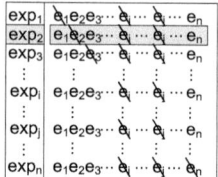

Fig. 8.2: Pre-computed values held by the TTP

The table holds the pre-computed value for each subscription, which is the product (modulo $\phi(n)$) of all public exponents except those from the revoked users and also that of the requesting user. Consider the non-revoked subscription 2, for which the corresponding smart card holds the value g^{e_2} MOD $\phi(n)$. On request, the TTP searches the corresponding exponent for subscription 2 in the table and answers with the pre-computed value $exp_2 = e_T \cdot d_2$ MOD $\phi(n)$. With this value, the smart card holding subscription 2 can compute $h(s_u^{exp_2}$ MOD $n)$, which is k_r. Finally the key $k_{p,t,r}$ is computed by $k_{p,t} \oplus k_r$.

8.3.3 Framework for Header-based Revoking Schemes

In the following, a framework is described to which existing revocation schemes based on header information can be applied (see next section). Similar to the previous section, the encryption key is expanded by a further component k_r. However, now k_r is randomly selected and no relationship to the RSA problem is given. The framework allows to realize stronger requirements than 1-resiliency.

In the pay TV scenario, long latencies will occur when programs are switched, unless header information is immediately available. Hence, the header information needs to be sent frequently. Wool [Wool00] suggests two mechanisms to solve this problem. Either the STB is always switched on so that it is able to receive and scan header information continuously. Corresponding encrypted header information is stored in an unprotected memory. Another possibility is to install a fixed channel, which transmits the current header information of the programs to the receivers. In this section subsequent considerations assume to have a fixed channel.

Due to the fact that the presented subscription models do not need any header information, the header size of the combined schemes, which result from the following framework, is determined by the utilized revocation scheme.

8.3 Revocation

Setup: In the setup phase the following steps are performed.

1. Create G_P and G_T following the subscription model.

2. According to the revocation scheme, create a binary user tree T_U where the users are represented as leaves; eventually the number of leaves is extended to a power of 2. The users are equipped with their corresponding keys.

Broadcast: To broadcast the data, the center performs the following steps.

1. According to the selected header-based revocation scheme, divide the non-revoked users from T_U into subtrees $T_1, \ldots, T_m$.

2. Choose a random key k_r.

3. For each non-revoked user group encompassed by T_i with $1 \leq i \leq m$, separately encrypt k_r with the key, which is assigned to the root node of T_i.

4. Create a list that holds the identifiers of the legitimate groups and together with the ciphertexts (due to Step 3) broadcast the list.

5. Let $k_{p,t}$ be the key, which is produced by the chosen subscription model for encrypting the item p at time t. Encrypt the content p with the key $k_{p,t,r} = k_{p,t} \oplus k_r$.

For computing the key $k_{p,t,r}$ also the key k_r is necessary. Thus, the encryption key consists of a further component that restricts access to legitimate users. When only legitimate users are served with k_r, unwanted users can be excluded.

Decryption: A valid non-revoked subscription enables to generate the decryption key as follows. According to the subscription model, from valid subscriptions the key $k_{p,t}$ can be produced. Unless revoked, the encrypted key k_r can be retrieved from the broadcast channel and decrypted by the key associated with a node from the transmitted index list. With $k_{p,t}$ and k_r the decryption key $k_{p,t,r} = k_{p,t} \oplus k_r$ can be computed, which enables to decrypt the encrypted messages.

8.3.4 Applying the CS/SD Revocation Schemes

In this section the integration of the Complete Subset and the Subset Difference revocation schemes into the framework described above is considered. Instead of single users, the revocation of single subscriptions is addressed. It is expected that the applied revocation schemes hold subscriptions as leaves in their "user trees".

The fusion of a subscription model with a revocation scheme offers both, an ordinary subscription expiry and also an extraordinary subscription invalidation. This means that among regular time-outs of subscriptions, an exclusion of single subscriptions is also provided. As a benefit, the pairing of a subscription model with a revocation scheme requires the same storage complexity as it is already given by the applied revocation scheme. The latter one determines the groups that en bloc cover all non-revoked subscriptions. For these groups, header information is created so that computing the encryption key $k_{p,t,r}$ (see previous section) requires the knowledge of the secret component k_r which is accredited to and reserved for non-revoked subscriptions. The header information covers the list of legitimate subscription groups and the ciphertexts that result from encrypting the session key with each legitimate group key separately. In the following example only the necessary "raw data" of the header is reflected. It should be remarked that additional storage for data encoding and data padding and others may be necessary.

Suppose that $1,000$ from $1,000\,000$ subscriptions are to be revoked. Recall that the header size of the CS revocation scheme is bound by $O(r \cdot log(\frac{n}{r}))$ for r revoked subscriptions out of n. Hence the broadcast center must consider to create and send $1,000 \cdot log(\frac{1,000,000}{1,000}) \cdot 128$ bits for distributing a 128-bit session key. For this example, approximately 156 kB of ciphertexts (encrypted decryption key) is expected. A single subscription must hold 20 secret keys.

In comparison to the CS scheme, the header size in the SD scheme only depends on r (at most $2r - 1$). Hence it requires less than $2 \cdot 1,000 \cdot 128 \approx 31$ kB of encrypted keys. However, a subscription must manage $O(log^2(n))$ secret keys. In the given scenario approximately 400 secret keys per subscription are necessary.

Since the resulting subscription keys, which are generated by the subscription model, are used to produce the encryption/decryption key, the resiliency based on computational security depends on the underlying schemes.

Corollary 8.2: The combination of the TSM with either the CS or the SD scheme is computationally secure against an unlimited number of collaborators.

8.3 Revocation

If the FSM$^-$ is used, the security depends on the difficulty of breaking tamper-proof devices that are used to store the keys. However, revoked users cannot collaborate to produce valid decryption keys. This is guaranteed by the underlying revocation scheme.

In contrast to subscription schemes that do not support extraordinary revoking mechanisms, these extensions allow to annul subscriptions before they would exceed ordinarily. From a security viewpoint, the revocation mechanism is independent on the number of involved subscriptions and on how powerful they are.

8.3.5 Comparison

Discussions on plain TSMs and FSMs (without the integration of extraordinary revoking mechanisms) are already given in Section 7.9.

To support ad hoc user revocation, we use the described framework and integrate approved existing revoking schemes into the subscription models. Thereby, we earn all advantages and also disadvantages from the applied schemes. The security of the transmitted ciphertexts is based on the used encryption function. As key derivation function HMAC is used. Therefore its security is based on HMAC.

When the CS revocation scheme is used, the broadcast center needs to send $O(r\,log(\frac{n}{r}))$ additional header data. A user has to store $log(n)$ secret keys. The TSM ensures that a collusion of legitimate subscribers is not able to produce new subscriptions. The CS revoking scheme provides resiliency against an arbitrary number of revoked and illegitimate users. When the SD scheme is used, the header data is restricted to $2r-1$ while the keys at user side are given by $O((log(n))^2)$.

Among the necessary header amount for the revocation scheme, combining a FSM-based subscription scheme with either CS or SD requires $O(|E_P|)$ additional information. The resiliency is given by the underlying revocation scheme. In case of CS and SD, the so constructed scheme withstands an arbitrary number of collaborators. As before, legitimate users cannot produce new subscriptions and the number of keys per subscription depends on the revocation scheme.

When the support of an ad hoc user revocation that does not produce additional header data is desired, the described 1-resilient revocation scheme based on the RSA encryption can be considered. However, it is only 1-resilient: two different secret subscriptions are necessary to undermine the entire revocation scheme.

Tab. 8.1: Comparison of the subscription schemes

Scheme	Header	Keys/User	Revocation	Resiliency	Security
TSM	–	$O(1)$	time-out	∞	E/H
FSM^-	–	$O(1)$	time-out	1	E/H
FSM	$O(|E_P|)$	$O(1)$	time-out	∞	E/H
TSM_{CS}	$O(r\,log(\frac{n}{r}))$	$O(log(n))$	time-out+adhoc	∞	E/H
FSM_{CS}	$O(r\,log(\frac{n}{r})) + O(|E_P|)$	$O(log(n))$	time-out+adhoc	∞	E/H
TSM_{SD}	$2r-1$	$O(log^2(n))$	time-out+adhoc	∞	E/H
FSM_{SD}	$(2r-1) + O(|E_P|)$	$O(log^2(n))$	time-out+adhoc	∞	E/H
$TSM^\dagger_{1r}$	–	$O(1)$	time-out+adhoc	1	E/H/R
$FSM^\dagger_{1r}$	–	$O(1)$	time-out+adhoc	1	E/H/R
Legend					
E	computationally bound by the used encryption function				
H	computationally bound by HMAC				
R	computationally bound by the RSA encryption scheme				
$\dagger$ requires a center that manages $O(n)$ exponents, which are delivered on request					

8.4 Subscription Upgrades

Until now, smart cards with "static" keys are considered, i.e. the secret information that is loaded on the card during the initialization process is never changing. When a subscription expires, the card becomes worthless. A prolongation of the validity period or an upgrade requires buying another card. Here a method is described, which allows to upgrade a subscription, while not disclosing the user identities.

Each privileged system user gets a smart card, which stores a unique identifier and a card key confidentially (see Figure 8.3). The card key k_{cid} is derived from the card identifier cid and the master key $k_{mk'}$ by using a key derivation function: $k_{cid} = f_{k_{mk'}}(cid)$. The key derivation function can be realized as described in Chapter 6. The system does not need to store the card key nor does it have to keep track of what is actually stored on the card. Only the master key $k_{mk'}$ has to be stored secretly from which all other card keys can be derived. Tasks at user side, which need a secret key, take place in the smart card only. Hence the decryption is performed by the smart card.

8.5 Inheritance of Rights 137

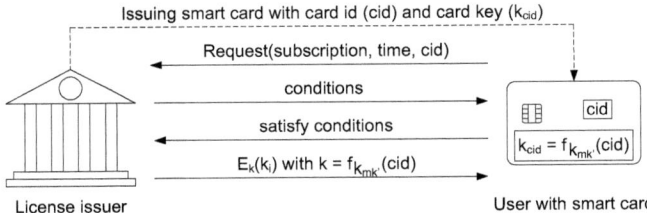

Fig. 8.3: Derived card key concept

When a user wants to upgrade an existing subscription, the user requests the new subscription with the desired validity period from the license issuer and indicates the existing card identifier. In general an upgrade requires fulfilling some conditions (e.g. financial transaction) specified by a trusted authority. After satisfying the requirements, the trusted authority derives the card specific key from the card identifier and the master key. Then the trusted authority encrypts (e.g. by using the AES) the secret information of the requested subscription with the card key and transmits the resulting ciphertext to the requester. Since the subscription is encrypted with the card specific key, only the smart card with the appropriate card key can decrypt the transmitted ciphertext. As mentioned above, the decryption is performed in the smart card so that keys are never revealed outside the smart card. This in turn prevents an illicit distribution of keys. Since there is no assignment of cards and users, this approach does not reveal the user's identity.

8.5 Inheritance of Rights

This section presents an extension for the key derivation concepts, which are described in Chapter 6. Here key pairs are investigated where one key is more powerful than the other. While the one key allows an inheritance of access rights for descendant nodes, the other key restricts access locally. To simplify key updates, it is assumed that only leaf nodes can be added into respectively removed from a given tree. This object of study seems to be very restrictive at the first glance. Even though, it enables to delete or insert whole subtrees. In case of an addition or deletion of subtrees, keys of existing nodes do not need to be updated.

Let T be a tree that incorporates the structure of a given hierarchy and let T' be a copy of T. It should be noted that these trees are virtual trees, i.e. they are generated on the fly (from the published hierarchy) and thus they do not need to be stored somewhere. Basically they are used for the key assignment whereas the hierarchical structure of them is supposed to be publicly known. Let $f_k(id)$ be an appropriate key derivation function that derives a key from a key k and an input id (cf. Chapter 6). For the key assignment the following steps are performed.

1. For each node v'_i in T' and for each node v_i in T, assign a distinct public integer id'_i and id_i respectively.

2. Select a random number k'_0 and assign it to the root node of T'.

3. From each key k'_i associated with a node v'_i in T', the key of its child node v'_j is computed as $f_{k'_i}(id'_j)$.

4. Each key k_i associated with v_i in T is computed from the key k'_i of the corresponding key v'_i in T' (located in the same hierarchical position): $f_{k'_i}(id_i)$.

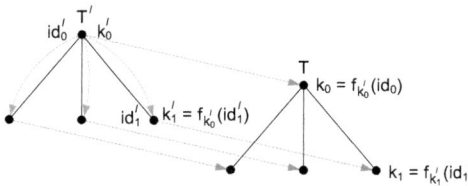

Fig. 8.4: Enabling (left tree) or disabling inheritance (right tree)

The contents, which are associated with a node v_i in T, are encrypted with the key k_i of node v_i. As depicted in Figure 8.4, a key associated with a node in T' allows to compute the keys for all its descendant nodes in T'. The relevant encryption key k_i of a node v_i in T is computed from the corresponding key k'_i associated with v'_i in T' as follows: $k_i = f_{k'_i}(id_i)$. From the key of any node in T, computing keys of subsequent nodes is not possible. Their use is restricted for encryption and decryption of the associated contents.

Let $G = (V, E)$ be the key derivation graph. Then V consists of all nodes from T' and all nodes from T. From the initially empty set of edges E, each key derivation from v'_i to v'_j according to Step 3 adds an edge to the key derivation graph: $E = E \cup \{(v'_i, v'_j)\}$. Additionally each key derivation from v'_i to v_i according to Step 4 contributes also an edge: $E = E \cup \{(v'_i, v_i)\}$.

8.5 Inheritance of Rights

This approach provides two different classifications of privileges. For a node v_i, a user can be endowed with a key that enables inheritance of rights for descendants. The other option is to give a user a key with restricted rights, i.e. rights to access the designated node only. For instance, consider temporary users or test users, who are assigned to nodes (security classes) such that access is restricted to a single node. These users could be equipped with keys that do not allow inheritance. Trusted users might get more powerful keys so that they can also access descendant nodes in the key derivation graph.

Insertion of new leaves: Suppose a new node v_j is inserted as a child node of an existing leaf node v_i. Since T' is a copy of T, the corresponding node v'_j is also inserted in T'. Then a unique public identifier id_j (resp. id'_j) is assigned to v_j (resp. v'_j). Both nodes are added to V. The key k'_j of the node v'_j is computed as $k'_j = f_{k'_i}(id'_j)$ and the key k_j of the node v_j is computed as $k_j = f_{k'_i}(id_j)$. The set of edges in the key derivation graph is extended by $E = E \cup \{(v'_i, v'_j), ((v'_j, v_j)\}$. Note that any other keys are not affected by the insertion.

Removing leaves or subtrees: Suppose that the leaf node v_j has to be removed. Then the corresponding nodes with their incoming and outgoing edges in G are removed. If repeated, whole subtrees can be deleted. Any other keys are not influenced by the removal in the key derivation graph.

Enabling and disabling inheritance: For each node v_i two keys k'_i and k_i are produced, which incorporate different kinds of privileges. More privileged users get k'_i, which enables inheritance of access rights; less privileged users get k_i.

Theorem 8.3: The key assignment scheme is complete.

Proof. It needs to be shown that the key associated with a node v'_i in T' enables to derive the encryption (resp. decryption) key of v_i and that of any descendant node. According to the key derivation graph, for each node v'_i in T' every child node v'_ℓ is connected by an edge (v'_i, v'_ℓ). Hence for any two nodes v'_i and v'_j in T' with $v'_j \in DoS(v'_i)$ there exists a path from v'_i to v'_j. Suppose that one has the key of node v'_i. Starting at v'_i and processing each edge (v'_x, v'_y) in that path, each subsequent key k'_y, and thus finally k'_j, can be computed by the key derivation function. The corresponding encryption (resp. decryption) key can be computed from k'_j according to Step 4. □

Theorem 8.4: The key assignment scheme is sound.

Proof. Let $G = (V, E)$ be the key derivation graph. Each node v'_i in T' adds an edge (v'_i, v_i) to E with v_i in T. Additionally, for two nodes v'_i, v'_j in T' with $v'_j \in Des(v'_i)$ in T', v'_j is reachable from v'_i in G. Since G encompasses only edges from nodes to their descendants in T' and from nodes in T' to their associated nodes in T, it is sufficient to show that from a key to any node (except the root) in G, it is not possible to compute the key of an ancestor node in G. Let $v_j \in V$ be a node different from the root and let $v_i \in V$ be a node such that $v_i \in Anc(v_j)$ in G. According to the applied key derivation, the key k_j of node v_j is derived from the key k_i of node v_i. Hence, if one wants to compute k_i from k_j, he or she must be able to invert the key derivation function which is intractable. □

Anonymity Aspects 9

> *Anonymity emphasizes the feeling for freedom.*
>
> ANONYMOUS

Especially in times where public places are monitored, profiles are created from people's habits, and collections and transmissions of data are at low cost, preserving the people's anonymity has evolved into a desired goal of the masses. Therefore, it is no surprise that anonymity has become a hot topic in the cryptographic community. However, access control is usually based on user authentication, where users show their identities to the verifiers. Ensuring anonymity, while guaranteeing that only legitimate users are served, is the main issue to address in this chapter.

9.1 Contribution and Structure

In this section anonymity aspects during the authentication process are discussed. New protocols are contributed that offer user authentication while ensuring the anonymity of the users. The main idea is that users demonstrate a priori the ability of decrypting requested ciphertexts. On the basis of the presented protocols, we relax the authentication mechanism of the Kerberos protocol to a kind of "anonymous Kerberos". The next chapter shows two concrete applications where some of the protocols are used as key components.

This section starts with a discussion about how anonymity of the users can be guaranteed when the subscription models are used. A solutions based on prepaid cards is presented. Then we leave the classic broadcast scenario and investigate how legitimate users can anonymously use services. Thereby we consider mechanisms to ensure anonymous authentication. Several protocols are specified that are able to classify legitimate and illegitimate users. Afterwards we address the problem when legitimate users answer questions in behalf of illegitimate ones. On the basis of the presented protocols, we specify an "anonymous Kerberos" protocol.

9.2 Anonymous Subscriptions

To ensure the users' anonymity, prepaid cards that are secure against eavesdropping could be taken into consideration. Particularly if the storage amount is kept low, cheap cards with low memory units can be used. For a subscription as described in Chapter 7, at most two secret keys of 256 bit each are necessary.

A DRM concept that offers users' anonymity is described in the following. The basic idea is that the content consumers do not authenticate at the service provider; but instead they use prepaid cards to decrypt the encrypted contents. The service provider, which broadcasts the encrypted contents, stores varied powerful subscription keys (at different prices) on prepaid cards in advance. Then, the prepaid cards are distributed to shops that offer the cards to their customers. According to their interest, customers buy such cards in shops and can use it at home to decrypt the broadcasted contents (see Figure 9.1).

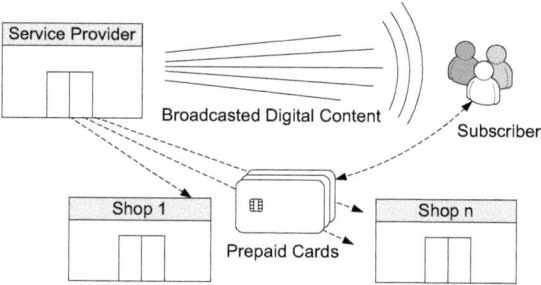

Fig. 9.1: Subscription keys on prepaid cards

This concept has benefits for both, the service provider and the user: the system is relieved of the effort of recording and billing individual user consumption and the user can consume the contents anonymously. Especially for the transmissions of live events for millions of people (e.g. soccer world championship, super bowl final, the Olympic Games etc.), it is decisive and essential that contents arrive at the users without remarkable time delays. Thus, the effort to manage countless keys and a huge amount of contents for millions of people, and also a concurrent authentication of an innumerable amount of users at the beginning of such a transmission, could easily overload a conventional key management scheme.

9.3 Anonymous Downloads

The subscription models, which are specified in Chapter 7, are suited for typical broadcast transmissions. This section considers classic internet services. Scenarios are shown, where files are retrieved from servers. Since the rise of peer-to-peer file sharing platforms, exchanging files through the internet has become very popular. Especially audio and video files are data types of special interest. Thereby the subscription models could serve as building blocks to realize flat rates.

A question, which often arises in the software sector, is how to supply licensed users with updates. Consider patches for operating systems or license services for anti-virus programs. The licensee may be able to refresh the operating system and anti-virus database respectively up to a specified time.

A traditional component to meet this requirement is user registration. After registering, users log into the websites of their software vendors and, there, they are able to download the updates, provided that their licenses are valid. Similar to the subscription models, subsets of privileged users emerge, which can claim for privileged services. However, this is different from the classic broadcast scenario, because the broadcast is "simulated" by several single connections following the client-server principle. To induce the service provider to transmit the software update, a user must first authenticate and request for it. Hence, users interact with the service provider. This in turn means that the service provider is exposed to denial of service attacks.

In this section, denial of service attacks on streaming servers, which transfer data to selected users, are considered. We expect to have massive payload as it is the case for multimedia data streams. For realizing time-bound access to the delivered data streams, they are encrypted with different keys depending on the time periods as described in previous sections. Then, only users with the corresponding keys can decrypt the transmitted ciphertexts and henceforth can access the contents. Protocols in this context are based on multicast transmissions, i.e. only selected users should be able to access the contents. Therefore, the users must authenticate themselves to the server. This allows the server to differentiate authorized users from unauthorized ones. A main goal, which we want to address in this section, is how to realize anonymous use of internet services.

9.3.1 Requirements

Anonymity: Accomplishing user authentication while assuring their anonymity are properties, which might be contradictory. However, we focus on scenarios, where the service provider does not need to know the users' identities. For these cases we assume that it suffice to demonstrate the ability of decrypting requested items, i.e. users prove that they are members of a legitimate group. The encrypted data streams are merely delivered to users, who can potentially decrypt the ciphertexts. This relaxation of a conventional user authentication into a recognition of legitimate users comes in handy: while the server does not need to take care of a user management, the users enjoy anonymity.

Also for non-real-time specific data transfers, this relaxation might become an interesting feature. Consider a server that offers encrypted software packages for download on the internet. Preemptive mechanisms ensure that only licensed users are able to download the items. Thus, they prohibit useless downloads, which are caused by illegitimate users. Besides saving bandwidth, it preserves the anonymity of the users.

Counteracting denial of service attacks: Streaming servers are especially highly vulnerable to denial of service attacks. Imagine an attacker who concurrently requests video streams from a streaming server. To cope with this type of attack, some measures must be taken in advance. One countermeasure is to initiate a data transmission only after users have proven that they can decrypt the encrypted data. It must be taken care that the described attack is not moved towards the user authentication process. Thus, the authentication process should be both, simple and quick.

It should be noted that Zero-Knowledge [GoMR85, QuGo89, Feig92] protocols are not well suited for the given requirements. The Zero-Knowledge property is based on the fact that the verifier must not gain any information about the prover's secret. In a Zero-Knowledge protocol, basically a further message is needed, which is called *commitment*. Typically, every user has a unique secret key and a public key component. The latter must be known to the verifier. Here the key management of a huge number of users may become a further problem. The assignment of public keys to users must be publicly accessible. This in turn requires assuring the integrity of the public entries.

9.3.2 Simple Protocol

This section presents a simple challenge-response protocol, whose goal is to hinder reserved downloads that are requested from non-privileged users. Hereby a user proves the possession of the key in the actual time period without revealing the time-bound key or showing the user's identity. It is achieved through the following protocol:

---

1. S selects $r \in_R \mathbb{Z}$
2. $S \rightarrow U$: r
3. U computes $c := E_{k_t}(r)$
4. $S \leftarrow U$: c
5. S verifies $E_{k_t}(r) = c$

Prot. 9.1: Proving the possession of an active time-bound key

Thereby, the server S sends a randomly chosen number r called *challenge* to a user U. The user encrypts r with the actual time-dependent key k_t and sends the ciphertext back to the server. Next, the server accomplishes in the same way, respectively it decrypts the response from the client. Finally, the server validates whether the output of the encryption is equal to the obtained ciphertext from the user, respectively whether or not the output of the decryption matches the challenge. If it is equal, the user is authenticated to the server and, henceforth, the user is served with the encrypted data; otherwise the authentication has failed and the server does not deliver contents to the user. As in other challenge-response protocols based on symmetric key encryption, a shared secret (active time-bound key) is necessary. In contrast to conventional challenge-response schemes, the shared secret differs from one time period to another.

The user proves the possession of the key, which is active in the actual time period. Instead of an encryption function, a keyed hash function could also be chosen: $\text{MAC}_{k_t}(r)$.

Clearly, a denial of service attack cannot be completely excluded. However, several techniques exist that at least diminish the success of such attacks. For instance, fraudulent clients, which have attacked or faked the server, may be added to some blacklists such that they are banned for future requests. The described protocol provides at least a countermeasure that addresses the problem of transmitting a huge amount of data to non-privileged users.

9.3.3 Enhanced Protocols

Users who successfully proof their legitimation are supplied with contents. Consider served users who have keys that have already been expired. This means that they are supplied with encrypted data, although they cannot decrypt them any longer. How can we avoid such scenarios? One way to handle such bandwidth misuse is to test whether the clients are further legitimized: the server sends challenges to the served users occasionally. When users come up with a valid response, the connection is continued and the transmission to other users is rejected. Another and more efficient strategy is to let users prove the key validity for the desired time periods.

Attesting keys for begin and end time: Consider a user wants to request a data stream from time period t_i until time period t_j. The server sends a randomly chosen challenge r to the user. The user's task is to prove the possession of valid keys by encrypting r with k_i and k_j (see protocol below).

---

1. S selects $r \in_R \mathbb{Z}$
2. $S \rightarrow U : r$
3. U computes $c_i = E_{k_{t_i}}(r)$, $c_j = E_{k_{t_j}}(r)$
4. $S \leftarrow U : c_i, c_j$
5. S evaluates c_i and c_j

Prot. 9.2: Proving the possession of k_{t_i} and k_{t_j}

To find out, whether the client is a legitimate user, the server decrypts the response and compares it with the challenge. In this way, the user proves the possession of k_{t_i} and k_{t_j}. To diminish the data overhead, the response can also be transmitted in a more compact manner: $E_{k_{t_j}}(E_{k_{t_i}}(r))$.

9.3 Anonymous Downloads

Further assurances: In the latter protocol, the user determines the two time positions, which have to be proven. Consider the case, when an illegitimate user accidentally knows k_{t_i} and k_{t_j}. The user may pass the legitimation verification process and is served with the encrypted contents. To reduce the chance for such an incident, the server picks at random a further time interval t_ℓ between t_i and t_j. The following protocol reflects this enhancement.

---

1. $U \to S$: t_i, t_j
2. S selects $r \in_R \mathbb{Z}$ and $t_m \in_R \{t_{i+1}, \ldots, t_{j-1}\}$
3. $S \to U : r, t_m, t_i, t_j$
4. U computes $c = E_{k_{t_j}}(E_{k_{t_\ell}}(E_{k_{t_i}}(r)))$
5. $S \leftarrow U : c$
6. S evaluates c

Prot. 9.3: Proving the possession of k_{t_i}, k_{t_j}, and k_{t_ℓ}

The addition of further challenges can be continued until the server is really convinced. However, a prolongation of this idea will also have consequences on the computation costs: the more such keys are taken at random, the more encryption operations have to be executed by both, server and client. The following protocol remedies the rise of encryption operations. Hereby, the keys are efficiently combined so that a single key is produced, with which a single encryption operation is executed.

---

1. $U \to S$: t_i, t_j
2. S selects $r \in_R \mathbb{Z}$, $t_{\ell_1}, \ldots, t_{\ell_n} \in_R \{t_i, \ldots, t_j\}$
3. $S \to U : r, t_{\ell_1}, \ldots, t_{\ell_n}$
4. $S \leftarrow U : E_k(r)$, with $k = k_{\ell_1} \oplus k_{\ell_2} \oplus \cdots \oplus k_{\ell_n}$
5. S evaluates c

Prot. 9.4: Users prove the possession of several keys

To be on the safe side, all keys in the corresponding time periods between t_i to t_j need to be taken. An improved way is to let the client prove the possession of a more privileged key, which can be used to derive keys for several continuous time periods. In this way the server can be sure that the client is able to derive all time-bound keys that are covered by that time period. Furthermore, the user and the server only need to operate a single key. Hereby, the simple protocol (as described above) can be used with the superior key. However, a legitimate user could respond to queries in behalf of illegitimate users. A measure against this attack is described in the next section.

9.4 Legitimate User in the Background

The goal of an illegitimate user is to mislead the validating instance such that it regards her as a legitimate user. A deception can be realized by a cooperation with a legitimate user. Consider an illegitimate user X who fools the verifier by pretending to be a legitimate user as follows (cf. Figure 9.2).

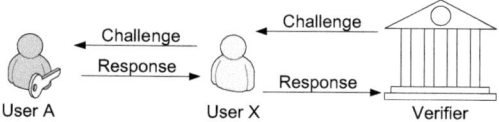

Fig. 9.2: Relay attack

The server sends a challenge to user X, who passes the challenge over to a legitimate user A. Since A is a legitimate user, he or she is able to respond to the challenge. She sends the right answer to X, who passes it further to the verifier. The verifier evaluates the response and accepts the user X as legitimate user, because the right answer was given. This attack is known as *relay attack* [KfWo05, Hanc05, Hanc06]. A similar attack is described in [DeGB87], which is referred to as the *Mafia Fraud*. Alice goes to a restaurant owned by a fraudulent person Fernando. Fernando collaborates with his accomplice Elisa and instruct her to buy at the jewellery Jim pretending to be Alice. Before Alice performs a challenge response protocol in order to pay her bill at the restaurant, Elisa starts a financial transaction at the jewellery. Then Jim starts to check the buyer's identity (who pretends to be Alice) by sending a challenge to Elisa. Elisa transmits the challenge from Jim to Fernando who passes it to Alice. Since Alice

9.4 Legitimate User in the Background

believes that she is paying her bill at the restaurant, she responds to the challenge. Fernando transmits the response to Elisa who passes it over to Jim. Jim verifies the response and believes to have sold the jewelry to Alice. Alice thinks to have paid her bill at the restaurant and does not know about her payment at the jewellery. Fernando and Elisa have betrayed Alice and Jim. Chen [ChCT04] suggests to extend the challenge response protocol such that in the end the prover and the verifier must send their identities encrypted with a session key that is fairly generated during the authentication process. However, the anonymity of the users is not protected by this approach.

Inspired from a story described in [Conw04] where a girl played against two chess grandmasters such that she copied the moves from one game to the other and finally won a game, Beth and Desmedt [BeDe90] introduced the *Chess Grandmaster Problem*. They propose a solution, which aims to detecting the time delays that a person in the middle needs for copying the moves. After three moves (at least), the fraud can be detected. However, it is based on precise clocks and its practical realization is rather questionable. Time delays are very likely in practice and, often, they occur due to technical problems (e.g. transmission and computation delays). Thus, one cannot be sure that time delays are always caused by fraud. Additionally, this solution is not transferable to our case, where we face the problem of a legitimate user in the background. The reason is that the server has no times to compare with each other.

Brands and Chaum [BrCh93] suggest a distance-bounding protocol that ensures that the prover is only a few meters away from the verifier. The idea is to send out a single-bit challenge to which the prover has to respond immediately. Repeating this procedure n times would limit the chance for cheating to 2^{-n}. Due to the fact that data cannot be transmitted faster than the speed of light, the distance can be computed from the time delays of the received responses.

In our case, a legitimate user responds in behalf of an illegitimate user (in full awareness). This attack has some similarities with the McCormac Hack [McCo98]: a legitimate card activates several receivers. The McCormac Hack is based on a distribution of secret information to others (one serves many) so that they can decrypt broadcasted contents. However, the general conditions are different because the Hack presumes the broadcast scenario. In our case the verifier fools the server during the challenge response authentication. To reduce the chance for this attack, we extend the concept of Section 9.2 by taking ICC numbers into considerations. Suppose that each ICC holds a unique and secret ICC number. For simplicity, we assume that the ICC numbers are long enough, so that the chance for guessing a valid ICC number is negligible. We adapt the challenge response protocol by redefining the response as the encryption of the challenge r and the ICC number of the subscription with the currently valid time key k_t: $E_{k_t}(r \parallel ICCNr)$. The server records the assignment of ICC numbers with their requested contents. During the verification, the server checks whether the ICC number is already taken for the request. Hence the server can at least react against double requests that are initiated by the same ICC. Since there is no assignment between user and ICC number, the user identities are not disclosed. In Chapter 10 we consider further countermeasures for each application separately.

9.5 Anonymous Kerberos

Kerberos [NeTs94, KNCT94] is the name of an authentication protocol that enables user authentication and establishes secure communication channels between participants in an insecure network. It is based on the Needham-Schroeder protocol [NeSc78]. Recently Version 5 is published as RFC 4120 [NYHR05]. The basic protocol assumes that each user shares a unique key with a trusted server S. To ensure the confidentiality of the transmitted data, it merely uses symmetric encryption. The basic protocol gets through the following steps (cf. [BoMa03]):

1. $A \to S : A, B, r_A$
2. $A \leftarrow S : E_{k_{AS}}(k, B, \ell, r_A, \ldots), E_{k_{BS}}(k, A, \ell, \ldots)$
3. $A \to B : E_k(A, t_A), E_{k_{BS}}(k, A, \ell, \ldots)$

Prot. 9.5: Basic Kerberos authentication protocol

When A wants to communicate with instance B, A requests appropriate keys from S first: together with a randomly chosen number r_A, A sends the identities of A and B to S. The server S generates a session key k for the desired communication. Then S encrypts k with the shared key k_{AS} between A and S together with B's identity, the lifetime ℓ, the random number r_A, and some optional data. Additionally k is encrypted with the shared key k_{BS} between B and S, including A's identity, the lifetime ℓ, and some optional data. The latter, resulting ciphertext is

9.5 Anonymous Kerberos

called *ticket*. Both ciphertexts are sent to A afterwards. User A decrypts the first ciphertext with k_{AS} and, thus, A gets the session key k. A encrypts her identity and timestamp t_A with k. Finally A transmits the resulting ciphertext and the received ticket to B.

We now apply the Basic Kerberos authentication protocol and adapt it according to our requirements (see Figure 9.3). As in the Kerberos protocol, the main task in the authentication process is shifted towards an authentication server. This concept unburdens the server from the authentication process.

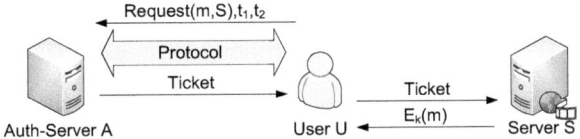

Fig. 9.3: Anonymous authentication protocol

To differentiate legitimate users from others, one of the protocols described in Section 9.3 can be deployed. The sub-protocol relaxes the user authentication in the Kerberos protocol. We define the *Anonymous Kerberos* protocol as follows:

---

1. $U \rightarrow A : Request(m, S), t_1, t_2$
2. <Apply a protocol of Section 9.3 between U and A; exit on errors>
3. $U \leftarrow A : ticket$
4. $U \rightarrow S : ticket$
5. $U \leftarrow S : E_k(m)$

Prot. 9.6: Anonymous Kerberos protocol

For the challenge-response authentication, the protocol requires selecting an adequate sub-protocol in advance (see Section 9.3). User U sends a request containing the desired item and the selected time interval to the authentication server A. To differentiate legitimate from illegitimate users, the selected sub-protocol is applied. With respect to a deception, we suggest that A sends a random number r to U, which in turn responds with $E_{k'_t}(r \,||\, ICCNr)$, where k'_t is defined by the used sub-protocol. A verifies the response. If the result is positive, A creates a ticket and sends it to U, otherwise the protocol fails and exits. The user U passes the ticket to the server S, which decrypts and verifies it afterwards. If the verification succeeds, S encrypts the requested contents with the key from the decrypted ticket and delivers the resulting ciphertext to U, otherwise the protocol halts.

Further Applications 10

> *Imagination is more important than knowledge.*
>
> ALBERT EINSTEIN

This section presents two selected applications of the the electronic subscriptions. It is assumed that the secret subscription information is stored in smart cards that are able to execute some fundamental cryptographic mechanisms like the AES, the HMAC, and the RSA.

10.1 Contribution and Structure

In this section new applications for the key management schemes are elaborated. First an electronic charging system is proposed where electronic subscriptions represent time-bound access authorizations for using highways. In another application financial transactions based on credit cards are investigated. Protocols are presented that contribute several security features.

10.2 Electronic Vignettes

Since 1997, driving on highways is subject to charges in Austria. Highway drivers have to buy so-called *vignettes* and stick them on the windshields inside their cars. These are stickers that allow to use national highways within some time periods. According to the validity time, three types are currently offered for sale. One is a license for a whole year's period, another is for two months and the third variant is for 10 days. The price for the vignettes depends on its validity time (currently, the vignette for a year costs 73.8 Euro, for two months 22.2 Euro and the price for 10 days is 7.7 Euro). Among others, vignettes are sold at customs offices, motorway restaurants, post offices and gas stations. Trucks are treated separately. Since 2004, they need to have a so-called *go box* on board, which is also referred to as *on board unit* (OBU). It is a battery powered communication unit whose size is similar to a cigarette pack. When passing through a section control station, the go box communicates via microwave transmission link with the station, which in turn charges a fee. Each section control station monitors trucks. In case of an evasion, the recorded material is used to trace traitors.

As already remarked in Chapter 1, even nowadays the complexity of toll systems is often underestimated. Providers may tend to solve everything but nothing satisfactory (cf. for example [Skro03]). In the following description we assume that section control units already exist on highways (as it is the case in Austria). Furthermore we presume that corresponding vehicles have OBUs installed that communicate with the section control units reliably under realistic conditions. We sketch out how an "electronic vignette" can be realized by applying the subscription models.

Realization: Conceptually a vignette is a time-bound authorization for using national highways. As such, we can take advantage from the electronic subscription models described in Chapter 7. An electronic vignette can be issued as a smart card holding a time-bound key, which incorporates the electronic subscription. For the three different time periods, we apply the TSM as shown in Figure 10.1.

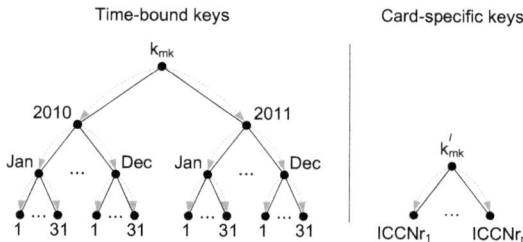

Fig. 10.1: The TSM applied on vignettes

A randomly chosen master key is assigned to each root separately. According to the key derivation graphs, the key of any further node is derived from the key of its parent node (see Section 7.6). While the left key derivation graph produces (card-independent) time-bound keys, the right one generates card-specific keys.

Consider the left key derivation graph first. A smart card, which holds the secret key of a year, represents an electronic vignette for that year. To realize a two-month authorization, a card is equipped with two secret keys, which correspond to the selected months. Analogously, the 10-days variant stores the ten keys, which

10.2 Electronic Vignettes

are associated with the desired days. For the authorization process, the simple protocol described in Chapter 9 is used: the verifier sends a random number to the card, which encrypts the challenge with the key of the current day.

Card-specific extension: As described in Section 9.4, a valid card could be misused such that it authorizes illegitimate users. Extending the response with the ICC number is not satisfactory, because a traitor could append an arbitrary ICC number. A mechanism is required that binds the response to the responding card. For this purpose, a second key derivation graph is created that takes the card-specific ICC numbers into consideration (see right graph in Figure 10.1). Keys generated by this graph are used for producing a MAC from the ICC number (and other parameters). Then, the correctness of the added ICC number can be verified. For a verification, the verifier needs the card-specific key. Instead of storing all card-specific keys separately, they can be generated from a master key k'_{mk} if required. Provided that a station records ICC numbers from the authentication process, it can detect multiple authorizations performed by a single card.

We denote k_t as the currently active time-bound key and k_{ICC} as the card-specific time-bound key. Suppose that a user U (actually the user's smart card) authenticates at the section control station S.

---

1. S randomly selects an integer r
2. $S \rightarrow U$: r, *date*, *time*
3. U computes $c := E_{k_t}(r \,||\, ICCNr \,||\, date \,||\, time)$ and
   $auth := \text{HMAC}_{k_{ICC}}(r \,||\, ICCNr \,||\, date \,||\, time)$
4. $S \leftarrow U$: c, *auth*
5. S verifies c and *auth*

Prot. 10.1: Authorization process

The Server S randomly chooses an integer r. Together with the current *date* and *time*, r is sent to the smart card from user U. The date helps the card to validate whether or not it can generate the desired time-bound key and hence can give the right answer. If so, it computes the time-bound key and, with it,

$r \,||\, ICCNr \,||\, date \,||\, time$ is encrypted. The resulting ciphertext is referred to as c. Additionally, the same input is hashed by the HMAC using the card-specific key k_{ICC}. The output is called *auth*. Next the card transmits c and *auth* to S who verifies the received data. For the verification, S decrypts c and compares the first component of the resulting plaintext with r. The second component enables the verifier to generate the card-specific key, provided that the verifier knows k'_{mk} (see right graph in Figure 10.1).

It should be noted that the binding of a response to a smart card could also be realized by digital signatures. However, this would require storing the public key of each card. In this scenario one might expect a huge number of cards. The verifier would continuously need to manage and query a huge number of public keys. Also one might keep in view that new cards are augmented in future, which would cause a refresh of the database. From this viewpoint, a decentralized local data storage, which could speed up the verification process, might be inadequate. To prevent unauthorized modifications, the assignment between public keys and cards needs to be certified. Besides, a signature verification usually requires costly computations.

10.2.1 Possible Extensions

Card upgrade: To prolong the validity of existing cards, the concept described in Section 8.4 can be applied. Hereby, the user requests further authorizations from the service provider. In the request the ICC number is appended. From the ICC number, the service provider can compute the card-specific key k_{ICC}. After payment, the service provider encrypts the requested time-bound key k_t by $E_{k_{ICC}}(k_t \,||\, validity)$ and transmits the resulting ciphertext to the card of the user. With the card-specific key, the card can decrypt the ciphertext and hence can read k_t. Then, the card is upgraded and ready to use the new key for further authorization proofs. The ciphertext is worthless for other cards, because they cannot decrypt it.

Signed input: In the protocol above, users can send challenges to the cards and they will get valid responses from their cards. To ensure that the challenge is produced by an authorized instance, public key cryptography can be used. Therefore, the challenges must be signed with the secret key sk of the vignette issuer. The card responds only after it has verified the signature of the input.

10.2 Electronic Vignettes

After a predefined number of wrong inputs, the card locks its services. As a precondition, every card stores the public key of the system in the card.

---

1. S randomly selects an integer r
2. S computes $s := sign(r \,\|\, date \,\|\, time, sk)$
3. $S \rightarrow U$: $r, date, time, s$
4. U verifies s; if the verifications fails, the protocol halts and exits
5. U computes $c := E_{k_t}(r \,\|\, ICCNr \,\|\, date \,\|\, time)$ and
   $\qquad\quad auth := \text{HMAC}_{k_{ICC}}(r \,\|\, ICCNr \,\|\, date \,\|\, time)$
6. $S \leftarrow U$: $c, auth$
7. S verifies c and $auth$

Prot. 10.2: Authentication process extended by digital signatures

However, the signature verification usually requires some extra resources. Therefore, this concept might be suitable for applications where it is not crucial when the evaluation takes some extra time.

10.2.2 Summary and Remarks

The presented challenge-response protocol based on time-bound keys ensure that only legitimate cards can produce valid responses. Application are shown whereby subscriptions are used for creating electronic vignettes. The presented realization does not reveal the identities of the users (only cards can be tracked). Even a disclosure of secret keys in a card would not undermine the system for several reasons. First, the stored time-bound keys are only valid for some time periods. In the given example the validity of such keys expire at most after a year. Second, for a valid response one needs also a valid card-specific key. Additionally, the system can react against published secret keys by recording compromised cards in a black list, which would disable them for further use. Furthermore, every day other time-bound keys are used in this example.

In many systems permissions are represented by some bits in smart cards whereby it is assumed that card-held data cannot be altered. As many examples showed, systems based on such assumptions have often been outsmarted [McCo98].

10.3 Credit Cards

David Chaum [Chau81] introduced blind signatures, which provided the basis for many electronic payment approaches. In a flash, new companies appeared establishing new markets concerning electronic cash. But as soon as they were built up, they disappeared: the electronic money was not accepted by the masses as initially supposed.

As Chaum [ChFN88] remarks, credit card payments are based on an "act of faith", where each participant is exposed to fraud by others. For financial transactions based on credit cards, it is sufficient to submit the card holder's name, the credit card number, and its expiration date. For payment, the customer reveals this information to the vendor. Some vendors require the *Card Validation Code* (CVC), respectively the *Card Verification Value* (CVV), which are 3-digit (respectively 4-digit) numbers that are printed on the backside of the credit card. These numbers do not provide a protection against credit card misuse. They can rather be considered as helpless attempts to stop the credit card piracy. Because not rarely, credit card data was corrupted, misused or sold to others.

Nowadays, credit cards are usually issued as smart cards. We assume that card services are authorized with a PIN validation whereas the smart card disables card functionalities after a series of wrong inputs. We consider credit cards as a kind of "shopping subscriptions", which enable card holders to buy offered goods within valid periods. The basic idea is to prove the authenticity of the financial transaction using time-bound keys. Figure 10.2 exemplarily illustrates the application of TSM on a credit card, which is valid between 2010 and 2012.

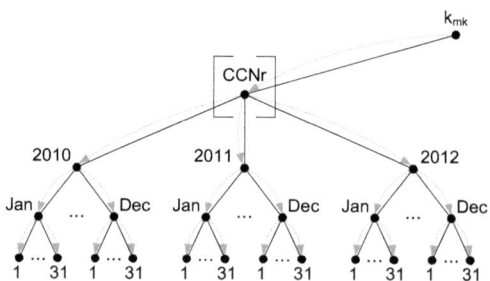

Fig. 10.2: TSM applied on credit cards

10.3 Credit Cards

The $CCNr$ node is marked, which stands for two different key derivation trees: one with node $CCNr$ and another tree without that node. Keys produced by the first variant are individual for each card because the card-specific $CCNr$ influences the resulting key. They are used for ensuring the authenticity of the transmitted data. The other derivation strategy leads to time-bound keys that are applied when data needs to be transferred confidentially between the credit card and its company. For these purposes the secret keys of their associated time periods of both derivation trees are stored in issued credit cards. Referring to the example in Figure 10.2, the credit card holds the secret keys of node 2010, node 2011, and node 2012 of both trees. From these keys any actual key (here it refers to the actual day) between 2010 and 2012 can be computed.

In the following protocols, the currently time-bound key is denoted by k_t and the currently time-bound card-specific key is named by k'_t. Furthermore, VID stands for the vendor identifier, TID is the transaction identifier, p the price, t the actual time, r_V the random number chosen by the vendor, and r_U denotes the random number selected by the user.

The following protocol specifies financial transactions based on time-bound keys and credit cards.

---

1. U selects items from vendor V
2. $V \rightarrow U : VID, TID, p, t, r_V$
3. U computes $c := E_{k_t}(CCNr \,||\, r_U)$ and
   $auth := \text{HMAC}_{k'_t}(CCNr \,||\, VID \,||\, TID \,||\, p \,||\, t \,||\, r_V \,||\, r_U)$
4. $V \leftarrow U : c, auth$
5. $V \rightarrow C : VID, TID, p, t, r_V, c, auth$

Prot. 10.3: Credit card payments based on time-bound keys

User U selects offered items from the online shop of a vendor V. The vendor sends its identifier VID, the transaction number TID, the price p, the timestamp t, and a random number r_V to user U. After user authorization (e.g. by PIN) and transmitting the data from the vendor to the credit card, it encrypts its card number and a randomly chosen number r_U with the actual time-bound key

k_t: $E_{k_t}(CCNr\,||\,r_U)$. We denote the resulting ciphertext by c. The credit card number, the vendor's data and the random number r_U are authenticated by the HMAC as follows: $\text{HMAC}_{k'_t}(CCNr\,||\,VID\,||\,TID\,||\,p\,||\,t\,||\,r_V\,||\,r_U)$. The resulting data is denoted by $auth$. The data c and $auth$ is sent to the vendor who passes the data together with the vendor's information to the credit card company C. Since C knows the actual key k_t, it can decrypt c and thus retrieve the credit card number and the random number r_U. After decrypting c the company recognizes whether $CCNr$ is valid or not: the time-bound key ensures the validity. Another option for the company is to verify the validity of the $CCNr$ by looking for it in its databases. From $CCNr$ the credit card company can compute the card-specific time-bound key k'_t, which enables to verify $auth$. The verification of $auth$ detects whether or not the transaction is valid.

However, anyone who knows the used time-bound key could reveal the anonymity of the financial transaction. A leakage of secret keys stored in credit cards will compromise the anonymity of those transactions. To reduce this threat, we suggest encrypting the data by the public key pk of the credit card company. Therefore, the credit card stores pk and encrypts data with it. A further information called lifetime ℓ is introduced that indicates whether data is expired or not. The following protocol ensures confidentiality with the public key of the credit card company.

---

1. U selects items from vendor V
2. $V \rightarrow U : VID, TID, p, t, r_V$
3. U computes $c := E_{pk}(CCNr\,||\,\ell\,||\,VID\,||\,TID\,||\,p\,||\,t\,||\,r_U)$ and $auth := \text{HMAC}_{k'_t}(CCNr\,||\,\ell\,||\,VID\,||\,TID\,||\,p\,||\,t\,||\,r_V\,||\,r_U)$
4. $V \leftarrow U : c, auth$
5. $V \rightarrow C : VID, TID, p, t, r_V, c, auth$

Prot. 10.4: Credit card payments based on time-bound keys and a public key

Note that only a single public key is needed, which is stored in the card during its personalization. No public key certificates and further public key services (e.g. public key directory) are needed. The confidential transmission of the payment and credit card information protects the payer's anonymity. Besides confidentiality, the payment is confirmed by a card-specific MAC. Since only the

10.3 Credit Cards

corresponding card can produce a valid MAC, the credit card company can be sure that the payment is authentic.

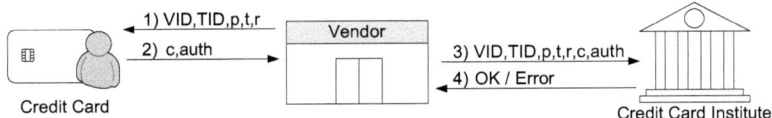

Fig. 10.3: Secure credit card payment

A credit card, which is valid from 2010 to 2012, would require storing the secret keys of node 2010, node 2011, and node 2012 of the depicted key derivation tree variant in Figure 10.2 that includes node $CCNr$. Additionally the public key pk of the credit card company needs to be stored.

Document Rights 11

> *Es ist nicht genug, zu wissen, man muss auch anwenden; es ist nicht genug, zu wollen, man muss auch tun.*
>
> J.W. VON GOETHE

Formulating and assuring rights are differently complex tasks. Solutions for the latter one are often unsatisfactory addressed. This section deals with publicly accessible documents. Notice that a document management system may become complex when the local document storage is shifted towards a global one. As observed in [VRTW01], the need for strong authentication, encryption, and scalability has to be evaluated. In many document management systems, rights are managed by a program. For instance, the web server only shows that information, which a user is allowed to see. The program evaluates those rights and it behaves according to specified rules. But what if the system is hacked and the rights management logic is bypassed? Generally, if someone has managed to shut off or to circumvent (e.g. the system administrator) such a component, the data behind that rights enforcement logic can be accessed in an unrestricted manner.

11.1 Contribution and Structure

This section presents new applications for the key derivation concept. In particular, key assignment schemes are presented that enable to force rights on documents locally. Aside access rights, also a realization of write permissions is given so that unauthorized modifications are detected. Additionally two key assignment variants are sketched out that establish a connection between read and write rights. It should be noted that the presented construction can be used for other rights as well. The primary goal is to reduce the amount of keys that have to be stored secretly. The presented concepts focus on published documents. It should be remembered that once documents are distributed, the control over them is lost. For assuring rights on documents, they need to be protected before they are made publicly. The concepts and ideas in this section are published in [Koll07c].

After a motivation and argumentation for partial encryption, key management schemes are discussed that use the key derivation concept to create differently powerful keys. One key offers superior rights, while the other enables inferior rights. This section focuses on write permissions, although also other rights could be addressed. Clearly, a technical write protection in the sense of prohibition cannot be accomplished for distributed electronic documents in the given scenarios. Unauthorized write operations will lead to invalid documents. Next we present several approaches to establish connections between read and write permissions. To detect impermissible modifications, the data integrity of contents and structures is assured. Afterwards that storage and security concerns are evaluated. Possible extensions conclude this section.

11.2 Motivation

Accessing data from a data storage is a traditional problem in computer science. Typically the data is stored in a data repository, which is usually a file system or a data base. To initialize a data transfer, the requesting instance queries the data holder. The execution unit evaluates the query and responds with some information accordingly. Thereby, the data repository may be consulted.

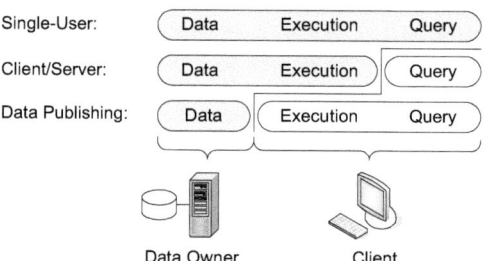

Fig. 11.1: Trust domains in data accessing systems (adapted from [MiSu03])

From a security point of view, the trivial case occurs when there is only a single user with no access limitation. Together with the query and execution unit, the data is located on a single-user machine (see first case in Figure 11.1). Usually, only one user with administrators' privileges has full access to all data stored in the system. Concerning the access control, this problem is a trivial one. The second case in Figure 11.1 shows two trust domains. This separation arises in typical web services, where the data owner, acting as a server, controls the data as well as the execution engine and waits for requests from the clients. Hereby the data owner does not trust the client who sends a query to the server. The data owner loses control over the data by the time it is published, since received data might be read, copied, and distributed. In [HILM02] the question of how to respond to queries without revealing protected data is discussed. Miklau and Crampton [MiSu03, Cram04] propose solutions based on partial encryption of documents. Depending on the keys, a user can decrypt encrypted parts.

11.3 Partial Encryption

The question of how to assure rights on digital contents is a main concern in the DRM leadership. A solution to this problem is to force permissions locally by cryptographic mechanisms. This can be realized by data encryption. Certainly, data encryption will only solve limited problems that arise in the context of document rights management. Nevertheless, the goal is to break down the 'all-or-nothing' encryption paradigm into partial encryption, where principals (e.g. authors) decide, which parts of a document need to be protected. This strategy provides the basis for a fine-grained access control. For example, some authors want their source code (and main idea respectively) in their documents to be accessible only by privileged users like those who pay for it (see Figure 11.2).

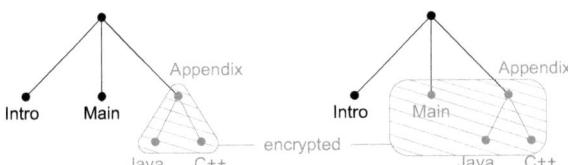

Fig. 11.2: Partial document encryption

An approach to enforce restrictive access in documents is to encrypt reserved document parts. It should be noted that different document parts may be reserved for distinct user groups. Therefore, different keys are assigned to distinct nodes. However, if every document has its own key and individual keys are assigned to the nodes in the structure of a document, the efforts to manage such keys would become a serious problem. Therefore, it is crucial that a key assignment scheme reduces the key storage significantly. In the ideal case, only one key is stored secretly by the system, respectively by a user. Other keys may be computable from those keys when needed. Hence, a key assignment scheme using key derivation mechanisms, which fit in the document structure, may be desirable.

11.4 Access Rights Management

Structured documents allow management at different levels in the document hierarchy. In particular we want to enforce rights on document parts in tree-structured documents. A special sort of this document type is defined by XML. It seems to be a very promising meta language that has been proved successfully in the document area. Emerging document standards are nowadays usually specified as XML (see Chapter A). The tree structure of such documents enables the providing of an easy and scalable rights administration. Rights inheritance can contribute an important impulse to disburden a key management. Thus, we desire that rights defined on nodes should be transferable to their descendants.

We want to consider a multi-layered rights access control on hierarchical structured documents. A key corresponding to a parent node should be more "powerful" than the key belonging to its child node. Therefore, a key derivation functionality that supports hierarchical dependencies is needed. In particular keys belonging to child nodes should be computable by keys belonging to their parent nodes. The other way, deriving a valid key for a parent from any key of its child nodes, must be practically impossible (see right tree in Figure 11.3). This requirement can be met by a publicly known key derivation function as described in Chapter 6.

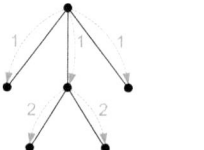
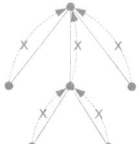

Fig. 11.3: One-way key derivation

Keys belonging to descendant nodes are recursively computed from those assigned to their parents. For example, keys assigned to grandchild nodes are first derived by keys associated with the child nodes, which are the parent nodes of the grandchild nodes. Afterwards the keys of the grandchild nodes are derived from the child nodes (left tree in Figure 11.3).

11.5 Read and Write Permissions

As a precondition, a unique public node identifier id_j is assigned to every node v_j in the tree structure of such documents. The encryption of a document at the root node means that the whole document is encrypted with the document key k_0. Only those who obtain k_0 (e.g. by purchase) can decrypt the document. From k_0 all other keys, belonging to any node in that document, can be computed (left tree in Figure 11.4). Generally, a key of a node allows to derive the keys in its subtree. Referring to k_1 in Figure 11.4, only k_3 can be derived from it.

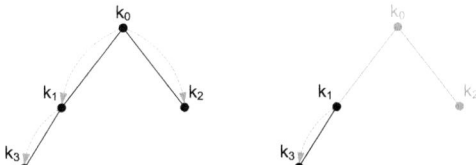

Fig. 11.4: Derived keys in a tree structure

Hierarchically structured data (like XML documents) can be encrypted at different nodes in the hierarchy, which allows a flexible and fine-granular encryption level. Consider, for instance, the case when an author of a document only wants the introduction to be read by the public. To disable access by the public, the author encrypts all nodes except the introduction (right tree in Figure 11.2). Only privileged users are served with the corresponding keys.

11.5 Read and Write Permissions

The following key management scheme focuses on realizations for read and write permissions for published documents (see also [Koll07c]). As already mentioned, the control over documents is lost once they are published. We assume that the documents are somehow distributed to the public. It is clear that a real write protection for such documents cannot be accomplished. In the following, a write permission to a node in a published tree structured document enables valid write operations to the contents in that node and all its subsequent nodes. If someone with no write permission modifies the document, it is detected by every system user. Similar to read permissions, write permissions of nodes are assigned to privileged members. These are users that have a corresponding write key. Any member of that group can make modifications. Each member of a privileged group is equally "powerful" in comparison to the other group members. It should be noted that user revocation, i.e. excluding former members from a group, is not addressed by this approach. Among modification of contents, the given approach supports valid extensions and deletions of leaf nodes, respectively subtrees. This is necessary, because otherwise impermissible deletions of document parts and structural additions may not be detected. To detect disallowed structural modifications, a further secret key is necessary. It should be mentioned that we do not want to realize a version control for documents (cf. [IwCA05]). The following schemes do not record which part was changed by which user. The scheme assures the originality of the document parts by giving answers to the following question: were the documents created or modified by a member of an authorized user group? The presented schemes fit in publicly accessible tree structured documents where equally powerful creators are grouped together and consumers are assigned to different document parts. For instance documents in electronic government may be applicable where officers can make entries into reserved parts. However also project reports, papers, newsfeeds, and podcasts are examples of such types. Generally it may be suited for scenarios where multiple users need to write into common documents.

Read permissions can be achieved with encryption. Allowing access to an encrypted content is equal to the possession of the decryption key. But how can write permissions be guaranteed? We cannot prevent unauthorized writing, but we can detect it. Digital signatures are mechanisms to ensure the authenticity of data. To assure the authenticity of data without decrypting the encrypted parts, whole ciphertexts are signed. For the signature verification, the public keys must be authentic and publicly available. The public keys are stored in corresponding nodes so that the authenticity can be locally verified. How to secure the public parameters and how to handle structural modifications is described in Section 11.6.

In order to support read and write permissions in a tree structured document, its tree structure is applied to the trees T_R and T_W. These trees are virtual trees incorporating the tree structure of a document: they get generated on the fly if required, so they are stored nowhere. T_R incorporates keys for read permissions and T_W for write permissions on the nodes of a tree structured document. For the key derivation (see Chapter 6) in T_R and T_W, the function f is used. To simplify discussions, we specify f as HMAC [KrBC97] with SHA-256 as its integrated hash functions. Furthermore it can be assumed that each node j in the document has an identifier id_j, which is an integer less than 2^{256}.

11.5 Read and Write Permissions

To reduce the key storage, a strategy is needed to avoid saving both, write and read keys of a node. In practice, write permission on an item often implies read permission on that item, although there are some scenarios where this is not a necessity. Thus write keys are generally "more powerful" than read keys. We want to apply the key derivation concept described in Chapter 6 to realize such a relationship between these rights. By constructing such dependencies, the following two derivation strategies arise (see Figure 11.5).

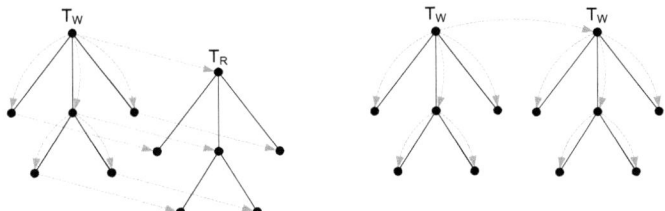

Fig. 11.5: Dependencies between write and read permissions

One possibility is to generate read keys by deriving them from their corresponding write keys (see left graph in Figure 11.5). The write keys are derived from those assigned to their parent nodes. With the write key of a node each write and read key corresponding to any node in the subtree rooted at that node can be computed. It should be noted that inheritance of read permissions is not supported by this variant, i.e. a read key does not support key derivation in this variant.

Another possibility is to provide inheritance of read permissions as well as write permissions (see right tree of Figure 11.5). In this case, the keys of the nodes in T_R and T_W, except the root, are derived from the keys assigned to their parents. Only the key of T_R's root is computed from the key assigned to T_W's root. Hence, inheritance of read permissions from write permissions is solely supported at the root level. The key of the root node in T_W is either chosen randomly or it is derived from a further key (master key) analogously to the key derivation concept. However, deriving read keys from the corresponding write keys, which is associated with a node different from the root, is not supported by this variant. In both strategies, only the write key of the root node of a document is necessary to have write and read permissions on the whole document.

In the sequel realizations of these two possibilities for deriving read keys from write keys are given. Afterwards a concept that combines both variants is presented.

11.5.1 Inheritance from Write Permissions

A realization of the left tree in Figure 11.5 can be performed by the following scheme. Choose $k_{W_0} \in_R \{0,1\}^{256}$ and assign it to the root node of T_W. Each write key k_{W_j} belonging to node id_j is derived from its parent node key k_{W_i}: $k_{W_j} = f_{k_{W_i}}(id_j)$. Each read key k_{R_j} belonging to node id_j is calculated from its write key k_{W_j}: $k_{R_j} = f_{k_{W_j}}(id_j)$. To encrypt the content associated with node id_j, the AES is used with key k_{R_j}.

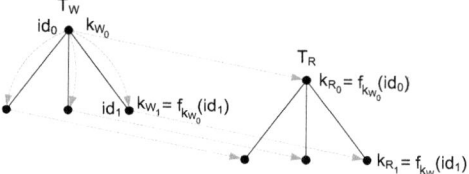

Fig. 11.6: Inheritance from write keys

This approach enables an inheritance of read permissions from write permissions. In particular it offers the following features:

- ✓ Recursive inheritance of write permissions
- ✓ Inheritance of read keys from write keys
- ✓ No additional data must be stored

The drawback of this variant is that no recursive inheritance of read permissions is supported. In the next section we will remedy this deficit.

11.5.2 Inheritance from Parent Nodes

A further possibility is to support both, inheritance of read and write permissions (see right graph in Figure 11.5). In this case each node in T_R and T_W, except the root node, is derived from its parent node. Choose $k_{W_0} \in_R \{0,1\}^{256}$ and assign it to the root node of T_W. Derive the read key of the root node in T_R from k_{W_0}: $k_{R_0} = f_{k_{W_0}}(id_0)$. This allows that read permission can be inherited from write permission at the root level. Let k_{W_i} and k_{R_i} be the write key and read

11.5 Read and Write Permissions

key respectively to the parent node of a node id_j other than the root node. Then $k_{W_j} = f_{k_{W_i}}(id_j)$ and $k_{R_j} = f_{k_{R_i}}(id_j)$. By having a write key of any node different from the root, corresponding read keys cannot be derived from it. Encrypt the content in node id_j by using the AES with k_{R_j} as encryption key.

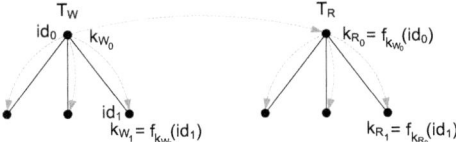

Fig. 11.7: Inheritance from parent nodes

This variant enables inheritance of read and write permissions. The benefits of this variant include:

- ✓ Recursive inheritance of write permissions
- ✓ Recursive inheritance of read permissions
- ✓ No additional data must be stored

A disadvantage of this variant is that inheritance of read permissions from write permissions is only supported at root node level.

11.5.3 Combined Inheritance

Combining both strategies means: on the one hand read keys and write keys are derived from the keys to their parent nodes separately while on the other hand a mechanism is necessary to compute read keys from their corresponding write keys. Figure 11.8 illustrates a realization of these requirements.

The read keys in T_R and write keys in T_W are derived separately. Additionally the read keys are encrypted with the corresponding write keys. The encrypted read key is stored appropriately in the document. Thus the read key k_{R_j} of a node id_j other than the root node can be derived from the key to its parent node id_i. Alternatively k_{R_j} can be computed by decrypting the encrypted read key with the write key k_{W_j}. The benefits of the combined key derivation variant are:

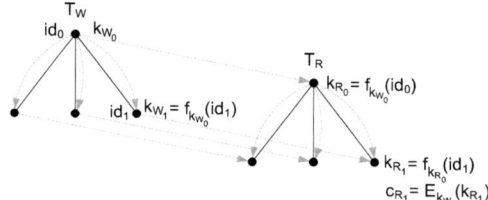

Fig. 11.8: Combined inheritance

✓ Recursive inheritance of write permissions

✓ Recursive inheritance of read permissions

✓ Inheritance of read permissions from write permissions

The drawback of this approach is that additional data (encrypted read keys) must be stored in each node. However, the following investigations refer to the combined key derivation variant, because it ensures the highest flexibility of the presented strategies with only a few extra cost for the storage of the encrypted read key. Since this variant acts as the basis for subsequent investigations, we give a detailed description of the procedure that realizes this concept:

1. Choose $k_{W_0} \in_R \{0,1\}^{256}$ and assign it to the root of T_W.

2. Each further write key k_{W_j} in T_W is derived from its parent node key k_{W_i}:
$k_{W_j} = f_{k_{W_i}}(id_j)$.

3. Derive the read key at root node of T_R from k_{W_0}:
$k_{R_0} = f_{k_{W_0}}(id_0)$.

4. Each other read key k_{R_j} in T_R assigned to node id_j is derived from its parent node key k_{R_i}: $k_{R_j} = f_{k_{R_i}}(id_j)$.

5. Encrypt each read key k_{R_i} to node id_i with its write key k_{W_i} by using the AES: $c_{R_i} = E_{k_{W_i}}(k_{R_i})$. Store c_{R_i} at node id_i in the document.

6. Encrypt the content in each node id_i with its read key k_{R_i} by using the AES and store the ciphertext at node id_i in the document.

11.5.4 Comparison

The following table shows a comparison of the features that are offered by the presented variants. Here W stands for recursive write inheritance, R for recursive read inheritance, and $W \to R$ for read permissions that are inherited from write permissions. *No data* indicates whether no additional data is necessary or some additional data has to be stored.

Tab. 11.1: Comparison of the inheritance strategies

Scheme\Feature	W	R	W→R	No Data
Variant 1	✓	–	✓	✓
Variant 2	✓	✓	–	✓
Variant 3	✓	✓	✓	–

Variant 1 is a prudent choice, when it is required that read permissions are inherited from corresponding write permissions, but recursive read inheritance is not necessary. Hereby, all read keys are limited to a single node. Each write key enables full read and write permissions to its associated subtree. The second variant is preferable when recursive read and write inheritance is required but it is sufficient that read permissions can only be inherited from the write key at the root node. The write key associated with the root node of a document endows full read and write permissions of that document. For all other keys, there are no cross connections between write and read permissions. Variant 3 combines both described inheritance strategies, but requires some additional data.

11.6 Authenticity of Contents and Structures

As remarked above, a real write protection for published documents cannot be provided. But invalid modifications can be detected. Modifications on both, contents and structures of documents, are reserved for authorized users. In order to detect invalid changes of the contents, they are signed as they are stored in the nodes: as ciphertexts or as plaintexts. The resulting signature and the public key are stored in the corresponding node. This enables everyone to verify the integrity of the contents in the document. To detect invalid modifications on the document structure, all public keys in the document are hashed, signed, and stored in the document as described later.

To reduce the storage capacity, the Elliptic Curve Digital Signature Algorithm (ECDSA) [dss] is used. Let E be an appropriately chosen elliptic curve, defined over a finite field $\mathbb{F}_p$, and P be a point in $E(\mathbb{F}_p)$, which has prime order n of 160 bit. The elliptic curve E, the prime p, the point P, and its order n are public parameters. Since the private key d can be randomly chosen from $\{1, \ldots, n-1\}$, d can be computed from k_{W_i}: $d = k_{W_i}$ MOD n. If $d = 0$ the value for the node id_i is changed, which causes a different write key. For each node id_i in a document, the following steps are performed:

1. Compute the private key $d = k_{W_i}$ MOD n
   if $d = 0$, then change the value for id_i and repeat

2. Compute the public key $Q = dP$

3. Select $k \in_R \{1, \ldots, n-1\}$

4. Compute $r = x_1$ MOD n, where $(x_1, y_1) = kP$, if $r = 0$ go to Step 3

5. Compute $e = h(c_i)$ with c_i as the content in node id_i

6. Compute $s = k^{-1}(e + dr)$ MOD n, if $s = 0$ go to Step 3

7. Store Q and (r, s) in the corresponding node

Here h denotes an appropriate hash function. Depending on whether or not the content in node id_i is symmetrically encrypted with read key k_{R_i}, c_i is the ciphertext or the plaintext of that content. The signature (r, s) guarantees that the content in node id_i was written or modified by someone who has write permission for that node. This is someone who has either d or the appropriate write key k_{W_i} with which d can be calculated. Since the corresponding public parameters are publicly known, the signature can be verified by each system user (see [HaMV04]).

Analogously, for each document a further key pair (Q_s, d_s) is generated, where only d_s allows structural changes in a document, i.e. adding or deleting leaf nodes or subtrees. The public key Q_s is signed by the secret key of the system called d_{sys}. Together with the signature, Q_s is stored in the root node of the document. Hence, by having the public key Q_{sys}, the authenticity of a document can be verified.

One further problem remains: one can delete or add whole subtrees or some nodes in a document, without being detected by other users. To prevent unauthorized structural modifications, all public keys $Q_1, \ldots, Q_t$ of a document are hashed by $h(Q_1 \,||\, Q_2 \,||\, \ldots \,||\, Q_t)$. Afterwards the hash value is signed by d_s. Finally the resulting signature pair is stored in the root node. To verify the authenticity of contents and structures of documents, one only needs Q_{sys}, which is the public key of the system.

11.7 Evaluation

In the following, the data storage for realizing the combined derivation strategy (cf. Section 11.5.3) is evaluated. Among read and write permissions also the necessary data for assuring the authenticity of contents and document structures is regarded. Furthermore security aspects of the proposed scheme are discussed. In the end, a comparison with Attalah's scheme [AtFB05] is given.

11.7.1 Storage

One should bear in mind that for data description, data padding, and data encoding (e.g. Base64) additional storage is needed, which is not reflected in the following considerations.

To realize the combined derivation concept, each node has to store the encrypted read keys of 256 bit each. In each node id_i the public parameter Q and the signature of the content are stored. With point compression 161 bits for Q and $2 \cdot 160$ bits for the signature pair are necessary. Thus, for each node, 93 Bytes are necessary. As described in Section 11.6, the private keys for signing the contents are derived from their write keys. This means that these private keys are stored nowhere. The root node covers two further signature pairs as well as the public key Q_s. Hence, the root node stores additionally 101 Bytes.

For instance, to ensure write and read permissions on a tree structured document with ten nodes, 1031 Bytes are necessary to store the signatures, public keys, and encrypted read keys in the document. 320 Bytes of the 1031 Bytes (approximately 31%) result from the encrypted read keys; the rest are caused by signatures and their public keys.

Consider a user with full write and read access to such a document. Then, the write key of the root node is encrypted with the user key and is stored in the root node (see Section 8.4). This means that there are additionally 32 Bytes necessary. For reading and modifying the contents in the document, the user only needs its user key. The system only needs to store the master key k_{mk}, the secret key d_{sys} ensuring the authenticity of structural changes in a document, and $k_{mk'}$ for deriving the user keys. All other keys in the system can be derived from them.

11.7.2 Security

The security of the proposed key management scheme for tree structured documents is based on the following cryptographic mechanisms:

- Message authentication codes (HMACs) to derive keys from others,
- ECDSA to ensure write permissions and
- Encryption of contents and read keys (AES).

Read permissions are assured by encryption using the AES. Choosing HMAC with SHA-256 as its hash function produces 256 bit keys, which are supported by the AES. The security of the encrypted contents is thus guaranteed by the AES with the highest possible key length. Since write permissions are ensured by digital signatures created by the ECDSA, their security is based on the ECDSA. The encrypted read keys do not make an attack more applicable because for a read key any integer less than 2^{256} is possible. An attacker knows the right read key, if the decryption of the ciphertext with this key results in a meaningful plaintext. Trying each key and checking the output of the decryption is equivalent to the brute force attack.

11.7.3 Comparison with Atallah's scheme

This section gives a brief comparison of the key management scheme described in [AtFB05] with the scheme described above regarding data storage. As already mentioned, the documents are given in a tree structure and only leaf nodes (resp. subtrees) can be inserted or deleted. More complex modifications will lead to a new document. The presented key management for such type of documents needs

11.8 Summary

less data than Atallah's scheme. Figure 11.9 shows the additional data, which has to be stored for the latter scheme.

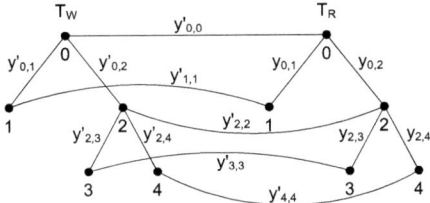

Fig. 11.9: Stored data in Atallah's scheme

In a tree structure each node except the root node has exactly one incoming edge. Let n be the number of nodes in the tree structure of a given document, then there are $n-1$ edges in each tree (T_R and T_W). Let the key size be ℓ bits long. Then a realization described in [AtFB05] would need $(n-1) \cdot \ell$ bits for each tree and additionally $n \cdot \ell$ bits for the edges connecting each node in T_W with its corresponding node in T_R. The public information of the edge (v_i, v_j) is referenced by $y_{i,j}$ in T_R, respectively $y'_{i,j}$ in T_W. Hence, $(3n-2) \cdot \ell$ bits are necessary to build such a structure. In comparison to the scheme presented in this paper, one only needs to store the encrypted read keys (see Figure 11.10), which require $n \cdot \ell$ bits.

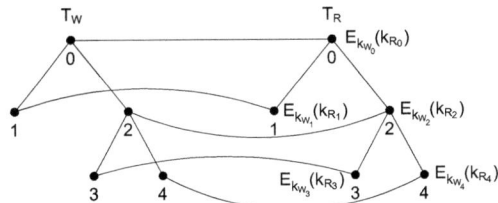

Fig. 11.10: Stored data in the given scheme

11.8 Summary

In the previous sections solutions are presented that assure read and write permissions on document parts such that a relationship is established between those rights. Read permissions are realized by data encryption. To detect illegitimate document entries and illicit document modifications, contents and structures are digitally signed. Based on the combined derivation strategy, an extended scheme is proposed that prevents unauthorized users from

- reading documents parts,
- writing unnoticeable into documents and
- modifying imperceptibly the structure of documents.

The scheme is designed such that the key storage at both, user and system side, is kept small. Inheritance of read and write permissions in a tree structured document is achieved through key derivation functions. Additionally, cross connections between those rights are realized. For a verification of the authenticity of such documents, only the public key of the system is needed. The problem of delivering keys to non-authorized users can be counteracted by protecting keys in smartcards (cf. Section 8.4). Certainly, a transmission of decrypted documents cannot be prohibited by the proposed approach. Once a document is decrypted, even special client software solutions cannot give a real protection against the transmission of decrypted documents. Although often afflicted with quality losses, there are usually possibilities to copy the source somehow (e.g. by a screenshot etc.). The whole DRM leadership works on solutions for this problem, often yielding in special hardware and software components.

11.9 Further Extensions

Suppose that write permission is divided into a subclass called *append*. In this context *append* denotes the right that allows a valid attachment of data in the corresponding location. Figure 11.11 demonstrates an example of a subclass relationship between *append* and *write* on the one hand, and *read* and *write* on the other hand.

In this example, an exclusive write permission on a single node allows valid write operations in the whole subtree, which is rooted at that node. The associated write key endows a user to append and read data in the assigned subtree. Consider to have *append* right to a node and someone modifies or deletes data, which is authenticated by digital signatures. Such attempts would lead to invalid documents, i.e. some signatures would be either invalid or missing.

11.9 Further Extensions

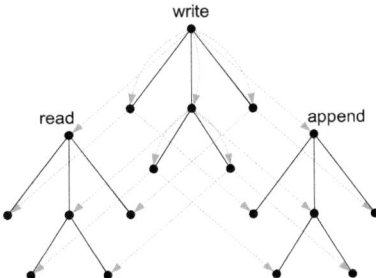

Fig. 11.11: Dependencies between several write permissions

In a similar manner, further rights classifications could be defined. For instance, the permissions *modify* and *delete* could be considered as further subclassifications of write permissions. A flexible document management system might make room for flexible extensions in future. In the following example *all permissions* denote a rights classification for belated integrations of further rights. For instance, the system administrator group could be equipped with such rights. Figure 11.12 illustrates the case where we have the following classifications of rights: all, write, and read permissions. Consider the case when *append* needs to be integrated later. Hereby, a similar relationship between *write* and *append* as shown in Figure 11.11 can be considered. Users that already have *all* rights do not need an update for further keys, because these users are able to derive them from their existing keys.

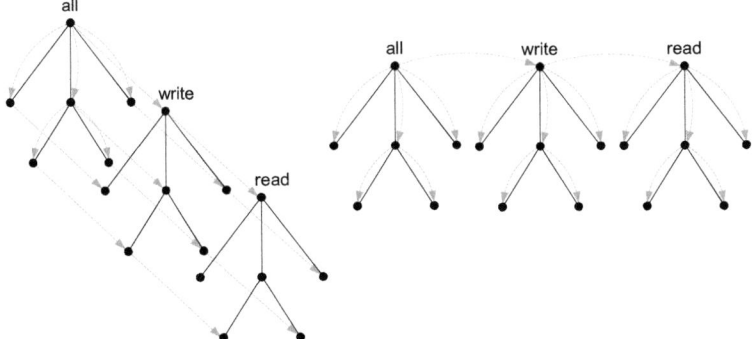

Fig. 11.12: Linking hierarchy classes together

According to the requirements, dependencies between those classes are established. Figure 11.12 shows two possibilities: the hierarchy classes are linked together on the root level (right graph) and on node level (left graph) respectively. This concept can be extended such that several chains of rights hierarchies evolve. Advantages and disadvantages of these two strategies are already discussed above. These are just a few examples that might give additional insight into the potential of such rights inheritance strategies. Approaches concerning XML security are appended to this work.

Summary 12

> *Perfection is achieved, not when there is nothing more to add, but when there is nothing left to take away.*
>
> ANTOINE DE SAINT EXUPERY

In this work electronic subscriptions are introduced. Conceptually subscriptions are considered as authorizations for utilizing corresponding items or services within a certain time period. Several subscription models are presented with respect to scalability, practicability, and security. The exclusive reservation of the broadcasted contents for subscribers is enforced by encryption. Therefore, the key management problem arises. Several strategies are examined that limit the key storage at the service provider as well as at user side to a constant number. Ideally only one key per subscription and broadcast center respectively is necessary.

In literature, related topics can be divided into either Broadcast Encryption or Key Management Schemes. The presented subscription models combine benefits from both research areas: an adequate key management for realizing time-bound keys and also mechanisms for restricting access of transmitted contents to intended receivers are required. Substantial work in both fields is summarized and compared in separate chapters. Also possible extensions concerning non-continuous time intervals as well as revocation and upgrade of existing subscriptions are discussed. Some relevant applications for the subscription models are sketched out. In particular protocols are defined for anonymous authentication where subscribers prove to have valid subscriptions but they do not show their identities. Additionally applications for realizing electronic vignettes and securing credit card based payments are shown. Finally, some applications of the key derivation function in context of document management are shown, which allow to realize dependencies between several rights in hierarchically structured documents like XML documents.

When we summarize the main points in this work, one might come to the conclusion that there is no single solution that is able to solve every problem. Therefore, analyzing the requirements is fundamental for designing and realizing a concrete key management model. It should be noted that the presented models and protocols leave much room for further research. For instance, there are several methods for implementing a key derivation function. Some of them might be inefficient, but they offer further functionalities (e.g. bidirectional derivations for special users). Pursuing such approaches and evaluating their practical relevance are topics for ongoing research.

In this work electronic subscriptions are defined as time-bound authorizations that allow access to specific objects. For proving one's authenticity, digital signatures have often been regarded as a universal solution. However, not rarely the practice has shown serious limitations and discrepancies when issues concerning certificates, public keys, and trusted authorities are insufficiently addressed.

For sure, electronic subscriptions can only solve a specific set of problems. However, for adequate problems they can really offer an interesting and efficient solution. Particularly when a huge number of users is expected, the advantages of electronic subscriptions can be overwhelming. In this work only a small outlook of the possibilities for electronic subscriptions is given. When integrated with other mechanisms, very complex requirements can be fulfilled. Hence, the real potential of electronic subscriptions remains an open issue and has to be investigated in more detail.

XML Security

XML security covers mechanisms for digital signatures and encryption of binary data resulting in valid XML documents. Recently, the World Wide Web Consortium (W3C) standardized XML Encryption and XML Signature. It should be noted that no new security mechanisms are introduced by these standards. These standards specify how binary data is signed and/or encrypted by using approved cryptographic mechanisms. In [Hirs] a good introduction to XML security standards is given. XML Security is often favored over comparable former specifications like ASN.1, because the latter is based on binary formats, which require special software for interpretation und usage. By using XML security one can benefit from all advantages of XML, including:

- World wide acceptance
- Platform and program independence
- Human and machine readable
- Flexibility and extensibility
- Unique names support (URI)
- Accessing techniques (XPath)
- Schema validation

Many program languages provide basic XML functionality like XML tree parsing. XML is an extensible standard and thus, supplementary extensions can be easier integrated than in binary standards. From the network point of view, XML security specifies end-to-end security. This means that applied security mechanisms like encryption and digital signature protect an XML document from the sender to the specified receiver. The following points characterize the features of XML security:

- Use of existing XML standards
- Use of existing security technologies
- End-to-end security
- Output is a valid XML document
- Applying security mechanisms

In [Naed03] a good overview of XML security standards is given. The standards are grouped together according to security goals (see Figure A.1). The illustrated security standards are explained in this work.

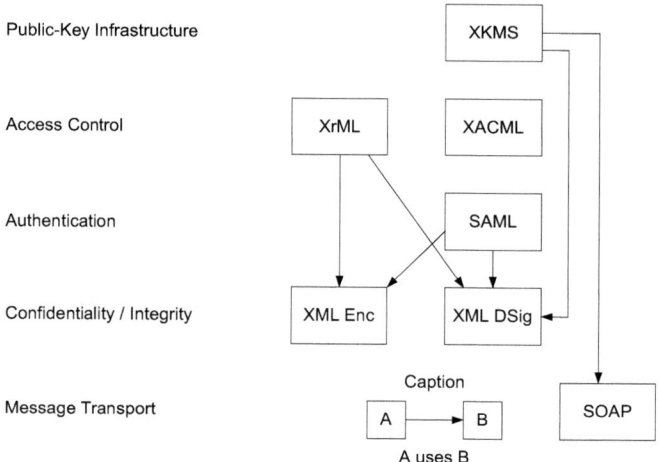

Fig. A.1: Security standards with their dependencies

It should be mentioned that the Simple Object Access Protocol (SOAP) does not provide any security mechanisms. It is a platform-independent protocol to exchange data in the structured XML format. For data transmission over the web, SOAP uses existing protocols like TCP/IP.

Sometimes XML is classified as the "ASCII of the web" (e.g. [Koch05]). Certainly, XML security is not revolutionary, because assuring the confidentiality and integrity is not a new invention. The only innovation is the adaption to the XML structure.

Several free available software solutions are offered, which support the W3C XML signature and the XML encryption standard. For instance, the IBM Security Suite or the IAIK XML Security Toolkit (XSECT) are such programs. Furthermore, there exist also free available XML security plug-ins for eclipse [Scha].

A.1 XML Access Control

The aim of access control is to regulate which resources can be accessed by which users under which conditions. Many access control approaches are based on the protection matrix model given in [HaRU76], where authorizations are encoded as triples given by (subject, object, access right). A subject is granted access to an object with some access permissions.

A.1.1 Server Side Evaluation

In [DVPS00] an access control model is given as 5-tuple, which is represented by (subject, object, action, sign, type). A *subject* is a triple, which is structured as (user id, IP address, symbolic address). The user id is the identity with which a user is authenticated in a system. Either the IP address or the symbolic address (e.g. *www.lab.com*) must be specified. Within the IP address and the symbolic name the wild card * (which matches any string) is allowed. An authorization *object* consists of a unique resource identifier (URI) possibly extended with an XPath expression (e.g.: doc.xml:docs[./@type=internal]). Dependent on the *sign*, which can be either plus or minus, an *action* (e.g.: read) is allowed or prohibited. The element *type* can be either local or recursive or local weak or recursive weak. For example ((admin, 62.114.136.18, *), doc.xml:sections[./@type=internal], read, +, R) allows a user authenticated as administrator from the given IP address to read sections and subsections in docs.xml marked as internal. Authorizations can be specified on single XML documents or on DTDs. In their approach they support two strategies: "most specific rules take precedence" (so-called non-weak authorizations) and "rules defined on schema level take precedence" (so-called weak authorizations). Thus, in the non-weak authorization mode more specific rules override less specific rules. In the weak authorization mode the same strategy is used (most specific principle) but with the exception that more specific rules can be overridden by rules defined on schema level. Authorizations can be marked as local or recursive. Locally defined rules are only valid on their elements' attributes, whereas recursive rules are valid on elements' attributes and their direct and indirect subelements. These strategies are indicated by the *type* element that can be either local or recursive or local-weak or recursive-weak. Similar to the approach from [DVPS00] a java implementation called Author-X to enforce access control on XML documents is introduced in [BeCF01].

A.1.2 Access Control based on Encryption

In contrast to systems with centralized right evaluation units, there exist other approaches as presented in [MiSu03], where access control policies are enforced by cryptography. In [Cram04] a role-based access control to XML documents is forced by encrypting XML nodes and distributing appropriate decryption keys to authorized users. A role becomes synonymous with a set of keys. Having a key to a node x does not imply full access to all elements rooted at node x. To overcome scenarios where access to node x is granted but access to some inner nodes rooted at x is reserved for more privileged users, nodes are encrypted several times. The number of encrypting per node does not exceed the tree hight. The authors suggest giving each recipient a single key (master key). In accordance to their roles and permissions users can generate decryption keys.

A.2 XML Encryption

XML Encryption is standardized by the W3C with the official web site at [Reag01]. The standard is given by the following syntax:

```
<EncryptedData Id? Type? MimeType? Encoding?>
    <EncryptionMethod/>?
    <ds:KeyInfo>
       <EncryptedKey>?
       <AgreementMethod>?
       <ds:KeyName>?
       <ds:RetrievalMethod>?
       <ds:*>?
    </ds:KeyInfo>?
    <CipherData>
       <CipherValue>?
       <CipherReference URI?>?
    </CipherData>
    <EncryptionProperties>?
  </EncryptedData>
```

Tags and attributes labeled with a question mark are optional; those marked with a star can occur zero or more times. The encrypted data is either stored within the `<CipherValue>` tag or is referenced by the `<CipherReference>` tag. The ciphertext is encoded as specified in the encoding attribute (i.e: Base64) given

A.2 XML Encryption

in the <EncryptedData> tag. There are three granularity types of encryption, declared by the attribute Type, which are supported by the XML Encryption standard: XML element, XML element content (elements) and XML element content (character data). In the first case a single node with all its subelements in it is encrypted (either a subtree rooted at that single node or the node is a leaf node). The second type addresses the encryption of several nodes at the same level in the hierarchy with all its subelements. Finally the last type covers the encryption of data contents within a tag. Furthermore the encryption of whole documents with arbitrary data as well as multiple encryption is provided by the standard. The <EncryptionMethod> allows to indicate the encryption algorithm, with which the cipher data is encrypted (i.e.: AES in CBC mode). With <ds:KeyInfo> it is possible to attach the encryption/decryption key in encrypted manner (i.e. encrypted with a public key).

The encryption/decryption of XML documents can be regarded as an XML document transformation process. In [BaCo03] a transforming is accomplished by XSLT (see Figure A.2). They point out that further programming functionality within stylesheets causes a significant increase of complexity. Therefore, they suggest extending the XSLT capabilities by using extension functions, which are encryption/decryption interfaces between cryptographic libraries and stylesheets. However, such a functionality is not supported by all XSLT processors.

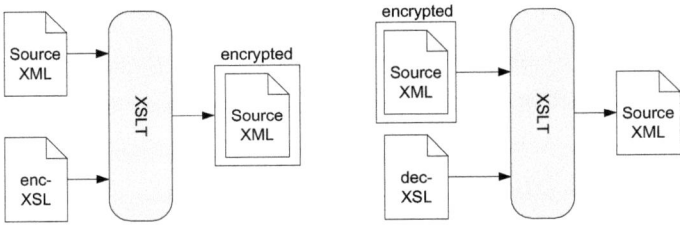

Fig. A.2: XML Encryption/Decryption using XSLT

In [ImMa00] some scenarios are given that emphasize the importance of element-wise encryption. A classic example is given by a purchase where the customer sends an XML document containing his or her credit card information to the the merchant. The merchant does not need to know the credit card number as long as the merchant gets the money. Encrypting only the credit card information with the public key of the credit card company would solve this problem. In [ImCM02] the authors illustrate how XML Encryption specification can be realized using a stream-based approach with XNI (Xerces Native Interface). They suggest implementing the encryption (respectively decryption) as a part of the parser (see Figure A.3). The parser for the decryption process first scans, next decrypts, and finally validates an encrypted XML file.

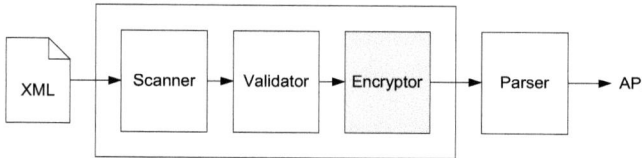

Fig. A.3: Stream based encryption of XML documents

With XML Encryption it is impossible to have parent nodes encrypted and its child nodes in plain text. In [Geue02] this problem is addressed by encrypting each node together with its position in the XML tree separately. The encrypted nodes are stored in a pool. According to the user rights users get decryption keys. Thus, the decryption can result in another document different from the original one (i.e. where some nodes are missing). This means that different users might get different views on a document depending on their keys. To convert the tree into a table structure, the Adjacency List Mode (ALM) has been adapted. In the ALM a recipient (respectively attacker) might get some information from the assigned numbers about how many nodes he or she is not allowed to see. Therefore, the encountering is performed in larger steps.

A.3 XML Signature

To ensure the integrity of binary data, W3C has standardized the XML Signature through following XML syntax (see [W3C02],[W3C06]):

```
<Signature ID?>
    <SignedInfo>
        <CanonicalizationMethod/>
        <SignatureMethod/>
        (<Reference URI? >
          (<Transforms>)?
          <DigestMethod>
          <DigestValue>
```

A.3 XML Signature

```
    </Reference>)+
  </SignedInfo>
  <SignatureValue>
  (<KeyInfo>)?
  (<Object ID?>)*
</Signature>
```

As above, "?" marks optional tags, "+" denotes one or more occurrences, and "*" denotes zero or more occurrences. The content to be signed is located in the `<SignatureInfo>` element. The data can be represented in many forms (different encoding scheme, carriage return/line feed etc.). To ensure that the same contents, which are encoded differently, map to a unified representation, the canonicalization process is used. The W3C has standardized "Canonical XML" which includes:

- UTF-8 encoding
- Normalizing line breaks
- Normalizing attributes
- Normalizing whitespaces
- Replacing char and entity references
- Replacing CDATA with char content
- Removing declarations
- Ensuring that start-tags have end-tags

In the `<CanonicalizationMethod>` element, the canonicalization algorithm can be specified. The cryptographic signature is covered in the `<SignatureValue>` element. XML Signatures can be applied to any digital content (including XML) and can cover one or more resources. The applied algorithm is specified in the `<SignatureMethod>` element (e.g. RSA-SHA1). The input data for the signing process is given under the `<Reference>` element. A reference can be XML data, binary data or a link to it. Optionally a transformation process can be applied to the data, which is defined in the `Transforms` tag. The output of each transformation step serves as an input to the next transform step resulting in the input for the algorithm specified in the `DigestMethod` element. This makes it possible to convert data or extract fragments from it. Optionally the key to validate the signature can be placed in the `KeyInfo` element.

There are three types of signatures: enveloped, enveloping, and detached (see Figure A.4). In the case of an enveloped or an enveloping signature, the signature and its resources are stored in the same XML document. Detached signatures are stored separately. In enveloped signatures the signature element covers all elements. Enveloped signatures are stored as subelements of the signed parts.

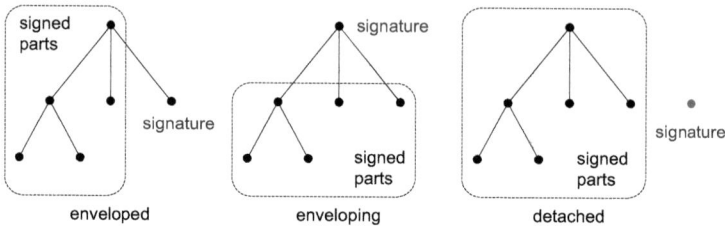

Fig. A.4: Digital signatures

A.4 XML Key Management Specification

XML Key Management Specification (XKMS) is a specification, which is supervised by the W3C (see [xkm]). In particular the specification defines protocols for distributing and registering public keys. In the following example someone sends a request for the public key of Alice Cryptographer:

```
<Locate>
   <Query>
      <ds:KeyInfo>
         <ds:KeyName>Alice Cryptographer</ds:KeyName>
      </ds:KeyInfo>
   </Query>
   <Respond>
      <string>KeyName</string>
      <string>KeyValue</string>
   </Respond>
</Locate>
```

If already registered, the TTP successfully responds with the public key:

```
<LocateResult>
   <Result>Success</Result>
   <Answer>
      <ds:KeyInfo>
         <ds:KeyName>Alice Cryptographer</ds:KeyName>
         <ds:KeyValue>...</ds:KeyValue>
      </ds:KeyInfo>
   </Answer>
</LocateResult>
```

A.4 XML Key Management Specification

In XKRSS a key is bound to a public key. A private/public key pair can be generated by either the client or the registration service. The following example shows a scenario for the first case:

```
<Register>
   <Prototype Id="keybinding">
      <Status>Valid</Status>
      <KeyID>mailto:alice@test.org</KeyID>
      <ds:KeyInfo>
         <ds:KeyValue>
            <ds:RSAKeyValue>
               <ds:Modulus>
               998/T2PUN8HQlnhf9YIKdMHHGM7HkJwA56UD0a1oYq7E
               fdxSXAidruAszNqBoOqfarJIsfcVKLob1hGnQ/16xw
               </ds:Modulus>
               <ds:Exponent>AQAB</ds:Exponent>
            </ds:RSAKeyValue>
         </ds:KeyValue>
         <ds:KeyName>mailto:alice@test.org</ds:KeyName>
      </ds:KeyInfo>
      <PassPhrase>Pass</PassPhrase>
   </Prototype>
   <AuthInfo>
      <AuthUserInfo>
         <ProofOfPossession>
            <ds:Signature URI="#keybinding"
                  [RSA-Sign (KeyBinding, Private)] />
         </ProofOfPossession>
         <KeyBindingAuth>
            <ds:Signature  URI="#keybinding"
                  [HMAC-SHA1 (KeyBinding, Auth)] />
         </KeyBindingAuth>
      </AuthUserInfo>
   </AuthInfo>
   <Respond>
      <string>KeyName<string>
      <string>KeyValue</string>
      <string>RetrievalMethod</string>
   </Respond>
</Register>
```

For example, the authentication information and the passphrase can be given as Auth = HMAC-SHA1 ("024837", 0x1) and Pass = HMAC-SHA1 (HMAC-SHA1 ("helpihaverevealedmykey", 0x2), 0x3). To prove the possession of the private key, a digital XML signature can be embedded. The registration service accepts the registration. Finally, the registration succeeds or fails with an error message. Moreover, the XKRSS protocol supports key revocation.

A.5 XrML

The Extensible Rights Markup Language ([xrm],[WLD⁺02]) originated from Xerox Palo Alto Research Center (PARC) is an XML-based language that allows to describe rights and conditions for digital resources.

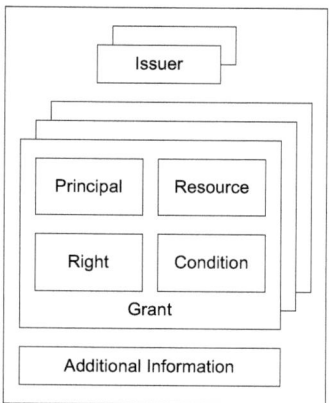

Fig. A.5: XrML license

Rights are specified as "Who is allowed to do what under which conditions on which digital resources?". In XrML a grant consists of the following elements:

- Principal: identification of a party to whom rights are granted
- Right: action/s that a principal may perform
- Resource: object like a digital content or a service to which rights are granted
- Condition: terms, conditions, and obligations under which rights are granted

A principal is usually a "KeyHolder" who is identified by a unique information like a private key of a public/private key pair. As depicted in Figure A.5, a license consists of at least one grant, which could further contains a set of grants. Optionally additional information (i.e. description or validity date) and an identification of the license issuer (issuers respectively), who can sign the bestowed grants, can be included. The following simple example shows a license, which certifies that the holder of the given public RSA key has the name "Alice Richardson".

```
<license>
   <grant>
      <keyHolder>
         <info>
            <dsig:KeyValue>
               <dsig:RSAKeyValue>
                  <dsig:Modulus>Ke7...==</dsig:Modulus>
                  <dsig:Exponent>AQABAA==</dsig:Exponent>
               </dsig:RSAKeyValue>
            </dsig:KeyValue>
         </info>
      </keyHolder>
      <possessProperty/>
         <sx:commonName>Alice Richardson</sx:commonName>
   </grant>
</license>
```

A.6 XACML

The Extensible Access Control Markup Language, which was developed by OASIS, is a general purpose policy system for expressing the rules so that authorizations are created [xac],[LPL+03]. It consists of request and response formats. The decision in the response can either be permit, deny, not applicable (rules could not be found) or indeterminate (an error occured).

As a precondition, the Policy Administration Point (PAP) makes policies available to the Policy Decision Point (PDP). The following data-flow steps are modeled by the XACML.

1. Application sends access request to the Policy Enforcement Point (PEP).

2. XACML request is generated and sent to the PDP.

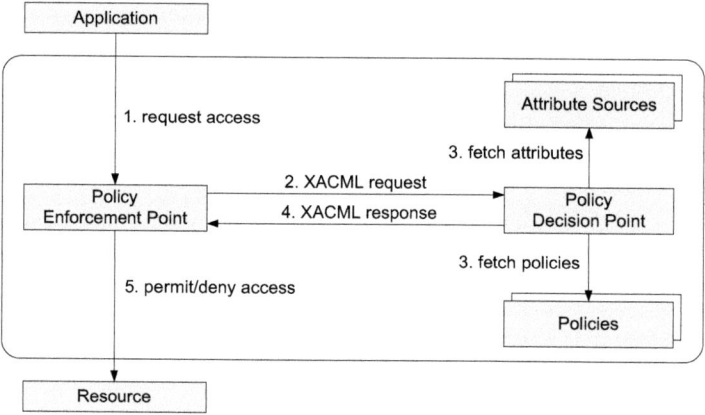

Fig. A.6: Overview of the XACML data-flow model

3. Additional subject, resource, action, and environment attributes are fetched.

4. The PDP evaluates the policy and returns the response (including the authorization decision) to the PEP.

5. According to the response access is permitted or denied.

For an example the policy "Any subject with an e-mail name in the medico.com domain can perform any action on any resource" can be described by the following XACML policy:

```
<Policy xmlns=...>
   <Description>Medico Access Control Policy</Description>
   <Target/>
   <Rule RuleId="Rule1" Effect="Permit">
      <Description>...</Description>
      <Target>
         <Subjects>
            <Subject>
               <SubjectMatch MatchId="rfc822Name-match">
                  <AttributeValue DataType="XMLSchema#string">
                     medico.com
                  </AttributeValue>
                  <SubjectAttributeDesignator
```

A.6 XACML

```
                    AttributeId="subject:subject-id"
                    DataType="data-type:rfc822Name"/>
              </SubjectMatch>
            </Subject>
         </Subjects>
      </Target>
   </Rule>
</Policy>
```

Abbreviations B

AES	Advanced Encryption Standard
Anc	Ancestors' function that determines the predecessors of a node.
AoS	Ancestors' or Self function, which outputs the ancestors of a node including the node itself.
CA	Central Authority
CAM	Conditional Access Module
CAS	Conditional Access System
CBC	Cipher Block Chaining
Chd	Children's function, that determines the direct successors of a node.
CI	Common Interface
CPPM	Content Protection for Prerecorded Media
CRL	Certificate Revocation List
CS	Complete Subset
CSA	Common Scrambling Algorithm
CVC	Card Validation Code
CVV	Card Verification Value
CW	Control Word
DCT	Discrete Cosine Transform

Des	Descendants' function, which outputs the successors of a node.
DLP	Discrete Logarithm Problem
DoS	Descendants' or Self function, which outputs the descendants of a node including the node itself.
DRM	Digital Rights Management
DTD	Document Type Definition
ECDSA	Elliptic Curve Digital Signature Algorithm
ETSI	European Telecommunications Standards Institute
FSM	Flexible Subscription Model
GPS	Global Positioning System
HDCP	High-bandwidth Digital Content Protection
HDMI	High Definition Multimedia Interface
ICC	Integrated Circuit Card
IV	Initial Vector
Leaves	Leaves' function, which determines the leaf nodes in a graph.
LMF	Local Media Format
LWDRM	Lightweight Digital Rights Management
MAC	Message Authentication Code
MHP	Multimedia Home Platform
MPEG	Motion Pictures Experts Group
NIST	National Institute of Standards and Technology
NSA	National Security Agency
OBU	On Board Unit
ODRL	Open Digital Rights Language

OWF	One-Way Functions
Par	Parent's function, which determines the parent nodes of a node.
PRNG	Pseudo-Random Number Generator
RSA	Rivest Shamir Adleman
SD	Subset Difference
SET	Secure Electronic Transaction
SK	Sealed Key
SMF	Signed Media Format
STB	Set-Top Box
STT	Set-Top Terminal
SVP	Secure Video Processor
TSM	Tailored Subscription Model
TTP	Trusted Third Party
URI	Unique Resource Identifier
XACML	Extensible Access Control Markup Language
XKMS	XML Key Management Specification
XKRSS	XML Key Registration Service Specification
XML	Extensible Markup Language
XrML	Extensible Rights Markup Language

Bibliography

[AAC06a] Advanced Access Content System (AACS): Introduction and Common Cryptographic Elements (2006), http://www.aacsla.com/specifications/.

[AAC06b] Advanced Access Content System: Pre-recorded Video Book (2006), http://www.aacsla.com/specifications/.

[AbSW00] M. Abdalla, Y. Shavitt, A. Wool: Key Management for Restricted Multicast Using Broadcast Encryption. In: S. Low (Hrsg.), IEEE/ACM Transactions on Networking (2000), Bd. 8.

[ACJT00] G. Ateniese, J. Camenisch, M. Joye, G. Tsudik: A Practical and Provably Secure Coalition-Resistant Group Signature Scheme. In: M. Bellare (Hrsg.), Advances in Cryptology (CRYPTO'00), August 20-24, Springer, Santa Barbara, CA (2000), Lecture Notes in Computer Science, Bd. 1880.

[AdGr05] A. Adelsbach, U. Greveler: A Broadcast Encryption Scheme with Free-Riders but Unconditional Security. In: R. Safavi-Naini, M. Yung (Hrsg.), First International Conference on Digital Rights Management:Technologies, Issues, Challenges and Systems (DRMTICS2005), Springer (2005), Lecture Notes in Computer Science, Bd. 3919.

[AkTa83] S. Akl, P. Taylor: Cryptographic Solutions to a Problem of Access Control in a Hierarchy. In: ACM Transactions on Computer Systems, ACM (1983), Bd. 1, 239–248.

[AnMa97] R. Anderson, C. Manifavas: Chameleon – A New Kind of Steam Cipher. In: Proceeedings of the 4th International Workshop on Fast Software Encryption (IWFSE), January 20-22, Springer, Haifa, Israel (1997), Lecture Notes in Computer Science, Bd. 1267, 107–113.

[ASFM06]   G. Ateniese, A. de Santis, A. Ferrara, B. Masucci: Provably-Secure Time-Bound Hierarchical Key Assignment Schemes. In: A. Juels, R. N. Wright, S. D. C. di Vimercati (Hrsg.), Proceedings of the 13th ACM Conference on Computer and Communications Security (CCS 2006), Okt 30 - Nov 3, Alexandria, VA, USA (2006).

[AtFB05]   M. J. Atallah, K. B. Frikken, M. Blanton: Dynamic and Efficient Key Management for Access Hierarchies. In: V. Atluri, C. Meadows, A. Juels (Hrsg.), Proceedings of the 12th ACM Conference on Computer and Communications Security (CCS 2005), Nov 7-11, ACM Press, Alexandria, VA, USA (2005), 190–202.

[BaCo03]   R. Bartlett, M. Cook: XML Security Using XSLT. In: Proceedings of the 36th Hawaii International Conference on System Sciences (HICSS03), January 6-9, IEEE Computer Society, Big Island, HI, USA (2003).

[Bar-04]   H. Bar-El: Known Attacks Against Smartcards. Discretix Technologies Ltd. (2004), http://discretix.com/wp.shtml, white Paper.

[BeCF01]   E. Bertino, S. Castano, E. Ferrari: Securing XML Documents with Author-X. In: IEEE Internet Computing, 5 (2001), 21–31.

[BeCK96]   M. Bellare, R. Canetti, H. Krawczyk: Keying Hash Functions for Message Authentication. In: N. Koblitz (Hrsg.), Advances in Cryptology (CRYPTO'96), August 18-22, Springer, Santa Barbara, CA, USA (1996), Lecture Notes in Computer Science, Bd. 1109, 1–15.

[BeDe90]   T. Beth, Y. Desmedt: Identification Tokens - or: Solving The Chess Grandmaster Problem. In: . A. V. A. J. Menezes (Hrsg.), Advances in Cryptology (CRYPTO'90), 11-15 August, Springer, Santa Barbara, CA, USA (1990), LNCS, Bd. 537.

[Bell06]   M. Bellare: New Proofs for NMAC and HMAC: Security without Collision-Resistance. In: C. Dwork (Hrsg.), Advances in Cryptology (CRYPTO'06), August 20-24, Springer, Santa Barbara, CA, USA (2006), Lecture Notes in Computer Science, Bd. 4117, 602–619.

[Blaz03]   M. Blaze: Rights Amplification in Master-Keyed Mechanical Locks. In: IEEE Security and Privacy, 1, 2 (2003), 24–32.

[BlMS96]   C. Blundo, L. Mattos, D. Stinson: Trade-offs Between Communication and Storage in Unconditionally Secure Schemes for Broadcast Encryption and Interactive Key Distribution. In: N. Koblitz (Hrsg.), Advances in Cryptology (CRYPTO'96), 18-22 August, Springer, Santa Barbara, CA, USA (1996), Lecture Notes in Computer Science, Bd. 1109, 387–400.

[BoBo04]   D. Boneh, X. Boyen: Secure Identity Based Encryption Without Random Oracles. In: M. Franklin (Hrsg.), Advances in Cryptology (CRYPTO'04), LNCS, Springer (2004).

[BoCY96]   B. Boesch, S. Crocker, M. Yesil: CyberCash Credit Card Protocol Version 0.8. RFC 1898 (1996), http://rools.ietf.org/html/rfc1898.txt.

[BoFr03]   D. Boneh, M. Franklin: Identity-Based Encryption from the Weil Pairing. In: SIAM Journal on Computing, 32, 3 (2003), 586–615.

[BoGV96]   A. Bosselaers, R. Govaerts, J. Vandewalle: Fast Hashing on the Pentium. In: N. Koblitz (Hrsg.), Advances in Cryptology (CRYPTO'96), August 18-22, Springer, Santa Barbara, CA, USA (1996), LNCS, Bd. 1109, 298–312.

[BoMa03]   C. Boyd, A. Mathuria: Protocols for Authentication and Key Establishment. Information Security and Cryptography, Springer (2003).

[BoSh95]   D. Boneh, J. Shaw: Collusion-Secure Fingerprinting for Digital Data. In: D. Coppersmith (Hrsg.), Advances in Cryptology (CRYPTO'95), Springer (1995), LNCS, Bd. 963, 452–465.

[BrCh93]   S. Brands, D. Chaum: Distance-Bounding Protocols. In: T. Helleseth (Hrsg.), Advances in Cryptology (EUROCRYPT'93), Springer, Lofthus, Norway (1993), Lecture Notes in Computer Science, Bd. 765, 344–359.

[Bris99]   B. Briscoe: MARKS: Zero Side Effect Multicast Key Management Using Arbitrarily Revealed Key Sequences. In: L. Rizzo, S. Fdida (Hrsg.), Proceedings of the First International COST264 Workshop on Networked Group Communication, Springer (1999), Bd. 1736.

[BrSe87]   Bronstein, Semendjajew: Taschenbuch der Mathematik. Nauka (1987).

[BSH+93] C. Blundo, A. de Santis, A. Herzberg, S. Kutten, U. Vaccaro, M. Yung: Perfectly-Secure Key Distribution for Dynamic Conferences. In: Lecture Notes in Computer Science, 740 (1993), 471–486.

[BuDe94] M. Burmester, Y. Desmedt: A Secure and Efficient Conference Key Distribution System. In: A. de Santis (Hrsg.), Advances in Cryptology (EUROCRYPT'94), May 9-12, Perugia, Italy (1994), Lecture Notes in Computer Science, Bd. 950, 277–286.

[CaGe98] D. Catalano, R. Gennaro: New Efficient and Secure Protocols for Verifiable Signature Sharing and Other Applications. In: H. Krawczyk (Hrsg.), Advances in Cryptology (CRYPTO'98), August 23-27, Springer, Santa Barbara, CA (1998), Lecture Notes in Computer Science, Bd. 1462.

[CGI+99] R. Canetti, J. Garay, G. Itkis, D. Micciancio, M. Naor, B. Pinkas: Multicast Security: A Taxonomy and Some Efficient Constructions. In: Proceedings of the 18th Annual Joint Conference of the IEEE Computer and Communications Societies (INFOCOM'99), March 21-25, New York, NY, USA (1999), Bd. 2, 708–716.

[Chau81] D. Chaum: Untraceable Electronic Mail, Return Address, and Digital Pseudonyms. In: Communications of the ACM, 24, 2 (1981), 84–88.

[ChCT04] T. Chen, Y. Chung, C. Tian: A Novel Key Management Scheme for Dynamic Access Control in a User Hierarchy. In: Proceedings of the 28th Annual International Computer Software and Applications Conference (COMPSAC'04), September 27-30, IEEE Computer Society, Hong Kong, China (2004).

[ChFN88] D. Chaum, A. Fiat, M. Naor: Untraceable Electronic Cash. In: Advances in Cryptology (CRYPTO'88) (1988).

[Chie04] H.-Y. Chien: Efficient Time-Bound Hierarchical Key Assignment Scheme. In: IEEE Transactions on Knowledge and Data Engineering (2004), Bd. 16, 1301–1304.

[CLTW04] C. Chang, I. Lin, H. Tsai, H. Wang: A Key Assignment Scheme for Controlling Access in Partially Ordered User Hierarchies. In: Proceedings of the 18th International Conference on Advanced Information Networking and Application (AINA'04), March 29-31, IEEE Computer Society, Fukuoka, Japan (2004).

[CoDF06] I. Cox, G. Doerr, T. Furon: Watermarking is not Cryptography. In: Y.-Q. Shi, B. Jeon (Hrsg.), Proceedings of the 5-th International Workshop on Digital Watermarking (IWDM'06), Springer, Jeju Island, Korea (2006), LNCS, Bd. 4283.

[CoLR90] T. H. Cormen, C. E. Leiserson, R. L. Rivest: Introduction to Algorithms. MIT Press/McGraw-Hill (1990).

[Conw04] J. H. Conway: On Numbers and Games. Peters, second Aufl. (2004).

[Cram04] J. Crampton: Applying Hierarchical and Role-Based Access Control to XML Documents. In: ACM Workshop on Secure Web Services, ACM (2004).

[CrMW06] J. Crampton, K. Martin, P. Wild: On Key Assignment for Hierarchical Access Control. In: 19th IEEE Computer Security Foundations Workshop (CSFW'06) (2006).

[Dai07] W. Dai: Crypto++ 5.5 Benchmarks (2007), http://www.cryptopp.com/benchmarks.html.

[Damg89] I. B. Damgård: A Design Principle for Hash Functions. In: G. Brassard (Hrsg.), Advances in Cryptology (CRYPTO'89), Springer (1989), LNCS, Bd. 435.

[DeGB87] Y. Desmedt, C. Gouties, S. Bengio: Special Uses and Abuses of the Fiat-Shamir Passport Protocol. In: C. Pomerance (Hrsg.), Advances in Cryptology (CRYPTO'87), 16-20 August, Springer, Santa Barbara, CA, USA (1987), LNCS, Bd. 293, 21–39.

[Denn82] D. E. Denning: Cryptography and Data Security. Addison-Wesley (1982).

[Ditt00] J. Dittmann: Digitale Wasserzeichen. Springer Xpert.press (2000).

[DoBP96] H. Dobbertin, A. Bosselaers, B. Preneel: The hash function RIPEMD-160 (1996), http://homes.esat.kuleuven.be/~bosselae/ripemd160.html.

[DoFa02]   Y. Dodis, N. Fazio: Public Key Broadcast Encryption for Stateless Receivers. In: J. Feigenbaum (Hrsg.), Digital Rights Management (DRM2002), ACM CCS-9 Workshop, LNCS, Springer (2002), 61–80.

[DoOs97]   S. Dolev, R. Ostrovsky: Efficient Anonymous Multicast and Reception. In: B. Kaliski (Hrsg.), Advances in Cryptology (CRYPTO'97), August 17-21, Springer, Santa Barbara, CA, USA (1997), Lecture Notes in Computer Science, Bd. 1294, 395–409.

[DRF08]   Digitaler Rundfunk (2008), http://www.digitaler-rundfunk.at.

[dss]   Digital Signature Standard (DSS). http://www.itl.nist.gov/fipspubs/fip186.htm.

[DVB08]   DVB-T: Das Digitale Antennenfernsehen (2008), http://www.dvb-t.at.

[DVPS00]   E. Daminani, S. D. C. di Vimercati, S. Paraboschi, P. Samarati: Securing XML Documents. In: Proceedings of the 2000 International Conference on Extending Database Technology (EDBT2000), March 27-31, Springer, Konstanz, Germany, (2000), 121–135.

[EaJo01]   D. Eastlake, P. Jones: RFC 3174 - US Secure Hash Algorithm 1 (SHA1) (2001), http://www.faqs.org/rfcs/rfc3174.html.

[enga05]   engadget: DVD-Audio CPPM encryption broken (2005), http://www.engadget.com/2005/07/07/dvd-audio-cppm-encryption-broken/.

[Feig92]   J. Feigenbaum: Overview of Interactive Proof Systems and Zero-Knowledge. In: G. J. Simmons (Hrsg.), Contemporary Cryptology – The Science of Information Integrity, IEEE Press, Kap. 8 (1992).

[FeSc03]   N. Ferguson, B. Schneier: Practical Cryptography. Wiley Publishing (2003).

[FiNa94]   A. Fiat, M. Naor: Broadcast Encryption. In: Advances in Cryptology (CRYPTO'93), Springer-Verlag (1994), Bd. 773, 480–491.

[Geue02]   C. Geuer-Pollmann: XML Pool Encryption. In: Proceedings of the ACM Workshop on XML Security 2002, ACM (2002).

BIBLIOGRAPHY

[GoGM86] O. Goldreich, S. Goldwasser, S. Micali: How to construct random functions. In: Journal of the ACM (JACM), 33 (1986), 792–807.

[GoMR85] S. Goldwasser, S. Micali, C. Rackoff: The Knowledge Complexity of Interactive Proof-Systems. In: Proceedings of 17th Symposium on the Theory of Computation (1985).

[gps] U.S. Governemnt: Global Positioning System. http://www.gps.gov.

[GrAi04] R. Grimm, P. Aichroth: Privacy Protection for Signed Media Files: A Separation-of-Duty Approach to the Lightweight DRM (LWDRM) System. In: Proceedings of the 2004 Workshop on Multimedia and Security (2004), 93–99.

[Grev06] U. Greveler: Applications of Broadcast Encryption Schemes and Related Technical Mechanisms for Digital Rights Management of Multimedia Broadcasts. Dissertation, Ruhr-Universität Bochum (2006).

[HaMV04] D. Hankerson, A. Menezes, S. Vanstone: Guide to Elliptic Curve Cryptography. Springer (2004).

[Hanc05] G. Hancke: A Practical Relay Attack on ISO 14443 Proximity Cards (2005), http://www.cl.cam.ac.uk/~gh275/relay.pdf.

[Hanc06] G. Hancke: Practical Attacks on Proximity Identification Systems. In: Proceedings of the Symposium on Security and Privacy (S&P'06), 21-24 May, Oakland, CA, USA (2006).

[HaRU76] M. Harrison, W. Ruzzo, J. Ullman: Protection in Operating Systems. In: Communications of the ACM Vol. 19 Number 8 (1976), 461–471.

[HaSh02] D. Halevy, A. Shamir: The LSD Broadcast Encryption Scheme. In: M. Yung (Hrsg.), Advances in Cryptology (CRYPTO'02), Springer (2002), Lecture Notes in Computer Science (LNCS), Bd. 2442, 47–60.

[Håst90] J. Håstad: Pseudo-random generators under uniform assumptions. In: Proceedings of the 22nd Annual ACM Symposium on Theory of Computing, ACM Press (1990).

[HILM02] H. Hacigümüs, B. Iyer, C. Li, S. Mehrotra: Executing SQL over Encrypted Data in the Database Service Provider Model. In: SIGMOD Conference, ACM (2002).

[Hirs] F. Hirsch: Getting Started with XML Security. http://www.sitepoint.com/article/getting-started-xml-security.

[ImCM02] T. Imamura, A. Clark, H. Maruyama: A Stream-based Implementation of XML Encryption. In: Proceedings of the ACM Workshop on XML Security 2002, ACM (2002).

[ImMa00] T. Imamura, H. Maruyama: Element-Wise XML Encryption (2000), http://lists.w3.org/Archives/Public/xml-encryption/2000Apr/att-0005/01-xmlenc.

[ird] irdeto. http://www.irdeto.com.

[IwCA05] M. Iwaihara, S. Chatvichienchai, C. Anutariya: Relevancy Based Access Control of Versioned XML Documents. In: Proceedings of the 10th ACM Conference on Access Control Models and Technologies (SACMAT'05), ACM, Stockholm (2005).

[KaAm01] W. Kanjanarin, T. Amornraksa: Scrambling and Key Distribution Scheme fo Digital Television. In: Proceedings of the 9-th IEEE International Conference on Networks (ICON'01) (2001).

[Kalv06] H. Kalva: The H.264 Video Coding Standard. In: IEEE MultiMedia, 13, 4 (2006), 86–90.

[KaRo95] B. Kaliski, M. Robshaw: Message Authentication with MD5. In: CryptoBytes, 1, 1 (1995), 5–8.

[KBPH06] J. Kim, A. Biryukov, B. Preneel, S. Hong: On the Security of HMAC and NMAC Based on HAVAL, MD4, MD5, SHA-0 and SHA-1. In: R. de Prisco, M. Yung (Hrsg.), Proceedings of the Security and Cryptography for Networks Conference (SCN2006), Springer (2006), LNCS, Bd. 4116.

[Kerc83] A. Kerckhoffs: La cryptographie militaire. In: Journal des sciences militaires, IX (1883), 5–38.

[KfWo05] Z. Kfir, A. Wool: Picking Virtual Pockets using Realy Attacks on Contactless Smartcard Systems. In: Proceedings of the First International Conference on Security and Privacy for Emerging Areas in Communications Networks (SECURECOMM'05), 5-th - 9-th September 2005, Athens, Greece (2005).

BIBLIOGRAPHY 211

[KNCT94] J. T. Kohl, B. C. Neuman, B. Clifford, T. Y. T'so: The Evolution of the Kerberos Authentication Service. In: Distributed Open Systems (1994), 78–94.

[Knut97] D. E. Knuth: Fundamental Algorithms, Addison-Wesley, The Art of Computer Programming, Bd. 1, Kap. 1.2. Third Aufl. (1997), 650.

[Knut98] D. E. Knuth: Seminumerical Algorithms, Addison-Wesley, Kap. 3.4. Third Aufl. (1998), 762.

[Koch05] D. Koch: Klammerheimlich. In: iX, 10 (2005), 130–132.

[Koll06] F. Kollmann: Key-Management für partielle Verschlüsselung von XML-Dokumenten. In: P. Horster (Hrsg.), DACH Security 2006, syssec (2006).

[Koll07a] F. Kollmann: Abonnements für elektonische Zeitungen mit statischer Baumstruktur. In: P. Horster (Hrsg.), DACH Security 2007, syssec (2007).

[Koll07b] F. Kollmann: A Flexible Subscription Model for Broadcasted Digital Contents. In: Y. Wang, Y. Cheung, Q. Zhang, P. Wang (Hrsg.), International Conference on Computational Intelligence and Security (CIS'07), IEEE Computer Society, Harbin, China (2007), 589–593.

[Koll07c] F. Kollmann: Realizing fine-granular Read and Write Rights on Tree Structured Documents. In: Second International Conference on Availability, Reliability and Security (ARES'07), IEEE Computer Society (2007), 517–523.

[KrBC97] H. Krawczyk, M. Bellare, R. Canetti: RFC 2104 - HMAC: Keyed-Hashing for Message Authentication (1997), http://www.ietf.org/rfc/rfc2104.txt.

[LaOd91] B. A. LaMacchia, A. M. Odlyzko: Computation of Discrete Logarithms in Prime Fields. In: Lecture Notes in Computer Science, 537 (1991), 616–618.

[Lens05] A. Lenstra: Further progress in hashing cryptanalysis (2005), http://cm.bell-labs.com/who/akl/hash.pdf.

[LeVe00]   A. Lenstra, E. Verheul: Selecting Cryptographic Key Sizes. In: H. Imai, Y. Zheng (Hrsg.), Public Key Cryptography (PKC2000), Springer, Melbourne, Australia (2000), LNCS, Bd. 1751.

[LPL+03]   M. Lorch, S. Proctor, R. Lepro, D. Kafura, S. Shah: First Experiences Using XACML for Access Control in Distributed Systems. In: Proceedings of the ACM Workshop on XML Security 2003, ACM (2003).

[MaVI97]   Mastercard, VISA: SET Secure Electronic Transaction Specification (1997), http://citeseer.ist.psu.edu/289529.html, version 1.0.

[McCo98]   J. McCormac: European Scrambling Systems : Circuits, Tactics and Techniques. Waterford University Press (1998).

[McCu90]   K. McCurley: The Discrete Logarithm Problem. In: C. Pommerance (Hrsg.), Cryptology and Computation Number Theory, American Mathematical Society (1990), Proceedings of Symbosia in Applied Mathematics, Bd. 42, 49–74.

[MCMM06]   R. McEvoy, F. Crowe, C. Murphy, W. Marnane: Optimisation of the SHA-2 Family of Hash Functions on FPGAs. In: Annual Symposium on VLSI (ISVLSI2006), 2-3 March, IEEE Computer Society, Karlsruhe, Germany (2006).

[McSh98]   D. A. McGrew, A. T. Sherman: Key Establishment in Large Dynamic Groups Using One-Way Function Trees. Tech. Rep., TIS Report No. 755 (1998).

[MeOV96]   A. Menezes, P. van Oorschot, S. Vanstone: Handbook of Applied Cryptography. CRC Press (1996).

[Merk89]   R. C. Merkle: One Way Hash Functions and DES. In: G. Brassard (Hrsg.), Advances in Cryptology (CRYPTO'89), Springer (1989), LNCS, Bd. 435.

[MeSi95]   P. Metzger, W. Simpson: RFC 1828 - IP Authentication using Keyed MD5 (1995), http://www.faqs.org/rfcs/rfc1828.html.

[Meye82]   C. H. Meyer: Cryptography: A New Dimension in Computer Data Security - A Guide for the Design and Implementation of Secure Systems. John Wiley and Sons (1982).

[MiSu03]   G. Miklau, D. Suciu: Controlling Access to Published Data Using Cryptography. In: Proceedings of the 29th VLDB Conference, Berlin, Germany (2003).

[MTMA85] S. J. MacKinnon, P. D. Taylor, H. Meijer, S. G. Akl: An Optimal Algorithm for Assigning Cryptographic Keys to a Control Access in a Hierarchy. In: IEEE Transactions on Computers, 34(9), IEEE (1985), 797–802.

[NaDW00] K. Nahrstedt, J. Dittmann, P. Wohlmacher: Approaches to Multimedia and Security. In: IEEE International Conference on Multimedia and Expo, 30 July - 2 August, IEEE, New York, USA (2000), Bd. III, 1275–1278.

[Naed03]   M. Naedele: Standards for XML and Web Service Security. In: Computer, 36, 4 (2003), 96–98.

[NaNL01]   D. Naor, M. Naor, J. Lotspiech: Revocation and Tracing Schemes for Stateless Receivers. In: Lecture Notes in Computer Science, 2139 (2001), 41–73.

[NeSc78]   R. M. Needham, M. D. Schroeder: Using Encryption for Authentication in Large Networks of Computers. In: Communications of the ACM, 21, 12 (1978), 993–999.

[NeTs94]   C. Neuman, T. Ts'o: Kerberos: An Authentication Service for Computer Networks. In: IEEE Communications, 32, 9 (1994), 33–38.

[news]   heise online news: Österreicher bevorzugen Satelliten-TV. http://www.heise.de/newsticker/meldung/87694/from/rss09.

[News05]   H. O. News: Kopierschutz für DVD-Audio ausgehebelt (2005), http://www.heise.de/newsticker/meldung/61455.

[NüGr03]   J. Nützel, R. Grimm: Potato System and Signed Media Format - an Alternative Approach to Online Music Business. In: Proceedings of the Third International Conference WEB Delivering of Music (WEDELMUSIC03) (2003).

[NIST02]   NIST: Secure Hash Standard (2002), http://csrc.nist.gov/publications/fips/fips180-2/fips180-2.pdf, fIPS 180-2.

[NYHR05] C. Neuman, T. Yu, S. Hartman, K. Raeburn: The Kerberos Network Authentication System (RFC4120) (2005), http://www.ietf.org/rfc/rfc4120.txt.

[Odly00] A. M. Odlyzko: Discrete logarithms: The past and the future. In: Designs, Codes and Cryptography, 19 (2000), 129–145.

[OtWi96] T. Ottmann, P. Widmayer: Algorithmen und Datenstrukturen. Spektrum (1996).

[PrOo95] B. Preneel, P. C. van Oorschot: MDx-MAC and Building Fast MACs from Hash Functions. In: D. Coppersmith (Hrsg.), Advances in Cryptology (CRYPTO'95), Springer (1995), LNCS, Bd. 963, 1–14.

[PrOo96] B. Preneel, P. C. van Oorschot: On the Security of Two MAC Algorithms. In: U. Maurer (Hrsg.), Advances in Cryptology (EUROCRYPT'96), Springer (1996), LNCS, Bd. 1070, 19–32.

[QuGo89] J. J. Quisquater, L. Gouillou: How to Explain Zero-Knowledge Protocols to Your Children. In: G. Brassard (Hrsg.), Advances in Cryptology (CRYPTO'89), Springer (1989), LNCS, Bd. 435, 628–631.

[RaEf99] W. Rankl, W. Effing: Handbuch der Chipkarten. Hanser, 3 Aufl. (1999).

[Reag01] J. Reagle: W3C XML Encryption WG (2001), http://www.w3.org/Encryption/2001/.

[Rijm04] V. Rijmen: The block cipher Rijndael (2004), http://www.iaik.tu-graz.ac.at/research/krypto/AES/.

[RiKa03] R. L. Rivest, B. Kaliski: RSA Problem (2003), http://people.csail.mit.edu/rivest/RivestKaliski-RSAProblem.pdf.

[RiSA77] R. L. Rivest, A. Shamir, L. M. Adelman: A Method for Obtaining Digital Signatures and Public-Key Cryptosystems. Tech. Rep. MIT/LCS/TM-82, MIT (1977).

[Rive92] R. Rivest: RFC 1321 - The MD5 Message-Digest-Algorithm (1992), http://www.faqs.org/rfcs/rfc1321.html.

BIBLIOGRAPHY

[RoDy03] B. Rosenblatt, G. Dykstra: Integrating Content Management with Digital Rights Management (2003), http://www.xrml.org/reference/CM-DRMwhitepaper.pdf.

[RoTM01] B. Rosenblatt, B. Truppe, S. Mooney: Digital Rights Management: Business and Technology. John Wiley ans Sons (2001).

[RSN+00] A. Rukhin, J. Soto, J. Nechvatal, M. Smid, E. Barker, S. Leigh, M. Levenson, M. Vangel, D. Banks, A. Heckert, J. Dray, S. Vo: A Statistical Test Suite for Random and Pseudorandom Number Generators for Cryptographic Applications. NIST, nist special publication 800-22 Aufl. (2000).

[SaIn05] A. Satoh, T. Inoue: ASIC-Hardware-Focused Comparison for Hash Functions MD5, RIPEMD-160, and SHS. In: International Conference on Information Technology: Coding and Computing (ITCC'05), 4-6 April 2005, IEEE Computer Society, Las Vegas, USA (2005), Bd. 1, 532–537.

[Sand87] R. S. Sandhu: On Some Cryptographic Solutions for Access Control in a Tree Hierarchy. In: Proceedings of the 1987 Fall Joint Computer Conference on Exploring technology: today and tomorrow, IEEE (1987), 405–410.

[SaSa96] R. Sandhu, P. Samarati: Authentication, Access Control, and Audit. In: ACM Computing Surveys, 28, 1 (1996), 241–243.

[SCFY96] R. Sandhu, E. Coyne, H. Feinstein, C. Youman: Role-Based Access Control Models. In: IEEE Computer, 29, 2 (1996), 38–47.

[Scha] D. Schadow: Eclipse XML-Security Plug-In. http://www.xml-sicherheit.de/.

[Schn96] B. Schneier: Applied Cryptography. John Wiley and sons (1996).

[Sedg03] R. Sedgewick: Algorithms in Java. Addison-Wesley (2003).

[Sham79] A. Shamir: How to Share a Secret. In: Communications of the ACM, 22, 11 (1979), 612–613.

[Sham84] A. Shamir: Identity-based Cryptosystems and Signature Schemes. In: Advances in Cryptology (CRYPTO'84), LNCS, Springer (1984).

[Shan49]	C. E. Shannon: Communication Theory of Secrecy Systems. In: Bell System Technical Journal, 28 (1949), 656–715.
[Skro03]	D. Skrobotz: Das Maut-Dilemma (2003), http://www.berlinews.de/artikel.php?13849.
[Stei00]	R. Steinmetz: Multimedia-Technologie: Grundlagen, Komponenten uns Systeme. Springer (2000).
[Stin95]	D. R. Stinson: Cryptography: Theory and Practice. Discrete Mathematics and its Applications, CRC Press (1995).
[svp]	Secure Video Processor. http://www.svpalliance.org.
[TLYL04]	Z. Tan, C. Lin, H. Yin, B. Li: Optimization and Benchmark of Cryptographic Algorithms on Network Processors. In: IEEE Micro, 24, 5 (2004), 55–69.
[Tsud92]	G. Tsudik: Message Authentication with One-Way Hash Functions. In: ACM SIGCOMM Computer Communication Review, ACM Press (1992), Bd. 22.
[Tzen02]	W.-G. Tzeng: A Time-Bound Cryptographic Key Assignment Scheme for Access Control in a Hierarchy. In: IEEE Transactions on Knowledge and Data Engineering, 14, 1 (2002), 182–188.
[UhPo05]	A. Uhl, A. Pommer: Image and Video Encryption: From Digital Rights Management to Secured Personal Communication, Bd. 15. Springer, advances in information security Aufl. (2005).
[VRTW01]	A. Veitch, E. Riedel, S. Towers, J. Wilkes: Position Summary - Towards Global Storage Management and Data Placement. In: Proceedings of the Eighth Workshop on Hot Topics in Operating Systems (HotOS-VIII'01), IEEE Computer Society (2001).
[W3C02]	W3C: IETF/W3C XML-Signature Syntax and Processing (2002), http://www.w3.org/TR/xmldsig-core/.
[W3C06]	W3C: IETF/W3C XML Signature WG (2006), http://www.w3.org/Signature/.

[WaHA98] D. Wallner, E. Harder, R. Agee: Key Management for Multicast: Issues and Architectures (1998), http://tools.ietf.org/id/draft-wallner-key-arch-01.txt.

[WaYY05] X. Wang, Y. L. Yin, H. Yu: Collision Search Attacks on SHA1 (2005), http://cryptome.org/sha1-attacks.htm.

[WeWi04] R. P. Weinmann, K. Wirt: Analysis of the DVB Scrambling Algorithm. In: Conference on Communications and Multimedia Security, Kluwer Academic Publishers (2004).

[Wirt05] K. Wirt: Fault attack on the DVB Common Scrambling Algorithm. In: LNCS 3481, Proceedings of the International Conference on Computational Science and its Applications, Springer (2005).

[WLD+02] X. Wang, G. Lao, T. DeMartini, H. Reddy, M. Nguyen, E. Valenzuela: XrML – eXtensible rights Markup Language. In: Proceedings of the 2002 ACM Symposium on Document Engineering, ACM (2002).

[WoGL98] C. K. Wong, M. Gouda, S. S. Lam: Secure Group Communications Using Key Graphs. In: Proceedings of the ACM SIGCOMM'98 (1998), 68–79.

[Wool00] A. Wool: Key Management for Encrypted Broadcast. In: ACM Transactions on Information and System Security (TISSEC'00), 3, 2 (2000), 107–134.

[xac] eXtensible Access Control Markup Language. http://www.xacml.org.

[xkm] XML Key Management Specification (XKMS). http://www.w3.org/TR/xkms/.

[xrm] eXtensible rights Markup Language. http://www.xrml.org/.

[Yeh05] J. Yeh: An RSA-Based Time-Bound Hierarchical Key Assignment Scheme for Electronic Article Subscription. In: Proceedings of the 14th ACM International Conference on Information and Knowledge Management (CIKM'05) (2005).

[Yeh07] J. Yeh: A Time-Bound Hierarchical Key Assignment Cryptosystem with No Lifetime Limit. In: Proceedings of the 2007 International Conference on Security and Management (SAM'07) (2007).

[Yi05]	X. Yi: Security of Chien's Efficient Time-Bound Hierarchical Key Assignment Scheme. In: IEEE Transactions on Knowledge and Data Engineering (2005), Bd. 17, 1298–1299.
[YiYe03]	X. Yi, Y. Ye: Security of Tzeng's Time-Bound Key Assignment Scheme for Access Control in a Hierarchy. In: IEEE Transactions on Knowledge and Data Engineering (2003), Bd. 15, 1054–1055.
[ZhHS93]	Y. Zheng, T. Hardjono, J. Seberry: New Solutions to the Problem of Access Control in a Hierarchy. Tech. Rep., University of Wollongong (1993).
[Zhon02]	S. Zhong: A Practical Key Management Scheme for Access Control in a User Hierarchy. In: Computers ans Security, 21, 8 (2002), 750–759.
[ZXHJ07]	L. Zhitang, M. Xiaojing, T. Hao, Z. Jiping: A Scalable Multicast Key Management Scheme combined MARKS and TR-LKH (2007), http://www.ietf.org/internet-drafts/draft-li-marks-trlkh-00.txt, internet Draft.

Die VDM Verlagsservicegesellschaft sucht für wissenschaftliche Verlage abgeschlossene und herausragende

Dissertationen, Habilitationen, Diplomarbeiten, Master Theses, Magisterarbeiten usw.

für die kostenlose Publikation als Fachbuch.

Sie verfügen über eine Arbeit, die hohen inhaltlichen und formalen Ansprüchen genügt, und haben Interesse an einer honorarvergüteten Publikation?

Dann senden Sie bitte erste Informationen über sich und Ihre Arbeit per Email an *info@vdm-vsg.de*.

Sie erhalten kurzfristig unser Feedback!

VDM Verlagsservicegesellschaft mbH
Dudweiler Landstr. 99   Telefon +49 681 3720 174
D - 66123 Saarbrücken   Fax   +49 681 3720 1749
www.vdm-vsg.de

Die VDM Verlagsservicegesellschaft mbH vertritt

Printed by Books on Demand GmbH, Norderstedt / Germany